Raising The Curtain On Raising Children

[signature]

BOOKS BY FLORENCE LITTAUER

After Every Wedding Comes a Marriage
Blow Away the Black Clouds
How to Get Along with Difficult People
It Takes So Little to Be Above Average
Hope for Hurting Women
Out of the Cabbage Patch
Personality Plus
The Pursuit of Happiness
Say It with CLASS
Shades of Beauty (co-authored with Marita Littauer)
Your Personality Tree
Looking for God in All the Right Places

Florence Littauer

RAISING THE CURTAIN ON RAISING CHILDREN

WORD PUBLISHING

Word (UK) Ltd
Milton Keynes, England

WORD AUSTRALIA
Heathmont, Victoria, Australia
STRUIK CHRISTIAN BOOKS (PTY) LTD
Salt River, South Africa
ALBY COMMERCIAL ENTERPRISES PTE LTD
Balmoral Road, Singapore
CONCORDE DISTRIBUTORS LTD
Havelock North, New Zealand

RAISING THE CURTAIN ON RAISING CHILDREN

Copyright © 1988 by Florence Littauer

First published in the U.S.A. by Word Incorporated, Dallas, Texas.

First U.K. edition 1989.

ISBN 0–85009–314–7

Unless otherwise indicated, Scripture quotations are from the authorised King James Version. Those marked:

>NASB are from the New American Standard Bible, copyright © 1960, 1962, 1963, 1968, 1971 by the Lockman Foundation.
>
>NIV are from the New International Version of the Bible, published by Zondervan Corporation, copyright © 1973 by New York Bible Society International.
>
>AMP are from The Amplified Bible, copyright © 1965 by Zondervan Publishing House.
>
>TLB are from The Living Bible, copyright 1971 by Tyndale House Publishers, Wheaton, IL. Used by permission.

Reproduced, printed and bound in Great Britain for Word (UK) Ltd., by Cox & Wyman Ltd., Reading.

92 93 94 / 10 9 8 7 6 5 4 3 2

Contents

Program Notes
by Florence

Did you ever wonder where all those people who write child-raising books have been all their lives? Have they had model children or perhaps none at all? So many of their ideas sound so sweet and spiritual that you wonder what they would have done if they'd spent twenty-four hours in your house with your kids. When I was a child there was a lady up the street from our store who wrote books on bringing up children. Since she worked at home, the children obviously put a cramp in her creativity and so each morning she would pack a little lunch for these pre-schoolers and send them out to play. Since this scene was in Massachusetts, half the year the weather was freezing with frequent blizzards. On really bad days these two little ones would knock on neighbors' doors and be taken inside by concerned friends who didn't want to find little corpses on the cement.

When questioned on her un-motherly practices, the author said she was teaching her children to fend for themselves and become responsible—and surely she was forcing them to be creative in self-preservation. These children never forgot to wear their boots, scarves, or mittens, for they knew that one forgetful moment might mean frostbite in the big freezer of life.

When no neighbors were home, the little ones would wander down to our store with their bag lunches and my mother would give them hot chocolate to go with their sandwiches. My father would shake his head and mutter, "and she tells people how to raise children."

With the memory of these moppets in mind, I never dared write on child-raising until I had all of my own children grown, educated, and established in their careers.

I didn't want to be the author who wrote on raising children while her own were out in the snow. Nor did I want to be mouthing platitudes of spirituality prematurely. I've been in the mothering mode for thirty-three years and when people ask me how many children I have, I hesitate because I've given birth to four, lost two, adopted one, and ended up with three.

I remember one day when young Fred was in the sixth grade, Marita a freshman in college, and Lauren a new bride. In every mother's life there are those days that you say you will never forget and yet as time goes by, the details blur and the impact decreases. The reason I can still hold this day in mind is that I took notes on it and made a tape of the happenings. Recently this twelve-year-old tape was played on a Los Angeles radio station and we were inundated with calls. Somehow my experiences of that twenty-four hours struck a responsive chord in the memories of my listeners.

It was on a Sunday evening when I entered Marita's room to discover her lying in a bathing suit under an ultra-violet lamp. Since this was not a normal family function I asked what she was doing.

"I'm getting a tan," she replied.

"Shouldn't you have your eyes covered or be wearing sunglasses?" I asked.

She was disgusted at my lack of understanding. "This light can't hurt me. Anybody would know that."

At that point her friend Terry arrived and asked how long she'd been under the lamp. When Marita said over an hour both Terry and I were stunned and Terry added, "I had a friend whose mother's cousin stayed under one of those bulbs for an hour. Her skin burned up and she went blind."

With this cheerful thought I insisted Marita get up before she burned up. In checking her "tan lines" we found there were none. The bulb had lost its power and Marita didn't go blind or get a tan.

I next went in to our adopted son, Fred's, room to see if he had done his homework or if he needed any help. He assured me he was completely caught up on his work and the last thing he needed was for me to check up on him.

At that point Terry left and I encouraged Marita to get a nap before she went to her job as an all-night waitress in a coffee shop. This was hardly my idea of an occupation with a future, but I had told her when she was eighteen she could take any position she chose as long as she still went to college. Her schedule was: Work from 10 to 6, home for breakfast, sleep from 7:30 to 9:30, college from 10 to 4, and then a variety of sleep, study, and socializing until 10, when the whole cycle started again.

Marita assured me she was not tired and was going to read until time for work. I left her and went to the family room where I found Richard doing push-ups. Richard was a twenty-five-year-old Campus Crusade staff member who had needed a place to stay for a weekend six months before. He had not yet even thought of looking for an apartment where he would have to pay rent. Richard was exercising and amusing twenty-four-year-old Brenda who was also on Crusade staff. Months before she had come to stay for two weeks to care for young Fred while I was on a trip. The trip ended but Brenda remained with us for years. She had chosen 8:30 Sunday evening to make cookies for everyone and soon we were all having a party. About 9:30 Marita put on her mini-skirted waitress uniform, drove off to work, and the rest of us went to bed.

In the morning when young Fred attempted to make his sandwich for his school lunch, I realized I had the remains of a turkey in the refrigerator. Wanting to be a noble mother, I decided to slice some up for him. In lifting the platter off the shelf, I caught my finger on a pointed skewer sticking out of the bird's rear, thus puncturing myself and dropping blood on the turkey. I figured Fred would never notice, but then as I started to slice a piece off the bird, I missed. The butcher knife cut right into my thumb and drops of blood fell onto the white bread.

Fred noticed and asked, "What are those red spots on my sandwich?" I told him I had cut my thumb and that his lunch was now a blood sacrifice. I felt a mother willing to make such a sacrifice for her son was a spiritual giant, but Fred was not impressed. Later I found out that Fred had swapped this treat with a boy who didn't like what his mother had made him for lunch. "He didn't know you'd bled all over the turkey," Fred explained.

By the time Fred was off to school and I had done the dishes, I noticed two bananas that were turning black. I don't know about your children, but mine only like the first day of anything. The minute they see something getting soggy, stale, or limp, they'd starve to death before eating it. They did not inherit my mother's dedication to cleaning up one's plate because of the starving children in China. Being the link between these two generations, I decided to make banana bread. This way I wouldn't be wasteful or feel guilty, yet the children wouldn't recognize they were eating old black bananas. Exhilarated over my solution, I mashed up the bananas and made bread. By this time the kitchen was a mess again and I decided, in some burst of forethought, to make a cake for dessert that night.

As I was cleaning up from my culinary experiments, the phone rang and it was my daughter Lauren. For those of you who think once you marry them off you are through with their problems, I have bad news. If you are within reach of the phone, you can become easily involved. With a sense of urgency Lauren explained that neither her car nor Randy's would start. She had called two garages but neither one would help her. She couldn't find my husband anywhere and Randy was going to be late for work if I didn't drop everything and drive twenty miles to bring jumper cables. When I asked why she hadn't bought jumper cables or new batteries (since their cars frequently wouldn't start), she burst into tears over my heartless approach to life. Her sobbing brought the desired guilt and I agreed to come as soon as my cake and banana bread were out of the oven. I couldn't be so sacrificial as to burn my baked goods to play mechanic and make a speedy house call at no charge!

Before leaving on this mission of mercy, I had to be prepared for my busy day as there would be no time to return. I had to gather my Bible study outlines to bring to the printer, find my maps of Jerusalem to use at Fred's school (where I was giving a lecture to his class on the history of the Hebrew race), collect my nail polish, remover, and cotton in hopes I could do my nails somewhere along the way, get dressed for the day, do my hair and make-up, remove the cake and bread from the oven, lock up the house, and leave. All this was accomplished in twelve minutes and I was on my way to rescue my damsel in distress.

I opened the garage door and surprise, Marita's car was parked in the driveway right behind mine! There was no way I could jockey around it, so I went in to wake her up and get her keys. She had come home from her waitressing exhausted and complained that her eyes hurt. She had no idea where her keys were so I started a search with her sleepy suggestions. I soon found her keys in her uniform pocket along with a multitude of quarters, her nightly tips.

After moving her car out of the way, I put her keys back on the proper hook in the garage where Father Fred had designated they belonged and reached for mine. They were missing. I remembered that Richard had borrowed my car for an errand the night before and had not returned the keys. I called him at Campus Crusade and he confirmed that he had the keys but that Dr. Bright had him on such an important assignment that the evangelization of the entire lost world would come to a screeching halt if I insisted he drop everything just to bring me my keys. It did seem like a trivial errand when he compared it to winning the world for Christ, so I told him to forget my problems and go back to boxing up the Four Laws in twelve languages.

I called my husband who always had an extra set of keys hidden in his closet but never in the same place twice. When I had begged him to put them in one simple spot, he'd said that if I knew where they were I'd lose them, too, and then there would be no reserve set. There was some dim logic to this secretive placing of the keys, so I had to call him for new clues each time I misplaced them. With his help I located the keys in the toe of his left loafer

and started out again. At least I *thought* I would start out again—
except that the car wouldn't start at all. In checking around I found
the lights had been left on and the battery was dead. At that point I
was not very happy with Richard, in spite of his zeal for lost souls. I
put my keys back on the hook and took Marita's. I transferred all
my printing, maps, and nail polish into Marita's car, and drove off.
As I glanced at the dashboard I noticed the gas gauge was below
empty. She never liked to have money tied up in gas she wasn't
going to use within the next hour. Gratefully it was down hill to the
gas station, so I coasted hopefully along.

Loud rock music was blaring from the radio and when I
fumbled around trying to find the knob I could feel it was missing, so I had no choice but to drive into the station like an aging
adolescent with my tunes preceding me.

The attendant asked how much gas I wanted and I took out
my wallet to see what I had, only to find there were no bills at all.
I then remembered I'd given young Fred all my money for a field
trip deposit and I was left only with change. While the man
waited I got out of the car to count out my change for him and in
doing so I missed his hand and dumped the money onto the
ground. He was not about to help me pick it up, so I got down on
my knees to crawl under the car and retrieve the quarters and
dimes. As I did so I wondered what I was doing in my white skirt
scrounging for change in an oily driveway in order to save Lauren
and Randy the price of a set of jumper cables.

I came up with $2.50 which didn't excite the man who was
standing dutifully holding the hose, but he did put the gas in and at
my request he turned the music down with a set of pliers. When I
finally arrived at Lauren's, she and Randy were standing woefully
in the driveway and wanted to know why I was so late. When I ran
through a review of my morning, they laughed and I cried. We got
their cars started, Randy left for work, and Lauren drove to a
nature walk as part of her college geology class assignment.

I went to the printer's and arrived at Mountain View Christian School early enough to do my nails in the car before going in
to give my Hebrew history talk. As I sat in Fred's classroom waiting
to begin my message with my maps of Jerusalem, the teacher an-

nounced that some pupils had not passed in the only written assignment of the term. This was inexcusable and would mean a zero. She read four names and one of them was Fred's. This had not been one of my better days and I just looked at him and mouthed one word, "why?" He whispered simply, "I didn't do it." That was obvious.

The teacher introduced me and I did my best to brighten up and interest these sleepy children in the Wailing Wall and the Dome of the Rock. When I finished my moving message, two boys were asleep and several, including Fred, were yawning. I decided to check in on his other teachers while I was there. Miss Twila reported he had a low test score he had not made up, and Miss Wenger showed me he had flunked his English test and had to do it over again at recess.

Luckily, I couldn't find Fred's math teacher, saving me one more set of grim statistics. I drove home quickly and arrived just in time to see Marita standing bewildered in the driveway, wondering where her car had gone without her.

I did live through the day and at dinner the whole family wolfed down the bread as if it had been made from fresh bananas.

With this report of twenty-four hours in the life of an ordinary mother, I'm sure you can realize why Fred and I, on young Fred's eighteenth birthday, raised our orange juice glasses at breakfast, clicked them together, and toasted our success. We had three children over eighteen who weren't on drugs, didn't smoke, hadn't run off to live with someone, and were still in the church. It's now six years later and we can write that by the grace of God, we have raised Christians and not just children.

To set the stage for this book I've asked one of the cast, our daughter, Marita, to give a synopsis of some of her life experiences. In reading about a few of the situations she got into, you will see that our script has not been a romantic comedy with a happy-ever-after conclusion, but a steady shift of one realistic scene after another. What has kept us going is that we know the Author and believe that He knows how it's all going to turn out in the end.

So let's start *Raising the Curtain on Raising Children.*

Program Notes
by Marita

Being a parent is not something that people ever feel confident or secure about . . . we've always been a step behind in bringing you up."[1] So said Garrison Keillor, noted humorist and author, at graduation ceremonies for Gettysburg College in 1987.

Garrison Keillor sums it up well. Parenting is a tough job. It is something that very few parents ever feel secure or confident about and as advice and trends change, parents often fall a step behind. I hope that by reading this book you'll move a giant step ahead!

The fact that confidence and parenting are two words usually not grouped together is evident in the plethora of parenting books seen in any bookstore across the country. Some are written by psychologists who don't have children of their own but spend a great deal of time counseling disturbed children and heart-broken parents. They have facts and research to quote, but many have very little personal or practical experience. You wonder what they would do in the middle of the night if a child woke up screaming with a tummy ache.

Some of these authors produce such wonderful children on paper that you conclude their child and your children are an entirely different species. Maybe you've read one of those deep books full of psychological research and struggled to stick with it.

The book may have had helpful ideas buried in it somewhere but you found that a few seconds of it before bed worked better than Sominex.

Some Christian books on bringing up children are written by parents who have been successful. They have raised decent healthy kids who have stayed out of trouble, have eagerly gone to church and Pioneer Girls, and were always at the top of their class. Any mother who has this feather in her cap deserves to have a book to testify that it is still possible to raise decent children in an indecent world. She deserves a star in her crown or maybe even a statue to celebrate her success. Parenting today is tough and someone who has done it well definitely has something to say to others.

We hope this book will be a perfect blend of both approaches. It is written by my mother, Florence Littauer. She has spent thirty-three years as a mother, over twenty years in study, research, and teaching, and has ten years of informal marriage and family counseling to her credit. Most importantly, she has three success stories of her own. She always said she was going to write a book on bringing up children when she was through with it, when she could look back and see that she'd done a good job. Mom, look back, you've done a good job.

My sister, Lauren, is thirty-three and four years older than I. She was a model child who got high grades, never cut classes, and was a cheerleader in high school. She graduated from college with a degree in psychology and business, worked in my father's office and married an exceptional young man when she was twenty. Now thirteen years later, she and Randy have a lovely home, three wonderful boys, and a Schnauzer dog. She is involved in various volunteer projects, she is a grief counselor, a speaker and an author of the book *What You Can Say When You Don't Know What to Say*. Besides all that she works with her husband in his stamp and coin business. Lauren has done well; she fills the traditional role as wife and mother, and she is the one who enables my mother to add "grandmother" to her resume.

Then I came along! I was more of a challenge to raise, for I was the one who didn't want to follow the rules. My report cards always came home with comments like "talks too much," "disrupts class," and "can't sit still." I made adequate grades and managed to skate through school on more charm than real work. In junior high school, I wore black leather motorcycle riding boots, jeans that hung off my hips, and oversized men's t-shirts. I rode motor-cycles and stood on the street corner before and after school and smoked with the rest of the "cool" kids, although I never let my parents know.

By high school I'd straightened out. I was never really ac-cepted by the fast set because I got grades that were too high and lived in a house that was too nice. I started waitressing in my father's restaurant when I was thirteen and continued through high school. I worked every night and on weekends so I never had time to go to parties or football games. Thus I managed to steer clear of drugs and drinking. In an effort to be grown up, however, I did run around with older kids. This was during the "Saturday Night Fever" era when everyone went to the discos except me because, at eighteen, I wasn't old enough. One of the girls I worked with, knowing how much I wanted to be part of the gang, taught me how to get an official ID through the Cali-fornia Department of Motor Vehicles. All I had to do was find a girl who looked similar to me and who was about my height and weight. I took her license number, address, and statistics and went into the Motor Vehicles office. I told them I had lost my license and they took my picture and printed me up her license. It was mailed to her home and she gave it to me when it arrived. There I was in print with a legitimate license that said I was twenty-two. I could go anywhere I wanted to go.

My foolproof method had, as do all illegal operations, a few loopholes. First was that I waited on policemen in the restaurant and had dated some of them, much to my parents' dismay. The policemen called me "Miss Jail Bait."

Second was, in my eagerness to be mature, I didn't consider the fact that this signing another girl's name on a legal document was both forgery and perjury. Like all daring teenagers, I knew I'd never get caught. I could hardly wait for that first Saturday night to come when we'd all go to Bobby McGee's. One good thing in my favor was that I didn't drink, so I only had orange juice in front of me when a vice-squad officer that I knew spotted me. He asked the manager to check my ID. I was thrilled that I could quickly prove I was twenty-two but the officer knew better and he took my license away and told me to leave. Suddenly, I was no longer twenty-two, but at least I hadn't been arrested.

The next day while I was out, two officers came to our home. When my mother opened the door and saw two men in uniform she was surprised. When she found out they had come to arrest me, she was shocked! What had her adorable daughter done? They wouldn't tell her but she had to promise I'd show up at the police station on Monday morning. When I came home that night I was met by a fearful mother and a questioning father. I thought I'd gotten away with it but I had to tell them I'd used a false ID. They couldn't believe their daughter had done any such thing, but neither one of them yelled or called me names. They both were supportive and pointed out that part of growing up was learning that bad choices produced bad consequences.

On Monday morning my father took me to the San Bernardino Police Station where they booked me, fingerprinted me, and took "mugshots." They put handcuffs on me and placed me in a police car with a shirtless man with big scars on his face and chest. As they drove me away to jail I wondered, *What is a good girl like you doing in a place like this?*

Surely I never thought what I'd done in fun would end up with me in jail. But there I was behind bars in a "holding pen." After two hours they let me out of the cell and did the fingerprinting and mugshots again, this time for the county. My father paid $600 bail and they set a trial date. With a lawyer's help, we were able to get the DA to lower my felony charges to misdemeanors and I was fined $300 that I had to pay back to my father. The case never went to court and the DA told me they had made an example of me because I was a nice girl from a nice family, and they wanted to teach me a lesson. He said, "If you were an ordinary low class kid, we'd have just taken the license and let it go at that."

At the time I felt that extra punishment for being a nice girl was unfair, but I realize now that the severity of the two hours in jail and the view of life behind bars did jolt me into the stark reality of life. I did learn that bad choices had *very* bad consequences.

My mother didn't speak on child-raising for several years after that experience, but neither she nor my father berated me or said "How could our child do a thing like that? What will our friends think?" Instead, my mother periodically took me out of college and brought me with her on speaking trips. One day she said positively, "I picture that sometime in the future we'll be working together." I thought to myself, *That will be the day that I spend my life in churches with women.*

As I did go with my mother to "the churches with women," I only went for the traveling and the sociability. I didn't want to get involved in religious work. Often I didn't dress in a way to make my mother proud of me and some people criticized her for taking me out of classes, but she defended her actions and showed me that even though I'd been far from perfect, she was on my side. Her support of me and her ability to forget the past and have fun at the present spoke to me of Christian love in a stronger way than preaching or moralizing could have done. Today I gladly spend my time in churches with women!

When I was twenty-one, on the way home from the Arizona Women's Retreat where my mother had been the speaker, I came up with the idea to start a similar retreat in Southern California. Instead of saying, "You're too young to do that" or "Where do you think you're going to get the money?" my parents encouraged me to form the Southern California Women's Retreat. The first year we had 100 women attend and this year (1988) we had 700 at the seventh retreat. We turned away another 100 who wanted to be part of the excitement.

When my mother started her Christian Leaders and Speakers Seminars in January 1981, I was an eager participant. I've been with CLASS ever since and now work full time training, booking, and promoting CLASS speakers and authors. I wasn't the model Christian child, but my parents never gave up on me, never looked down on me. They let me know they believed in me as a person of worth. I never did finish college, but my mother poured her love and information into me so I learned things I never would have gathered from worldly professors.

At CLASS I often say, "I'm the youngest member of the staff, but I'm the only one who has had twenty-nine years of Florence Littauer's private training." Yes, there is hope. They do grow up eventually.

The other member of our family is my brother, Fred. After my parents lost their two sons, they adopted Fred when he was three months old. Lauren and I adored him with his big brown eyes and thick dark brown curly hair. Fred was always well behaved and didn't have the hyperactivity that seemed to go with being a Littauer.

In high school, Fred had lots of friends and was more interested in a good time than good grades. He and his buddies came up with many wonderful schemes during those years. We only know about the ones he got caught for, but I suspect there were many more. One time he and his friends painted over the room numbers on all the classroom doors the day before high school started. The new students were horribly confused trying to figure out where their classes were.

The other great prank involved one of his favorite classes— "Office." Since Fred worked in the school office for one period a day, he knew what went on in the attendance department. On the eve of "Senior Ditch Day" Fred and his friends broke into the school office, grabbed the bag with all the cards of the absent students and were gone by the time the police responded to the alarm. When he showed me the bag of cards hidden in his closet I thought he was quite clever, but not everyone did. Someone turned them all in and he and his friends had to clean the campus for several Saturdays!

College was not a major event in Fred's life as it wasn't with me. He worked as a "bagger" in a local grocery store while going to the community college and when that got old he packed up and joined some of his buddies at Utah State. That time proved to be more of an opportunity for great skiing than higher learning and when my parents got his report card saying he'd flunked music (because he'd failed to listen to the records), they decided he'd been in Utah long enough.

Although he never graduated, Fred has taken my father's auto repair business from neglect to near profit. The customers respect him and the employees respond to him. Fred runs my dad's three shops and maintains the family home while my parents are on the road. He has grown from an adorable little boy and an active teen to a productive adult.

Perhaps your family is like ours. Maybe your children aren't the "Father Knows Best" type. You may have a perfect one—be grateful for your blessings. Others may be more spirited and more of a challenge to raise as I was. Or maybe you have one like my brother, Fred, who is so different from you that you don't know what to do with him. Read on. My parents were not without faults and we kids certainly presented them with problems, but through lots of love, plenty of attention and positive discipline, we all grew up to be responsible adults.

Being a parent isn't easy, but now that my mother has three success stories on record, she can write a book, *Raising the Curtain on Raising Children.*

Part I

THE AUTHOR

Looking unto Jesus the author and finisher of our faith.
(Hebrews 12:2a)

> Unless the Lord builds a house,
> the builders' work is useless.
> (Psalm 127:1 TLB)

I

The Author

From the time I was a child I loved being on the stage. I memorized little poems to recite in the church talent shows and tried out for every local play. In high school I won the poetry reading contest by delivering "Constancy" by Edna St. Vincent Millay and had the part of Cuckoo in the Senior Class Play. In college I was on the debate team, was a winner at the Model Congress, and participated in many dramatic presentations.

As a speech teacher, I directed high school shows, started a drama club, and made my wedding into a theatrical production. Later I directed musical comedies such as *Oklahoma, South Pacific, Guys and Dolls,* and *Call Me Madam* for a local theatre group, won a New England award with my version of *The Boyfriend,* and was on the founding staff of the Long Wharf Theatre in New Haven, Connecticut.

Our daughter Lauren was first on the stage at the age of 4 when I cast her as the one little child in a high school Christmas pageant. She followed this up with bit parts in each production I directed, including a role in *South Pacific,* where she spoke and sang in French. Marita was a Polynesian child in the same show and a Sunbonnet Sue in *Oklahoma.* My husband Fred became an actor and sang the lead role in *Call Me Madam.*

Throughout all these years I loved anything connected with theatricals. I enjoyed taking the raw materials of human lives, moving them around a stage, motivating them to occasional brilliance and thrilling to the opening night performance.

What I did not realize at the time was that my whole life had become an act. Fred and I played roles at home as well as on stage; we each portrayed the picture of a perfect parent. We lived on the right side of the tracks, surrounded our children with luxuries and dressed them in appropriate costumes. Our home became a stage set with each room having its own theme. Everything had to be kept in perfect order so that if anyone came to the front door I could give them a house tour with full confidence.

It was in the midst of what we now call "Mother's Stage Phase" that my musical comedies turned into tragedy. My two little sons were diagnosed with a fatal brain disease and there was nothing any of us could do about it. There was no happy ending for the Littauer show.

As I sat holding my first little boy and a year later my second, both of whom had frequent convulsions and screamed round the clock, reality fell heavily upon me. There were no changes of scenery and surely no supporting cast. I was alone on the stage and the lights were out.

It was at that point, at a Christian Women's Club, that I first met the Author of my life, the Lord Jesus. The speaker told me that Jesus could transform my mind and give me a role that would go on forever. Gradually, I took off the old costumes and put on the new clothes. My eyes were opened and I saw for the first time that I wasn't much of a mother. I had placed my children in a beautiful setting and I knew the right lines, but I had no understanding of selfless love. I was depressed over my losses, disheartened that friends no longer came to visit, and in disbelief that a merciful God would let two tragedies happen to a good person like me. Gradually my attention shifted from my own self-pity to the lives of my two daughters. We started going to a Bible-believing church and within a few months my husband committed his life to the Lord. As Fred began to study the Bible he found a verse in the Song of Solomon (1:6) that said, "They made me the keeper of the vineyards but mine own vineyard have I not kept."

To Fred, that statement was God saying "Fred you've been president of the Rotary Club and your own business but you haven't taken care of your family as you should." When he shared this verse with me and said he was sorry, he gave me the gift of hope. Perhaps our lives would change; perhaps we could become a real family. Suddenly we both saw that we had not been raising Christians but just children.

We adopted an adorable baby boy and named him Frederick Jr. No sooner had we started on our new Christian walk than the great Director of life moved us from comfortable Connecticut to the desert of Southern California. Fred became the Conference Services Director at Campus Crusade for Christ headquarters in the historic Arrowhead Springs Hotel, and we were assigned to live in Bungalow One, a dilapidated old motel unit with no kitchen. As I cooked on a hotplate on the porch, I wondered why God had uprooted us, given us an unlikely setting, and cast us in totally new roles.

As I look back twenty years later, I can see that God used our tragic circumstances to get my attention and get me off the stage where I was starring in my own show. He humbled me as He took my hand and led me from my twelve-room Connecticut home into shabby, old Bungalow One which was falling in around me. I tried to be optimistic by realizing that in the line of old bungalows it was at least Number One!

We plastered the holes in the ceilings, replaced the dripping "swamp coolers" with air conditioners, and made the porch into a kitchen. We had a new setting for our new life.

We studied God's Word, listened to every visiting lecturer, and began to teach an adult Sunday school class called "Harmony in the Home." We had a new script.

We instituted a daily prayer time, had family meetings, and began to raise Christians instead of just children. We had a whole new theme.

We searched the Scriptures for information on parenting, called to God for direction in discipline, and concentrated on building a Christian home. We had a new plot, God's plan for our life.

Most important of all, we recognized that we had a new Author, a Lord who knew the beginning from the end, the Alpha from the Omega, because He had written both the words and the music.

In 1 Corinthians 14:33 Paul says, "God is not the author of confusion, but of peace." Our lives had been in confusion, even in turmoil, but as we studied our new roles our Author gave us peace.

As we appropriated the power of the Spirit daily and walked in the path prepared by our Lord, we learned that "He became the author of eternal salvation unto all them that obey Him" (Hebrews 5:9).

Isaiah told us to "Lift up your eyes on high and behold who has created these things" (Isaiah 40:26). As we studied the Bible and then the four basic personality patterns, we allowed our God to change our weaknesses into strengths. He showed us how to examine ourselves and accept each other as He had made us to be. We saw how creative He could be when we weren't looking for the credit.

As fast as Fred and I received instruction from classes and from God himself, we taught others what we had learned; first in Sunday school, then in our home, then for retreats. People asked, "Do you have this information in print?" so we wrote up our study plans and outlines. Soon they requested a book and so I sat down and told my life story, *The Pursuit of Happiness*. Now, fourteen books later, I could be considered an author, but not *the* Author, for Jesus is "the author and finisher of our faith" (Hebrews 12:2).

When I sit down to write a book, I don't start until I have a plan and know how it's going to end. I don't just put words on paper and hope it will turn out all right. Jesus is our author and He knows every moment of our life before it happens. He has a plan, a plot, a theme, a setting for each one of us and when we believe in His infinite wisdom, He will not be the author of confusion but He will write the word peace upon our hearts.

Jesus is also our "finisher"; one who perfects or polishes, one who completes the labor, one who cultivates manner, speech, and social skills, one who brings us to maturity. Jesus is our Author and the instructor at our finishing school.

As our Author, He has written our script; it is now up to us to read it and be willing to obey His scriptural directives for family life. Fred and I have played it both ways. We've raised children by giving them what we thought they would appreciate, and by trying to bring them up according to our plan. Gratefully, the Lord showed us our self-centered natures before it was too late. When we accepted the Lord, Lauren was 11, Marita 7, and Fred 2. From that time on we changed our direction and began to raise Christians and not just children.

If you are a parent, a grandparent, or know someone who is, this book will give practical suggestions based on biblical truth and consistent with the words of "the author and finisher of our faith."

Part II

THE CAST

Honor your father and mother . . . Parents, don't keep on scolding and nagging your children, making them angry and resentful. Rather, bring them up with the loving discipline the Lord himself approves, with suggestions and godly advice.

(Ephesians 6:2–4 TLB)

Many are called, but few are chosen.
(Matthew 22:14)

II

The Cast

In any production there has to be a cast, the people who make it happen. For a Broadway show the job of casting director is extremely important. Many come to try out, but few can be chosen.

The first requirement is that the individual selected for the role already created by the author will fit the part in looks, voice, style, and talent. Miscasting can be costly. The second need is that the whole group blend together, that they have what is called "chemistry." No show can be successful even with a string of excellent actors if, when you put them together, nothing happens. The whole is the sum of its parts set on fire.

Unfortunately, our family productions don't have casting directors. We meet and marry without the guidance of an experienced selection committee and when our children come along we have to take what we get whether or not they blend in and sing harmoniously.

When I counsel a couple before they marry, they have the optimistic expectation that they will be the exception. They believe that by some miracle their two lives will truly become one, that they will think alike and each be submitted to the other's desires. Those of us who have been married know better; even a great union takes cooperative skill to achieve harmony.

For the last twenty years, Fred and I have had the opportunity to introduce thousands of people to the four basic temperaments. Originally labeled by Hippocrates, the four personalities have been the foundation for almost all personality teaching for 2,000 years, surely standing the test of time. As long as we keep the theory in perspective and teach it as a tool, not a theology, we can reap its benefits in our family lives as we begin to understand our cast.

The Bible instructs us to examine ourselves, and put ourselves to the test, but it doesn't give us a test to take so that we can examine ourselves. We could study God's Word carefully and pull out all the positive traits we should have as displayed in the Bible characters. We could make lists of sins, problems, and weaknesses—and measure ourselves against them. But few of us will use either of these methods. Instead we tend to bumble along hoping all those other people will someday shape up and see the light.

We need a casting director who will put the right people into the perfect roles, but since we don't have one, the next best thing is to understand the cast we already have.

In this book I will show you and your cast how to use the concept of the four basic temperaments to understand yourselves and to learn how to get along in the family with each other.

Since you, as the Director, cannot predetermine the personality each child will have, your goal should be to find out as quickly as possible what tendencies each one has. Based on that, you can train up your child in the way he should go, not the way you might dream up or desire. Most parents, not aware of the different personalities, bring up all their children in approximately the same manner. They wonder why Suzy Sanguine talks all the time and forgets her chores, why Charlie Choleric bosses his friends around and even seems to have control of you. Why Martin Melancholy is so neat and organized and gets hurt so easily, why Phyllis Phlegmatic is so relaxed and doesn't seem to care one way or another about any of your exciting plans.

In the last few years, studies have shown that children are born with pre-packaged personalities. Obviously, environment can alter what God has created, but our aim as parents is to accept the basic inborn traits and not to try to change them. The University of Minnesota study, "Twins Reared Apart," produced convincing proof of inherited personality by testing identical twins separated at birth and brought up in different homes. When invited to participate, these twins came together and were dumb-founded to meet face to face with a replica of themselves in looks, mannerisms, attitudes, sociability, and personality.

In my seminars, as I have used the Minnesota study and a comparable one done at Indiana University, I have had identical twins give me personal evidence of their similarities. Janette and Annette were born seven minutes apart, both married evangelists, and twice gave birth to babies at the same time. Although they live 800 miles apart, they frequently do the same things on the same day and later in a phone call make startling connections.

Lana and Lorna, separated at birth and later reunited, found when they visited each other that they had the same wallpaper in their master bedrooms and many of the same outfits in their closets. Another pair told me that they had been apart thirty years and when brought together they discovered that both wrote and illustrated children's books. Jean and Joan were brought up to-gether and had many similarities. They think alike and say the same things simultaneously. They like the same colors and chose the same kind of cars independently. They even fell in love with the same man, but Joan was the one who married him. When they buy the family presents and cards, they frequently choose exactly the same one.

Brenda and Linda each weighed 5 pounds and 13 ounces at birth and their mother dressed them alike for eighteen years. They both had hernia surgery and became ill at the same time even when apart. They both are Melancholy and both married Phlegmatics in a double wedding. When people first meet them they are struck as much by their identical gestures as their dupli-cate looks. They have been apart fifteen years, but in a reunion last summer they both arrived in the same green dress and identi-cal shoes. They like the same food and people, and their favorite candy bar is Baby Ruth.

From my personal study of these case histories and many others I have confirmed that we do inherit our personalities as well as our looks, hair color, and body size. To make our personal-ity review applicable to our own cast, let's turn to the *Personality*

Profiles on pages 78 to 81 of the book and check off one trait on each line for ourselves. Transfer your marks to the same word on the scoring sheet and add up your totals. Have all the teens and adults take the same profile and estimate the younger children's personalities by reading over the Personality Patterns on the next page.

Your children will not have to be very old before you can sense their personalities. The *Popular Sanguine* will laugh a lot, love fun, and enjoy being with people. Marita was the life of the party from the time she was two years old.

The *Powerful Choleric* will give orders as soon as he can talk. Our little grandson, Bryan, at 21 months looked up at my husband one night, pointed in front of him with his finger and stated clearly, "Poppa, here!" Fred moved immediately to his side and Bryan knew he had Poppa under firm control.

The *Perfect Melancholy*, who is well-behaved and can be disciplined by a disapproving glance, will start lining up his toys in rows when he is still a toddler. Our son Fred put all his stuffed animals in a certain order on his bed each day and if anyone moved one of them, he knew.

The *Peaceful Phlegmatic* is the child most eager to please as he wants to conform to your wishes and will do whatever makes people happy. My son-in-law, Randy, as a Phlegmatic child went out with his parents many nights a week and sat quietly wherever they placed him, causing them no trouble.

As we become acquainted with the different personalities, we will find explanations for the behavior of ourselves and others. We will develop a new tolerance for those people who aren't like us and begin to accept our children as God made them to be, not as we might want them to become.

Let's look now at how the cast of characters interact. We'll take the *Popular Parent* who wants life to be one big party, the *Powerful Parent* who automatically takes charge of any given situation, the *Perfect Parent* who feels anything worth doing is worth doing right, and the *Peaceful Parent* who is consistently pleasant and wants to avoid conflict. We'll explain the probable relationship between each type of parent and the different kinds of children. As you read these next chapters and integrate the information from your Personality Profile, you will find your role as a parent and then see the cast description of each one of your children.

Let's raise the curtain on your personal production of raising children.

> Help me, Lord, to keep my
> mouth shut and my lips sealed.
> (Psalm 141:3 TLB)

1. The Popular Parent
   (The Sanguine)

The *Popular Parent* loves to have fun and thrives on an audience. Often the children become the audience and the Sanguine mother will really turn on her stage personality when a group of little friends arrive who think she's so much more entertaining than their own mother. As long as the Popular mother gets attention, she will play games with the children, but since the Sanguines all get their self-worth from the response of those around them, a disinterested group will cause them to turn off their charm. Why bother being cute and adorable if no one cares?

Recently I met Yole at a party and she reminded me of the time ten years ago that she had come to me asking for help. She had heard me speak on the personalities and she wondered why she couldn't get along with her son. The minute she mentioned that we had met at a coffee shop on the freeway, I remembered the situation. Yole, a bright-eyed, adorable Sanguine, had a Melancholy son of six and as we talked about him I could see that he did not respond to Yole's humor. She would get angry when she'd tell me what hilarious thing she had done that he had refused even to notice. She wanted to be the clever comedienne but her audience appeared to be bored.

There is no worse punishment for the Popular Parent than being ignored by the family. As I shared this discouraging thought with Yole, she realized that she was killing herself performing for a son who didn't think she was cute; yet the less he applauded, the harder she tried. As she explained to me at the party, once she saw what she was doing and toned down her approach, her son began to respond to her. Now he is sixteen and they both understand each other. Without a knowledge of the four personalities, we only find people who see things our way one time out of four. With this learning we can get along with people whether or not they are like us. Let's not depend upon the law of averages to help us.

Ever the showman, the Popular Parent would like to have the starring role and have an eternal position on center stage without being responsible for any of the hard work or details. Responsibility is not a plus in the Popular Parent's mind and frequently the other personalities call them air-heads. However, the mistakes they make that would embarrass others become fascinating material for their ever-growing reservoir of entertaining stories.

A light-hearted, possibly light-headed, Popular personality from Phoenix wrote me this story. If it had happened to a more serious person it would have been buried away in a box forever:

"My husband's nephew had his sixth birthday and I had gotten a darling tooth pillow for him to use after he pulled a tooth. Well, I boxed it all up, gift-wrapped it, and mailed it to Tennessee and was very proud of the 'different' gift I had sent. Later they called and said there was nothing in the box and they wondered what happened. Poor Aaron had looked and looked but found nothing. I couldn't figure out what happened as I even remembered putting the pillow in the box. Sure enough, back in the hall closet *in a box* was the pillow. Somehow I had mailed the wrong one! An empty one!"

This kind of a mother is most appreciated by children of a similar personality who can laugh along with them.

The Popular Parent with a Popular Child
(Sanguine with Sanguine)

The Popular Parent will relate well with the Sanguine children as they can all make life into a game and leave the chores for those other people who like to work. As long as the child is no competition, their mutual love of fun and sense of humor will bind them together. However, in teen years the Popular Parent may enter into competition with the Popular child. When the teen girl brings home a boy friend, mother may divert his attention to herself, causing the insecure child to be jealous. If the daughter complains, the Popular Parent, always wide-eyed and innocent, will respond, "What did I do wrong? I was only being pleasant to your friend."

Since Sanguines bounce back quickly from any defeat, don't hold grudges, and can't remember what happened yesterday, they seldom get depressed and are usually optimistic. They bring a ray of sunshine into any room they enter.

The strength in this relationship is the mutual sense of humor, the zest for life, and the ability to give profuse compliments to each other. Marita and I had what we called our mutual admiration society. Indeed, any time we need a pick-up today, we call each other.

The weakness here is that in their pursuit of happiness Populars may never get life pulled together at one time. Popular students are frequently voted Miss Congeniality or Most Likely to Succeed, but without forcing themselves to set goals and get organized they may miss their potential mark.

Popular Parent with the Powerful Child
(Sanguine with Choleric)

Popular Parents will enjoy the strengths of the high-achieving Powerful children, brag about their achievements, and share the spotlight in any honors. The problem comes when the child, sensing the parent's lack of resolve and follow-through, takes control of the parent's life, dictates the time when they wish to be picked up, and reprimands the parent for being late.

Popular Parents often unconsciously allow this shift of control because they don't like to work, so desperately need to be loved and will do anything to avoid problem situations where they might be unpopular. When the Powerful teen is a boy, he becomes protective of poor, mixed-up mother, but when it's a girl, she may look at mother in despair, take over control of the house and become father's best friend.

If the Popular Parent is the father, the Powerful child will enjoy him until he sees his father's vulnerability and cleverly flatters him into getting his own way.

The strength in this relationship lies in the double optimistic outlook of both and in the parent's giving the praise for achievement that the Powerful child so desires.

The weakness comes in the gradual shifting of roles and control. The Popular Parent must always be aware that the Powerful child is out to capture new territories, slay a few dragons, and take over the throne.

Popular Parent with the Perfect Child
(Sanguine with Melancholy)

Popular Parents will have the least understanding for their Perfect Melancholy children who don't respond well to their parents' bubbling humor. Since response is what Popular Parents need, this deeply intuitive child makes an inner decision not to give them what they want. They take secret pleasure in their quiet power to unnerve mother by refusing to applaud her antics. My Melancholy son once said, "It's amazing that people pay money to hear you speak. I guess that's because they don't have to listen to you for nothing."

This Perfect child not only doesn't appreciate the humor of the Popular Parent but, because he takes everything to heart, he is easily hurt by the flip comments the parent makes in the attempt to be funny.

The other major problem with this combination is their opposite concept of time. The Melancholy child has a mental clock-calendar combination that keeps him on time and records the failures of the Popular Parent who doesn't know what day it is and has no sense of timing. I'm convinced that if a child prodigy were born to a Sanguine mother, the child's talent would die on the vine because the mother would forget to get him to his lessons and not have the discipline to sit by his side during hours of practice. That just wouldn't be much fun.

My ten-year-old grandson Randy is a Perfect child. He has the Melancholy strengths in that he is quiet, studious, well-behaved, and musical. He can memorize his piano pieces easily, and testing shows he has a genius IQ in math and science. As with every one of us, his strengths are accompanied by some weaknesses. He wants all of life to be in order and withdraws to his room when his noisy brothers get on his nerves. He does not have a high tolerance level for confusion and he doesn't adjust easily to schedule changes. He tends to be critical and notice mistakes.

Overriding his memory of the negatives is a sweet sensitive spirit, a loving nature, and a desire to become a doctor. He and I are the Popular/Perfect Grandparent/Grandson combination and because we understand each other and the personality strengths and weaknesses, we have a close relationship and he is my "special boy."

One day I took him to Carl's Jr. for lunch and he ordered a hamburger. We sat down with our food and he took the top off his burger. He looked up with a sad face and said, "Do you know what I don't like about this place, Grammie?" I didn't think we'd been there long enough to give a review, but I dutifully asked, "What?"

"They don't even center the hamburger on the roll! All they do is throw down a roll, drop the burger on any old way, plop on two pickles and this lettuce leaf and they call this a hamburger!"

Because he looked so depressed, I added, "Randy, there are some restaurants where if you knew what went on in the kitchen you wouldn't eat there."

"Well, Grammie, this is one of them."

He then centered his hamburger on the roll, took off the pickles and ate his meal in a resigned fashion. When he had finished he began to tell me how difficult it was living with little brother Jonathan. "He sneaks into my room when I'm not around, he takes my toys out of the boxes and doesn't return them, and he steals my batteries."

As I tried to commiserate, he brightened up and said, "There's one good thing about having a new little brother."

"What's that?" I asked.

"Now Jonathan's going to find out what it's like to have a little brother."

His glee soon turned to horror as he added, "I just realized. If Jonathan has a little brother that means I have *two* of them!"

This so did him in that he could hardly get enough energy to walk to the car.

If I didn't understand the personalities, I would have felt our luncheon was a failure but the fact that I had listened and not tried to jolly him up gave him a feeling of acceptance. When I dropped him off at home he thanked me for a "very nice time."

The Popular Parent or grandparent has to accept the Perfect child as he is and not try to make him over.

Once we understand and use our new-found knowledge there is hope! One Popular Sanguine mother who was divorced and trying to raise her children alone came to hear me speak on the personalities. She went home to put what she'd learned into practice. After several months Sally wrote me this letter about how she had learned to get along with her Melancholy son:

Dear Florence,

Developing a good relationship with my children has been something I have had to really work at, just like with any other person. Maybe even harder since I am so close to them and can see so many ways I'd like to change them. And, of course, in my present situation, my children have felt such a rejection from their father, I have felt it even more important for me to understand my children as well as work at forming good relationships with them.

The first step took place this summer when the Lord showed me I was not totally accepting my Melancholy son as he was. The sad part was he was feeling it long before I saw it, and we were constantly having verbal battles in which no one really won. He is a very gifted child with computers, the most important part of his life right now. I know nothing about them and furthermore really don't care to learn much about them. However, as I began to show interest in his interest and build him up in the areas he is good in, he began to blossom into a new person. Our battles have become further and further apart, which leads me to believe he is secure in my love and acceptance. I realize too I cannot be his Holy Spirit and have backed off on trying to help him become the spiritual giant I thought he should be at 14.

Once I began to let go, the Lord began to really work and it has been so exciting to see what He is doing with Jim.

One of the natural tendencies in child-raising is to try to make each little one to be like us. The Popular Parent wants them all to be light-hearted and fun, the Powerful wants them all to accept his goal and march straight for it, the Perfect wants everyone to do everything seriously and on time, and the Peaceful wants them all to calm down and relax. When we don't have any measuring stick and don't realize each child comes prepacked as an individual with strengths and weaknesses, we use up much of our own energy trying to convert the group to our way of thinking.

Speaker/author Bill Sanders of Kalamazoo, Michigan, wrote me after coming to CLASS and hearing about the personalities. His daughter Emily was four years old at the time and was a Perfect Melancholy. The night before coming to CLASS he had given her an ultimatum. In his words, "If you don't answer people when they talk to you I'm not going to take you any more places in public with me. You will have to stay home the rest of your life with the babysitter.' That was Sunday evening. After your class on Monday I ran in the house and said, 'Guess what Daddy learned today, Emily?' She said, 'What Daddy?' I said, 'You can be anyone you want to be. You don't have to talk like Mom and Dad. If you don't want to say goodbye or hello, you don't have to.' Her eyes brightened up and she said, 'Oh, thank you Daddy. I love you so much,' and she gave me a hug. I quizzed her a couple of days later and she hadn't forgotten a word of that lesson. Even though she was only four years old, I was trying to make her my jolly sanguine self."

The Popular Parent with a Peaceful Child
(Sanguine with Phlegmatic)

Popular Parents will enjoy the relaxed, unpressured attitude of the Peaceful Phlegmatic child, but will be disappointed when this child refuses to get excited over their numerous brilliant ideas. The more the Popular Parent pushes for energetic enthusiasm, the more stubborn this child will become. The two share a mutual disinterest in organization and they both are casual about appointments and time, but the differences become apparent in the area of enthusiasm. The Popular Parent lives for excitement and the Peaceful child wants to avoid it. The Popular Parent loves noise and confusion, the Peaceful child wants it quiet. Another conflict comes in the area of decision making. The Popular Parent loves to do things on the spur of the moment, while the Peaceful child has difficulty in making decisions in the best of times and becomes traumatized when an excited parent pushes for an instant decision.

Another problem Popular Parents have to understand is that their friendly, outgoing ways come across to their Peaceful and Perfect children as loud and aggressive and their sense of humor and spontaneous actions embarrass the more reticent natures. If we don't realize this and modify our manners and turn down our volume when we're with them, they will retreat into a humiliating depression.

Fred, Jr. didn't like to go marketing with me as I always spoke to absolute strangers whom he felt I had no business addressing. He asked me before his track meets that I not cheer, as hearing my voice unnerved him. All the other mothers were screaming but I had to be restrained. Peaceful Perfect children want us to be supportive but to keep quiet about it.

Debbie from Texas wrote me about how she had managed to get her family into the front row at a sell-out seminar I had done.

As a Popular Parent she had bragged to her children that she knew me. They drove over 100 miles to get to the church and arrived in the afternoon, hours before the scheduled time. True to her temperament, Debbie had not sent in for tickets ahead of time assuming there would be no problem picking them up at the door. She came into the empty church in the afternoon and put Bibles on the seats in the front row to reserve them.

When she returned in the evening she was given green pieces of construction paper cut in squares as tickets and told these tickets would allow her into the overflow room where she could watch on a monitor. Naturally, she was not about to sit in an overflow room so she went to the entrance with her green tickets and told the lady at the door that she knew me and had already saved seats in there. The lady was a Powerful who was addicted to her duty and she was not impressed or moved. "You can pick up your Bibles afterwards but you may not go in there now. To get in this room you need pink tickets and those are sold out."

Debbie looked around and saw people passing in pink pieces of paper. Sensing she was going to do something strange, her children begged her to go sit where she belonged, but as they were tugging on her, she spotted a pink poster on the wall. Without hesitation she pulled the poster down and asked her son for his pocket knife. She took her one Sanguine daughter to the ladies' room where they laid the poster on the counter and together they measured and cut out pink tickets the same size as their green ones. Some people looked at her strangely, but no one dared ask what she was doing. Sanguines exude confidence and no one thinks of questioning them.

Debbie threw her green tickets in the trash and emerged with pink ones as if she'd had them in her possession for weeks. Her Perfect and Peaceful children had been quietly huddled in the foyer awaiting her return and wondering what mother was up to now. She smiled and told them proudly, "We have pink tickets. Let's go." She pushed them all to a different entrance, obviously avoiding the lady who had refused to let her in. The next person took her pink tickets without question and she proceeded to the front where her Bibles and seats were awaiting her arrival. She was thrilled with her brilliant handling of the situation and didn't realize this whole procedure had made nervous wrecks of her children. Later, when she asked one Peaceful child how she'd enjoyed my speaking, the girl replied, "I didn't hear a word she said. I was scared to death any minute the police were going to come in and drag us away."

Naturally Debbie had to write and tell me this story, a perfect example of the Popular Parent functioning without thought as to the feelings of her more reticent children.

The strengths in the Popular Parent and Peaceful child are their love of wit, their casual attitude, and their lack of any compulsions for power or perfection. Left to their own devices, this pair will forget what they were supposed to do and not care enough to worry about it. What difference does it make as long as we're having a good time?

If you are a Popular Parent, realize your major strengths are in the personality area and your weaknesses in scheduling and follow-through. Enjoy your Popular children, be proud of your Powerfuls, accept the serious nature of your Perfect ones, and uplift your Peacefuls. Once you know who's in the cast, you may want to write a whole new script.

> Quick, Lord, answer me—
> for I have prayed.
> (Psalm 141:1 TLB)

2. The Powerful Parent (The Choleric)

Because the *Powerful Parent* instantly becomes commander-in-chief in any situation, being in charge of the family seems a natural for them. All they have to do is line up the troops and give orders. It all sounds so simple. Cholerics believe that if everyone would only do things their way now we could all live happily ever after. The Powerful father is accustomed to giving firm orders in the business world without anyone second-guessing him, and he expects the same respect at home. The Powerful mother, usually married to a Peaceful man who wouldn't dream of disagreeing with her, controls the family firmly, and her quick decisions are usually right. The home with a Powerful Parent is usually businesslike and fast-paced unless someone stages an insurrection.

Not only is the home under control but the Choleric parent is the one who can even make work out of leisure time. This individual doesn't like any rest and considers relaxing a sin that he will never fall into. One Powerful man took his children to

Disneyland. He felt noble to be giving up his productive time to humor the family. He bought the tickets and let everyone know how much they cost. Somehow the Powerful person seems unable to do anything without attaching a value to it and announcing it. (Every time my mother-in-law would give me a present she would say, "Be careful with that, it was very expensive.")

This man marched his children into Disneyland for a "fun-filled" day. After an hour a cloudburst hit the area and his wife and children wanted to head for the car. "What do you think you're doing?" he asked. "We paid good money to get into this place and we are not going to let a little rain spoil our fun. You will go on the rides and you will enjoy it. We are going to get our money's worth!"

When this man's Peaceful wife told me the story it was both pitiful and hilarious. "Can you imagine having fun on a roller-coaster in a pouring-down rain when you can't see a foot in front of you and the children are crying to go home!"

This Powerful man not only got his money's worth but he achieved another triumph. The family has never asked him to take them to Disneyland again!

The Powerful Parent with a Powerful Child— (Choleric with Choleric)

When two Powerfuls live together there are three alternatives. The most pleasant one is that they both agree and their march toward the goal is done to the same drumbeat. This is possible when, for example, a strong, athletic father produces a son who has similar desires and they mutually dedicate their lives to sports. Even though this provides a positive relationship with this pair, their mutual goals and admiration may be so close that the other children, and sometimes the wife, feel left out and inferior.

One family I counseled came to me with a homosexual son. "How did this happen?" they cried out. "We're good Christian people and we've brought them all up in the church." As the father talked of his first son, John, his namesake, he was seething with anger and bitterness. "How could he do this to me?" He had not a clue as to what had happened in the family and yet in a short time I could see the admiration he had for his second son, Rick. Obviously he and Rick were both Powerful people with the same interests. The father loved hunting and they lived in an area where this was considered the manly thing to do. From the time Rick was a little boy, he loved going out in the woods with his father and guns fascinated him. The fact that this sport helped bind these two together was a positive factor but it eliminated any relationship with his son John who was a Peaceful, hated anything to do with shooting, and was allergic to just about everything growing in the woods.

When I talked with John he informed me that his father had let him know from the beginning that he would never be a "real man" if he didn't love the outdoors. Every time the two hunters would head for the woods, John was told "It's too bad you aren't coming with us." This statement was made in a demeaning tone and John was made to feel like a wimp.

His mother, hurting for him, would baby him and console him and keep him in the house with her. John had musical talent and he was cast in singing roles in school productions. When I asked his father how supportive he'd been of John's talent, he scoffed at the possibility that being in plays had any positive aspects for a boy. "That's sissy stuff. Once I'd seen him in leotards dancing like an elf, I refused to go again. I couldn't stomach my son in that fruity stuff. His mother has made a fool out of him!"

Here was the typical setting to produce a homosexual son: A father who tells the boy he's not masculine according to his standards of manhood. A mother who makes up for this treatment by overprotecting the boy. He relates to the feminine side of his parents and yet emotionally he is desperate for his father's love and acceptance. When a man approaches him with warmth and understanding, he's vulnerable and open for male affection. The initial advance is not sexual but loving and paternal. However, once it advances to a sexual relationship the chances of a return to normalcy are remote, though not impossible.

Although this chapter is not in any way intended to be a thorough study of homosexuality, it is indicative of what I personally find in Christian families. The same results can come from a home where the father is deceased or divorced. It can stem from a passive father who doesn't enter into the mainstream of family life and leaves control up to his wife, or an aggressive father who is so dedicated to his work, his church, his sports, or all three that he ignores his children in any emotional relationship. (Obviously the reverse of this male problem can happen when a daughter has a negative relationship with the mother and is told by the father, "You should have been a man—you have a man's mind.")

John, Sr., was an example of a Powerful personality. He set up his own standards on what a real man did and had no peripheral vision. Either you fit his mold or you were wrong. Since he owned his own business, no one bucked him for control. His family had been dominating forces in his church for generations and were the largest single financial supporters, so he spoke with an unquestioned voice of authority in church.

His Peaceful, Phlegmatic wife had learned early in marriage to do things his way or suffer his wrath so she agreed with anything he said. Here was a strong, intellectual, successful businessman and church elder who had been able to control everything he touched in life but this one son. Typical of the choleric characteristics, he was without any insight as to what he might have done to contribute to what he called "the utter failure of this boy to grow up to be a man. I offered to take him with me. He had his chances and he's just going to have to live with the consequences of his choices."

Those of us who are Powerful Parents must learn to take off our single-minded blinders and realize that just because someone isn't "like me" it doesn't make him wrong. It is so natural for this strong personality to look at his successes and judge everyone who doesn't fit into one of his niches as a square peg. When this misfit is his own child, this attitude can have disastrous results.

We have looked at the first possibility in a Powerful/Powerful parent-child relationship. They can see eye-to-eye and agree on their goals in life. The cautious side of this positive connection is when, because of it, other family members are made to feel inferior, not masculine (or feminine), or hopeless.

The second path this similar parent-child union can take is constant friction and fighting. Each one is determined to win and they are often at each other's throats. Neither one will give in because each one knows he's right. Two Cholerics at war may provide sport for them but it keeps the rest of the family in a nervous emotional state and makes evenings at home seem like target practice. These two battling Powerful personalities, whether they are parent-child, both children, or both parents, must be brought to the bargaining table. Think of this meeting as "Peace Talks" with warring nations and set down some rules of conciliation. There may need to be an outside authority, sometimes called an intervention or confrontation therapist, to show these two what they're doing to themselves and how they are promoting dissension in the family unit. From my experience with this volatile combination, I seldom see them come to a meeting of the minds on their own initiative. Remember, "He that is soon angry dealeth foolishly" (Proverbs 15:17).

Choleric children are very hard to punish as they need to win so badly that they will never give you the satisfaction of letting you know you have made a point; yet, you cannot allow constant scrapping for control to become the norm. Discuss areas of dissension, set down working rules, and stick to them. Remember when you as the parent argue, the children have already won because they got you to enter the fray.

The third possibility in this situation is that one of the Cholerics gives up, puts on a Phlegmatic mask, and pretends not to care. This may appear to be a Peaceful solution for the one who wins control, but it so represses the other one that some unexpected day the lid will blow and everyone around will be hit by the flying pieces. I know one Powerful Parent who was in control of everything but her young daughter. The child was precocious and powerful and managed to overwhelm a strong mother. The child made decisions for herself, told her brothers and sisters what to wear each day, and chose the restaurants where the family ate.

One day when she reprimanded her mother for having failed to feed the dog on time, something snapped in the mother's mind. Suddenly she realized she had allowed this child to change positions with her. She became so instantly furious that she slapped the child around and banged her head against the wall. Obviously, the child couldn't imagine why the mother went wild when she had only mentioned the dog was hungry.

Whenever we totally sublimate our natural personality for any period of time, it will come bursting out when we least expect it. If the Powerful child is the one held down, and if he is made into a "yes man" at home, he will usually take his hostilities out on his peers at school or on his teachers. He will probably marry a Peaceful person and overcontrol that individual to make up for all the years he was held down without being able to express a heartfelt opinion.

It is obvious that two Powerful personalities are programmed for potential problems, but with an understanding of why they both desire control and a discussion of the division of authority, much grief can be spared. If you are already in this power struggle, read this section to your family, let them offer opinions without your second-guessing them, establish some guidelines, and ask them to help you abide by the rules.

The strengths in this powerful combination are in their drive for success, ability to achieve, and willingness to be responsible for the rest of the family. The weaknesses lie in their feisty, volatile natures and their absolute need to win every battle. If these two don't see eye to eye or compromise their positions, life becomes a battleground and other family members the casualties.

Powerful Parent with a Perfect Child
(Choleric with Melancholy)

When the controlling parent deals with the sensitive child, his main aim must be to lift up the spirit of this little one and not crush him. Because the Melancholy child is deeply emotional and likes to think things over rather than leap into instant responses, the Powerful Parent is apt to jump on this child and expect quick action. Since the Perfect child is easily intimidated, acts of aggression will immobilize his ability to move at all. Because the strong parent spouts off and then puts the incident behind him, he or she can't believe that three days later the Melancholy child is still brooding over something they've long forgotten.

When our Melancholy grandson Randy had his fifth birthday, I had an all-purpose party for him, his father, and my husband who all have February birthdays. Being practical and home very seldom, I felt this collective party was an admirable idea. Lauren and I, both Powerful Parents, felt we were killing three birds with one stone and were delighted with the pile of presents we had amassed for the occasion. In the middle of dinner, young Randy said he felt sick and he withdrew to the bedroom. We finally pulled him out to open his presents which he did mechanically with no enthusiasm. We pleaded with him to tell us what was wrong, but in typical Melancholy fashion, he would give us no clues. Several days later, after much questioning, Lauren finally got out of him that he didn't want to have a party for everyone at one time. "That is worse than no party at all," he cried.

He also was crushed that night when he realized the pile of presents was not all for him but had to be shared. "It's not fair to put the presents out there and then tell me they're not all mine." This double shock to his sensitive spirit had caused him to withdraw from his own party, and the typical Melancholy inability to bounce back quickly from his hurts kept him from enjoying the presents which were for him.

Without an understanding of the different personalities, the Powerfuls would be apt to seize upon this situation as a natural opportunity to give a lecture on the evils of selfishness when what was needed was a loving, soothing balm of understanding. One year later, when I had put this incident far behind me, little Randy came quietly up to me and whispered, "Could you give me a birthday party that's just for me?"

The Perfect child never forgets and doesn't respond to demeaning lectures. The positive side is that these children are introspective and are harder on themselves than on others. They rethink their various experiences and ultimately come up with the "right solution."

Two years later, without being asked any questions, Randy said to me, "Grammie, it's all right if you have a party for everybody together. I'm grown-up now and I'm not selfish any more."

If you are a Powerful Parent with a Perfect child, tone down your approach, be sensitive to his or her feelings, and know that, like elephants, such children never forget.

The strengths in this combination are that the Powerful Parent can motivate this reticent child who has so much ability. He can stimulate his creativity and pull him out of his shell. The negatives come when the parent is impatient with this child who wants to think things over for a while and then spouts off critical or angry words that devastate the child and put him into a depression. Speak softly and don't even carry a big stick.

Powerful Parent with a Peaceful Child
(Choleric with Phlegmatic)

The Powerful Parent loves the Peaceful child because by nature he is a follower and is most willing of all to do what the strong parent tells him. Since his inner desire is to avoid any sign of conflict, he wants to do what will make you happy. Since the Powerful Parent's aim is to keep people under control, he will rejoice in the child's spirit of obedience. This combination is what we tend to think of as the norm. Without an understanding of the personalities, we fall into the pattern of expecting all parents to be disciplined leaders working lovingly with obedient children. When we personally have neither of these norms, we think we are the only ones in the world who are failures; but as you can see, there are sixteen possible combinations and no two will function identically. Worse than that thought is that if you have four children, they may all be different! What you learned by trial and error with the first one may not work with the others! Once you grasp what personality each member of your family possesses, you will be able to look at each one separately, understand their strengths and weaknesses as well as your own and your mate's, and begin to pull the cast together.

The problem in this ideal parent-child blend comes not in arguing or depression, but in lack of motivation. Because the Powerful Parent is the most highly productive of all and thinks in units of work, he can't believe that normal people can exist who have no burning desire to "get up and at 'em." People without goals must be lazy. At some point, the Powerful Parent looks at his Peaceful child who has never caused him a moment's grief in his life and suddenly wonders when the child is going to get moving. Why isn't he going out for football? Why doesn't she want to run for class president? Without thinking, the parent begins to ask these questions, expecting them to spur the child on to action. Because the Peaceful person's greatest emotional need is to be made to feel of some value and worth, these pointed questions achieve exactly the opposite of what they were intended to do. The Phlegmatic child says to himself, *They don't think I'm any good just being myself. They'll only love me if I do some great and mighty deed.*

Instead of being goaded into action, this child shuts down what little motivation he might have had, retreats into lying around watching television, and further frustrates the parent.

Often I'm asked, "How do you motivate a Phlegmatic?" The answer is, "Not easily." If I could come up with a motivation pill guaranteed to work, I could grow rich and retire. There is no simple formula to arouse the Peaceful personality into dynamic action, whether it is for your child or your mate. The one thing for sure, however, is that making them feel worthless, slow, or dumb will make it worse. This reasoning is foreign to the Powerful who responds to adversity by saying to himself, *I'll show them.*

On this point alone we can see how valuable it is to understand those difficult people who don't function at all as we do.

Each Phlegmatic has some area of proficiency that can be cultivated but the parent may have to dig around to find it. Don't push this child into hot competition, but try some of the less strenuous sports. Don't *ever* compare him with his brothers and sisters and ask, "Why can't you be like them?"

Enjoy his sense of humor, praise his consistent behavior, and be glad you have at least one Peaceful person in the family!

The strengths here lie in the fact that the parent is the Powerful leader and the child is the Peaceful follower, providing a "normal" balance. The problems arise when the Powerful Parent overwhelms the Peaceful child, can't understand why he seems to have no ambition, and knocks him down in an effort to get him up and moving. This pattern of aggressive motivation won't work but a Powerful Parent who understands his child's nature and makes him feel capable and valuable will become a hero to this child looking for a dynamic role model.

Powerful Parent with a Popular Child
(Choleric with Sanguine)

The Powerful Parent with the fun-loving Popular child can be an excellent combination. One gets the work done while the other entertains. Since the Popular child is looking for love in both right and wrong places, the Powerful Parent with an understanding of this emotional need can win his child's undying affection if he lets him know clearly what is expected behavior and then praises him lavishly when he performs anywhere close to form. Sanguine, talkative children are motivated by compliments and approval and devastated by criticism. Appreciate their humor, don't make fun of them, and give them plenty of loving and "treat them kind," for a good child nowadays "is hard to find!"

Sometimes the Popular child with his winning ways becomes the pet of the Powerful Parent and is able to con the parent and get away with behavior for which the others would be punished. I can remember Marita as a child taking money from my wallet and buying me a present with it. I thought she was cute and adorable and for a while I didn't even see it as a negative action. Powerful Parents admire strength and abhor weakness and the Popular child knows how to become what the parent wants. Acting is fun, especially if it produces results.

The strengths of this relationship are in the mutual optimism and enjoyment of people along with a cheerful attitude toward accomplishments. The Sanguine child so desperately wants to please that he or she will follow the forceful leadership of the Powerful Parent until he or she drops doing it.

The weaknesses again only manifest themselves when the parents don't understand their own personalities and their compulsion for work and think everyone should be keeping up with them. Carried to an extreme this drive overwhelms the Popular child who in turn stays out of the parents' path and finds somewhere else to have fun.

A young girl named Sue came to CLASS and learned about the different personalities. She worked as a counselor in a home for underprivileged, abused, or orphaned children and when she went back, she began to categorize her group. Since they had all come from dysfunctional families, they had lower motivation than the average children would be expected to have. The counselor decided to do some case studies and she first divided them into four groups, according to their answers to some simple questions. One was, "If you could be any kind of person in the world, what or who would you choose to be?" She sent me some of their answers.

The Popular Sanguines wanted to be actors, comedians, TV stars in soap operas, cheerleaders, salesmen, Cinderella, or Miss Piggy.

The Powerfuls wanted to be kings and queens, president, Hitler, owners of big houses and limousines, highway patrolmen, and football players.

The Perfects dreamed of being musicians, artists, poets, bankers, Mozart in *Amadeus*, Garfield the cat.

The Peacefuls wanted to be rich so they didn't have to work, live on lakes with row boats and canoes, be golf pros, have long vacations, and more recess.

As she worked with the groups she found the Populars were motivated by abundant praise, Powerfuls by appreciation of all their achievements, Perfects by her encouragement and observation of how well they had done each task, and Peacefuls by a slow building of a trusting relationship where they were finally convinced she valued them.

The other counselors were so impressed by the new and growing excitement in Sue's group that they asked her to teach them how to work with the personalities. One of the unexpected byproducts of this division into groups according to their personalities was that this grouping gave insecure children an identity. For the first time in their lives they belonged to something positive; they became real people.

As I have counseled depressed teenagers, one of their consistent complaints is "I'm a nobody." They don't know who they are and they are sure their parents know even less about them. This lack of identity and self-worth is what propels some of them into cults where they are warmly welcomed and made to feel part of a group that stands for something and demands some kind of discipline.

How great it would be if we could help each one of our children to understand who they are, what their strengths are, what weaknesses they need to overcome, and that we accept them exactly as they are, not as we wished they would turn out to be.

As a Powerful Parent your strengths lie in your motivational and action skills. Your weakness is that you expect instant obedience from all around you. By learning to accept differences and by not just insisting on "your way," you can relax enough to tone down the tension your presence often brings into the home. Realize that ¾ of the population don't have your drive, zest, stamina, and love for work, but that doesn't make them wrong, just different.

> You chart the path ahead of me, and
> tell me where to stop and rest. Every
> moment you know where I am.
> (Psalm 139:3 TLB)

3. The Perfect Parent (The Melancholy)

The *Perfect Parent* is what all the others wish they were; clean, neat, organized, punctual, thoughtful, analytical, detail-conscious, compassionate, talented, dedicated, musical, patient, artistic, creative, poetic, sensitive, sincere, and steadfast. Could you ask for anything more? The Perfect Parent takes on the raising of children as a serious life-time project, and indeed it is, but no other personality so totally dedicates itself to producing Perfect children.

Often this parent resists using the four personalities as a tool because it seems too simple, seems to put unfair labels on people, and can't be found spelled out in Scripture. However, once they decide to give it a fair trial (since they are analytical people), they find the simplicity explains complex issues. They learn the labels are needed to break personality down into understandable units, and the theory becomes a useful tool to obey what the Bible commands in examining ourselves, finding our sins, failures, and weaknesses, and bringing them before the Lord for forgiveness and cleansing.

It's hard to ask the Lord for help in areas we don't know how to find because we have no simple tool with which to discover them. In my experience, once Perfect people examine the use of the four personalities with an open mind, they become excited over how easily they can communicate this skill to their family and others.

For the first time in his life, the deep Melancholy understands why other people don't all see things his way. Previously, he thought everyone should be a perfectionist like him and assumed everyone would want to be if they only knew how. Many had dedicated their lives to helping God conform others into what they perceived He wanted them to be. What an eye-opening experience to find only a fourth of the people in the world have the capacity or desire to do everything perfectly! The Powerfuls want to do it their way, whatever that might be at the moment, the Populars want to make a party out of doing it, and the Peacefuls hope someone else will do it and keep quiet while thus engaged.

Perfect Parent with a Perfect Child
(Melancholy with Melancholy)

When both parent and child are Perfect, everything is done "decently and in order." Rooms are neat, charts are checked, homework is completed on time, research projects are a positive experience. This combination produces child prodigies as each one is dedicated to intellectual pursuits and neither one minds if practice is boring or the routine's dull as long as the goal is a worthy one. What would be too slow for the Powerful, too dreary for the Popular, and too much work for the Peaceful, is just right for the Perfect.

David Feldman, Tufts University psychologist, in his book *Nature's Gambit*, says "A prodigy's talents will not be expressed unless the right conditions are there."[1] These conditions he points out include a child with exceptional ability and a parent who will take the time to find the talent and patiently develop it. The Perfect/Perfect combination is a natural one to produce prodigies.

An article in the *Houston Post* was titled "Child Prodigies, Precocious children are born not made but upbringing still makes a difference." Writer Art Levine said, "It's difficult enough raising children, but when a child proves smarter or more talented than his or her own parents, things become more complicated. Prodigies—people who perform at a high level in a demanding field at an early age—inspire awe, skepticism and even resentment from adults because little is known about why they are so brilliant."[2] He points out that we should spend time searching out each child's personal abilities and training him up according to his basic nature and talent. Parental discipline and a dedication to hard work are needed to produce an outstanding child.

Levine notes that the Jewish race has given birth to an unusually high percentage of prodigies and he credits this to their tradition of hard work and their need to emerge from their underdog persecuted past. Dorothy DeLay, an instructor at Julliard says, "I think it's their work ethic. American families don't give their kids the same motivation."[3]

Not every child will be a genius and not every parent would take the time to develop one if they recognized him, but of all the combinations the Perfect/Perfect would have the greatest chance of success.

Although Melancholy children are basically neat, they want to be neat in their own way and when this way conflicts with mother's way, they may go through a sloppy phase that belies their true personality. One reason may be a temporary rebellion. A teen boy told me that the only way to "really get to" his mother was to leave his room a mess each day. His mother would "go into a tear" and her reaction gave him a feeling of control. Once he'd flexed his independent muscles, he went back to his neat ways with a feeling of self-satisfaction.

The other reason a natural Melancholy child becomes sloppy is that his Perfect Parent has such impossibly high standards that he gives up on the whole program. Becky said, "No matter how hard I tried my mother was never pleased and always told me I could do better, so one day I said to myself, 'Why are you killing yourself cleaning this room all the time when you can't make her happy anyway? Forget it!'"

One of the hardest lessons for the Perfect Parent to learn is to keep the standards within reasonable reach. Help the child attain the goals and praise him when he does it correctly. Don't keep moving the target the minute he gets close to a bull's eye.

The strengths in this Perfect team can be the greatest of all combinations when both parent and child have mutual deep artistic talent of some kind, exceptional organizational skills, and enjoy working seriously together. Since they get hurt easily, if one senses the other is against him, he may withdraw and get depressed. But because they each have the same sensitivity, they will share a sympathy with each other that no other combination can understand. The weakness here would be if they both became depressed at the same time or if one is so perfectionistic that the other one gives up and quits trying.

Perfect Parent with a Peaceful Child
(Melancholy with Phlegmatic)

The uniting of a Perfect Parent with a Peaceful child will produce a low-key, reticent relationship. The parent will be grateful for the quiet, pleasant, agreeable traits that don't cause any noisy conflicts, but they will be discouraged when this child has no interest in serious dedication to any project in life and will assume that they must be a poor parent because they can't get this child excited over the violin.

If the Peaceful child has a Perfect brother who is admired by the parent, he will feel worthless in comparison and probably not try to compete. A parent who is sensitive to this possibility will lift up the Phlegmatic child and not let him die on the vine, but one who puts a high priority on talent and ignores the child without it will add to the Peaceful's feelings of inadequacy and low value.

The Peaceful child is the easiest to get along with but he needs the greatest encouragement of all to live up to his potential. Left to his own in a busy household, he could be the one to slip quietly through the cracks.

The strengths in this combination are that the Perfect Parent is most able to motivate the Peaceful child because the parent does not overwhelm him and because, if he understands the personalities, the parent can gently lead him in the right direction without making him feel stupid as the Powerful parent is apt to do. The caution is that the Perfect Parent may have standards that exhaust the Peaceful child when he looks at them. Remember that the Peaceful child measures all activity by how much energy it will take. If it looks too much like work, he won't try it at all.

Perfect Parent with a Popular Child (Melancholy with Sanguine)

Without a knowledge of the different personalities, this combination could produce disaster. The Perfect Parent expects each child to do things on time and correctly, and can't understand when he discovers this child doesn't have a serious thought or an organized mind. Whatever the parent says, the child has a funny answer and he refuses to get deeply involved in anything. These two tend to bring out the worst in each other. The Perfect Parent gets depressed and feels like a failure when he can't locate this child on a chart. When this Sanguine child gets none of the praise he so desperately needs for survival, he loses any will to perform. His lack of organization and indifferent attitude toward schedules further depresses his parent who becomes critical and nitpicking. These negatives make him feel hopeless, he shuts down his bubbling personality, and saves his humor for people who will appreciate him.

The Perfect Parent must realize that once you've wiped out the Sanguine humor in the Popular child, you have little left. Without an appreciative audience at home, this child feels worthless and his need for approval may cause him to become the class clown or a discipline problem. The Popular child will get attention in any way he can either positive or negative. For the Perfect

Parent, discipline is based on "normal" behavior. The parent sets down the rules and puts up a chart; the children follow the rules, and check off the chart. It sounds simple but with the one child who forgets what he's doing while traveling from one room to the next, lives only for the moment, and can't see long-range consequences (and performs even menial tasks for the praise of an audience), the thought of making a bed alone in his room and then remembering to put a check on a chart borders on the impossible.

If you are the Perfect Parent who expected all your children to line up behind you like little ducks following the leader, you will save yourself migraine headaches if you can see your Sanguine child as a God-given court jester, presented to you for comic relief in a heavy world. Know he is probably not going to be a nuclear physicist but will somehow make a living on his charm and ability to tell a story better than anyone else. This thought may depress you, but when you accept it as a probability, you will help him emphasize his personality gifts.

My mother, a Peaceful with many Perfect talents as a violinist and cellist, wanted all of us to be musicians, but all three of us were, as she said, "all mouth." She put us into music lessons and with some effort I learned to play a few hymns on the piano. Jim took piano and singing lessons, and Ron played the trumpet well enough to be in the high school band. But our Popular personalities were more interested in being funny than in practicing notes.

When Ron was still in grammar school, he began to memorize the words on Spike Jones records. He was able to lip-sync them so perfectly that you would think he was the one singing the songs. He collected sound effect items to enhance his performance. He found an old galvanized tub and spent days filling a pail with broken glass. At a certain point in one record he would pour the glass chunks from the pail into the tub making a horrendous racket. Each time he did this, my mother screamed and grabbed onto a doorframe for support. She knew the world was coming to an end. She tried to dissuade him from "his tomfool pranks" but he happily persisted.

During high school he was in shows, wrote singing commercials, and became a disc-jockey, all instead of doing his homework. Mother knew he'd never amount to a "row of pins," but today he is the most popular radio personality in the Dallas/Fort Worth area. In April Ron asked his loyal audience to send him checks for $20 for no specific reason or cause. Because he has a 29-year track record of being an honest, upright, moral, and generous citizen of Dallas, he has earned the respect of his listening audience. Within three days of his suggesting that they send him $20, he had received almost a quarter of a million dollars! When he reported "that's enough," people still sent him money and were found slipping envelopes under the door at midnight to beat the deadline. Suddenly Ron was on the front page of the Dallas papers, in *People, Fortune, Newsweek,* and *Star,* on *Entertainment Tonight,* NBC, ABC, and CBS news. The Fox Network did a fifteen-minute *Current Affairs* special on him and the *National Enquirer* inquired.

TV evangelists marveled at his drawing power and everyone wondered what he'd do with the money. To this date he has given $100,000.00 to the Salvation Army to equip a clinic for battered wives, $14,000.00 to a school for the underprivileged for a new room, a new heavy-duty refrigerator truck for the Food Bank, and the rest to fix up old houses for the homeless.

Wouldn't Mother be amazed!

Jim became a career chaplain in the Air Force and retired as a full Colonel. I taught English and Speech and now write and speak. We have all made our livings with our mouths in spite of her hand-ringing and pessimistic prophecies.

Realize that not every child is going to do the "normal" things, but as you parents understand and use the Personality Principles you will be able to encourage each child differently according to his particular strengths, even if these don't conform to what you would have liked or expected. Don't try to jam little square pegs into round holes.

As a Perfect Parent you would like each child to be organized, serious, studious, artistic, and brilliant, but because of their own inherent personality children will not automatically conform. Accept this and don't make the child who isn't Perfect feel peculiar, don't make him an outcast from your tidy boat or you may never be able to pull him back in again.

Sherry came to a study group Marita was leading based on my family book, *Your Personality Tree*. She took the Personality Profile and came out Melancholy, the Perfect personality. As she followed the instructions each week and began to dig into her childhood she realized that she had originally been a happy-go-lucky child. Marita suggested she ask the Lord to show her when the shift came in her personality. When she returned the next week she was radiant and excited. She explained that her father was Pastor Perfect and that he obviously had no tolerance for any child who didn't fit the Perfect Christian mold of seriousness and silence. Every time she would be her cheery, funny self, he would say sternly, "Frivolity is a sin."

She learned that basic precept as one would memorize a scripture verse, and so she put away her unacceptable natural personality and put on a Melancholy mask to please her father. Now in her thirties, Sherry is beginning to become who God intended her to be.

Don't take the joy out of your Popular children or you'll have plastic phonies on your hands.

This Perfect/Popular combination can be either an exciting blend of opposite personalities filling in each other's empty spaces, or it can be a painfully misunderstood relationship. In this the Perfect Parent demands order from a child who can't give it and the child, receiving no accolades for what the parent sees as trivial and frivolous performances, shuts down his enthusiasm and excitement and saves his true personality for his friends.

Often a Perfect Parent says to me, "I can't understand why people are so drawn to her. She sure doesn't have much charm at home." Can you imagine why?

Perfect Parent with a Powerful Child
(Melancholy with Choleric)

The Powerful child wants to do what's right in his or her own sight and if that happens to coordinate with your perfectionistic nature, you two will do well. In contrast to the Popular child, the Powerful knows what day of the week it is and can usually out-think his parents automatically. The Powerful has a natural desire for control and your aim is not to shut down his leadership ability but to keep the two of you on the same side. If you hold this aim in mind you will emphasize whenever you agree and tell him constantly how much you appreciate his helping you to run the family. With steady affirmation of the work he is doing, he will become dedicated to high achievement, and he will do half your work for you. He will even remember to check off his chart and do odd jobs you didn't assign him!

Not understanding the Powerful's need for credit will bring trouble down upon you, for if the Powerful decides to set up an opposing team, you will enter into a battle that you may never win. This type of child can instantly become devious and manipulative and can inspire dedicated loyalty from those he selects to be on his side. If he determines to do you in, watch out.

Does this mean you throw up your hands in despair with this child? No, it means forewarned is forearmed. This super-achieving child needs to have daily challenges and constant affirmation. This treatment does not come naturally to the Perfect Parent who is short on praise unless the job is done perfectly. The Perfect Parent's compliments tend to be tinged with the negatives. "You brushed your teeth nicely but the next time, put the cap on the toothpaste."

Learn to separate your praise and instruction, and ask yourself, "Is insisting on perfection worth the risk?"

Some of you Perfect Parents may feel as my mother did that giving compliments will make the children have a "swelled head." Since your Populars eat praise for lunch and can't grow without it, and your Powerfuls will only stay on your side if they know you appreciate what they've done for you, the alternative to compliments is personality death to the first and mutiny to the latter.

When you look at these natures in perspective, you will see the value of meeting your children's emotional needs and keeping them on your team.

> How wonderful it is, how
> pleasant, when brothers
> live in harmony.
> (Psalm 133:1 TLB)

4. The Peaceful Parent
(The Phlegmatic)

The *Peaceful Parent* has the kind, low-key, relaxed, patient, sympathetic nature that we find so agreeable and acceptable in a father or mother. They don't argue or fight, they don't insist on high achievement, they roll with the punches, and they're never irrational or hysterical. What more could any child want?

How many little ones would be glad to turn in their dramatic, emotional, Popular mother, their dictatorial, temperamental, Powerful father, their critical, nitpicking Perfect parent for one Peaceful protector. Let's turn down the volume and take a rest!

Peaceful Parent with a Peaceful Child
(Phlegmatic with Phlegmatic)

The Peaceful/Peaceful combination is ideal in that both parent and child agree that life is "no big deal." There's nothing to get excited over. Let's not "sweat the small stuff."

One couple told me their baby was born so Phlegmatic that for the first month they thought she was in a coma. She didn't care whether she ate or not, and they sometimes woke her up to make sure she was still alive! Amazingly we can often tell the personality of a baby very early when we know what we're looking for.

The little Peaceful child is the easiest to raise, especially for a Peaceful Parent. My son-in-law Randy and his father are both Peacefuls. His father told me how as a child Randy was so adaptable that wherever they took him he would sit quietly and read. He would sleep anywhere and eat at any time.

The problem with this pair of Peacefuls comes later in life when the child is not motivated and the parent doesn't care, or the child wants to get into some sport and the parent feels it's just too much like work. One other weakness in these parents is their ability to overlook the truth if it will save them work. The Peaceful person often finds a little white lie a useful, if not admirable, tool.

When I asked a close friend, Ray, about his childhood relationship with his father, both of them being Peaceful people, he replied it was non-existent. "He listened to sports on the radio but he wouldn't play any with me even though he was a coach." Ray then told me how his father was an athletic director for a school for juvenile delinquents and spent all his available energy on them. Typical of the Peaceful personality, by the time he came home he had no heart for sports with his own son. This perceived neglect made Ray know in his heart that his father cared more for the "bad boys" than his own "good son."

At one point Ray wanted to be in Little League and he had to drag his father to the try-outs. A few days later his father told Ray the coach had called to say he had not qualified for the team. Ray peacefully accepted the fact that he wasn't good enough to play. A while later the coach said to Ray, "It's a shame your father couldn't help us in Little League so you could play." In dismay Ray listened while the coach explained it was not his lack of talent but his father's unwillingness to help coach or drive him to and from the games that had prevented his being accepted.

Ray was so depressed over this revelation that he never tried out for sports again. Typical of the Peaceful personality, Ray has not ever discussed this hurt with his father and his father, not aware that Ray knows the truth, has never brought up the subject. This problem of deception and unwillingness to bring up unpleasant topics is one that strangles relationships, especially between two Peacefuls who will do anything to avoid confrontations, including living a lifetime without any meaningful communications.

The strength in a double Peaceful relationship is that they will both relax with each other and remove the pressures that others are putting on them. They can kick back in their lounge chairs or spend the afternoon in a boat fishing without concern for time or telephone. The negatives are obvious. If the two of them get too happy with each other, they may tune out on the rest of the world and never get on with life, for neither one motivates the other.

Peaceful Parent with a Powerful Child
(Phlegmatic with Choleric)

On Easter Sunday as the family was gathered, I asked my Peaceful son-in-law Randy, "Can you think of any example of you as a Peaceful father with Bryan, a Powerful son?" He thought and said, "No I can't." At that point, two-year-old Bryan sat down on the grass next to Marita's two Schnauzer puppies and their dish of food. As Bryan began to feed them, I noticed he was putting one piece of kibble into each puppy's mouth and then one into his own little mouth. I pointed out to Randy, "Your son is eating dog food."

"Don't do that, Bryan. Don't eat the dog's food, little Bryan," Randy said softly.

Bryan looked him straight in the eye, picked up one more piece, stuck it in his mouth, and smiled at his father.

Typically Randy shrugged and replied, "Oh well, a little dog food won't kill him." I laughed and we both realized what a perfect example he'd given me of the Peaceful father who made token resistance to the strong child and when he found out that to implement his direction he'd have to get up and walk across the lawn, he found it wasn't worth the effort.

It is always easier for the Peaceful Parent not to buck the Powerful child, but this Choleric is a smart, aggressive child. If he can control at two, watch out when he hits thirteen! The Peaceful Parents are always the best loved because they are easy-going, pleasant to get along with, and they don't really care what the child is doing.

I remember my Peaceful mother saying, "I don't care what you do as long as I can't see it or hear it."

The problem with this combination is that the Peaceful Parent's weakness is in the area of discipline and the Powerful child doesn't need to know the meaning of the word "power" before he knows he has it and his parent doesn't.

Sharon shared with me that her first baby had been a Peaceful right from the beginning, totally undemanding and loving to sleep. Often when she was nursing him he would doze off and not wake up until the next feeding time. She was a Peaceful herself and she felt she was an excellent parent because she had this well-mannered, agreeable, flexible child.

Then she had her second baby who was controlling right from the start. He would only nurse out of one side and the minute she put him on the other breast he would push away and scream. Each feeding she would start him on the "wrong side" and he would yell and push. Then she'd shift him to the other side. Sharon said she would wait an extra hour until he was so hungry he was eating his fists and he still refused to nurse from the "wrong side." This Powerful baby was determined from birth that he would control his mother and he did. Sharon laughingly said, "For a whole year I looked like a lop-sided camel."

The major problem with a Peaceful Parent having a Powerful child is that the balance is tilted in the wrong direction. The child has an inner mechanism that tells him he can be in control if he is persistent in his determination and so he is. Without an understanding of this possibility, the Peaceful Parents throw up their hands in despair and wonder where they got this child.

Peaceful Brenda lived with us for several years and then married Peaceful/Perfect Ken. Seldom do two people of similar personalities marry but they did, and they established a very Peaceful household. Neither one ever raised a voice of opposition and they both enjoyed resting. All went well until Brenda gave birth to Michael. We all assumed he'd be calm and Phlegmatic but right from the beginning he surprised us all. Before he could talk he grunted and pointed directions with his finger. His first full sentence was "I can do it myself!" By the time Michael was two, he was in charge and they were checking decisions with him. One day Brenda was on the floor playing with him and she asked, "May I get up, Michael?" He replied instantly, "Just sit down and be a nice lady." Brenda sat down. By some genetic miracle their second baby is also Choleric. Not quite two, Heidi pulls her mother into the right spot and points to a seat. If Brenda sits somewhere else, Heidi tugs on her again until she gets her own way.

When I asked Brenda what she found the hardest in raising strong children, she replied, "The discipline. It's so much easier just to do it their way."

Perhaps the most exhausting combination is the Peaceful Parent who wants to stay calm, cool, and collected with the one or more Powerful children who want constant control and instant action.

Brenda said she has to force herself each morning to make strong statements and establish authority, setting the tone for the day. If she weakens anywhere along the line, Michael and Heidi are both poised for the kill. They don't have to think about it; they instinctively take control.

The best thing about Powerful children is that they are competent and willing workers from a very young age, and they sense when a parent needs help. Use this ability to your advantage and give this child some areas of control. The caution is, just make sure what he controls isn't you!

Peaceful Parent with a Perfect Child
(Phlegmatic with Melancholy)

The similarities in the Peaceful Parent and the Perfect child are that they are both natural introverts, they tend to be pessimistic, they don't initiate conversations, and they need to be inspired to get down to work. When you bestow upon the Peaceful Parent a Perfect child, the combination can be quiet and respectful because of their similarities, but when the quiet child withdraws and becomes depressed the Peaceful Parent prefers not to deal with the problem. It's easier to avoid it and hope it goes away.

One Peaceful father said, "When he clams up it takes too much effort to find out what's wrong. I give him a couple of chances and if he doesn't tell me, then I figure it's his problem." It is his problem but if he feels his father doesn't care, he will retreat further from him. By the time he's a teen the two of them will have no communication at all. The deep child needs a parent who is willing to dig deeply—all the way, all the time.

The positives here are that neither one is pushy and they can enjoy each other's company without having to say a word. Personality-wise, they don't seem to bring the best out in each other and the Perfect child is apt to get critical of the Peaceful Parent and try to get him organized. When the parent resists his suggestions, the child may pull back and give up on trying to communicate. If we can't do it right, let's not bother at all.

Peaceful Parent with a Popular Child
(Phlegmatic with Sanguine)

In contrast to the Perfect child, the Popular child usually brings out the humorous side of the Peaceful Parent who loves to have a good time as long as someone else is preparing the party. The Popular child loves to instigate parties as long as someone will come. The Populars are all a constant source of entertainment and they thrive on response; the Peacefuls are responders to the circumstances around them so they provide a perfect balance. Once the Peacefuls get involved in a humorous repartee, their dry wit often produces the funniest lines and they become downright Sanguine. Because they are responders and not initiators, the Peacefuls react to the people they are with more than any other type. They become whatever it's right to be today. The Peacefuls truly fit the verse, Romans 12:15, "Rejoice with them that do rejoice, and weep with them that weep."

This pair is the least apt to get anything accomplished that isn't downright fun. Neither one is very responsible and they both hope someone else will show up to do the work.

Personality Summary

In the area of household work and projects, any child can learn early in life which parent will do the job and which one will make *him* do it. An analytical child can see that the Popular mother only works if she gets credit and will often forget to check up on what she told you to do. Once the child senses this pattern, he relaxes and doesn't feel any pressure to do his chores because mother won't follow through at least 50 percent of the time and it's worth taking the chance. Even if she has a dramatic tantrum, she'll get over it and soon forget why she was upset.

When Powerful Father bursts in the door the child knows he had better give a quick account of his achievements and be prepared for due punishment if he has neglected his duties. This Powerful Parent often unwittingly causes his child to lie about his behavior rather than "face the music." In working together with a Powerful Parent, the child learns early in life that if you pretend you can't do the job the impatient parent will grab the work away and say, "Here, I can do it faster, let me do it." Chances are if the child is lucky, he'll not get such an assignment again. The smart child will praise the Powerful Parent's ability and speed, and stand in awe of his achievements, thus eliminating his ever being asked to perform these tasks himself.

The Perfect Parent usually communicates early in the child's life that he will never be able to do it right. "Let mother do it. I can do it better." Because of extremely high standards and a critical nature, the Perfect Parent often wipes out a child's desire to try new things and the child often resigns himself to inactivity around the house. "Even if I do it, she'll do it over again, so why bother?" This parent comes equipped with a built-in martyr complex and in a strange way likes to be left with all the work. This gives him or her an excuse for constant complaints of being over-burdened.

The Peaceful Parent doesn't have much inborn zeal for housework, repairs, or projects, and children sense quickly that you can "get away with murder" if you keep your contacts with laid-back father, instead of eager-beaver mother. Since the Powerful Parent is always pushing the Peaceful one into mowing the lawn or fixing the faucet, the children tend to line up in defense of the parent they perceive is being picked on. They know if they stick together the Powerful Parent will do the work after screaming a while about how lazy they all are. The Peaceful Parent would rather listen to the yelling than do the work. Besides, he's learned to tune the noise out with his unique mental volume control button. Peaceful Parents and children learn the value of procrastination. If you postpone doing it long enough, the project may lose its relevance or someone else will have done it. In either case, it's worth a try.

Whichever parent you are, realize that your children don't have to know a Melancholy from a melon to have you all figured out.

To help you figure them out, remember that the Popular Sanguine child will work if he gets enough praise for it, and if you can make the project sound like fun. The Powerful Choleric child will work round-the-clock if he feels appreciated and he will grab control if he can sense a leadership vacuum or a power struggle between his parents. The Perfect Melancholy child will be the first to sort you all out and he will do his projects perfectly as long as you recognize his ability and don't redo what he has accomplished. Let him work alone if he desires as those other people distract him and don't do anything right anyway. The Peaceful Phlegmatic child won't argue or give you trouble. He'll even agree to do what you ask, but he'll test you to see if you mean business. If you forget to check or do it yourself that tells him that as long as he keeps the peace and looks willing, he won't be expected to do much work.

As you understand yourself, your mate and your children, you will learn how to work together with wisdom and knowledge.

How grateful we should all be that once we care enough to understand what makes others tick, we can get along with just about anybody.

"Understanding is a wellspring of life unto him that hath it" (Proverbs 16:22).

5. Cast Instructions

1. Study the Personality Patterns.
2. Explain the concept to your children.
3. Tell them about your childhood.
4. Fill out your Personality Tree.
5. Create a Children's Chart as a teaching tool.
6. Make a Family Cast page with each child.

7. Discuss personal emotional needs.

8. Make this personality analysis a positive experience.

Now that we know the cast of our family production, how can we explain their roles so that they will understand each other?

How can the Personality Profile become of practical value to our family? How early can we teach these concepts to children? The first step is to study the material yourself until you have a working relationship with the different types and can confidently explain them to others. For more background material read my books, *Personality Plus* and *Your Personality Tree*, and do the suggested activities at the end of each chapter. If your children are old enough, have them work through your family research with you and fill out your family's Personality Tree. Share with them your childhood memories, especially when these stories show your own birth personality. My grandchildren love to look at the family tree I had painted on my wall and by looking at the pictures they have begun to learn the names of all their ancestors.

When Jonathan was five I first started teaching him the personalities. One day as we were driving down the freeway I told him, "Jonathan, you are Sanguine. That means you love to have fun."

He giggled and said, "I do love to have fun."

"You also like to go to parties."

"I like to go to parties. Everyone in my class invites me to their parties. They tell me if I didn't come to their party it wouldn't be any fun."

"Jonathan, do you like to stand up front and have people look at you?"

"Oh, I love to be up front. When the teacher asks who wants to come up and help her, I go right up."

We discussed some other traits and Jonathan was thrilled with all of them. Then I said, "Jonathan, Grammie is a Sanguine too." He threw his arms around my neck and squealed with delight. He was so happy to know we were the same. "And Aunt Marita is a Sanguine too," I added.

"Oh, I'm so glad. I love Aunt Marita."

I hadn't realized before how little children want to be somebody. They want to belong to something and know they are like some adult person. Using the personalities in the family gives them a "belonging tool."

I then moved on. "Your brother Randy is a Melancholy."

"Melancholy," he repeated seriously.

"That means he likes to keep his toys in the right boxes."

Wide-eyed, Jonathan exclaimed, "Oh, he likes to do that all right. He doesn't even want me to touch them."

"Poppa is a Melancholy too and he and Randy both like pens."

"They sure do like pens!"

"Uncle Chuck is a Melancholy."

We discussed the traits of the Sanguines and Melancholies and then I asked Jonathan to recite back what he'd learned. He stated proudly, "You and I and Aunt Marita are all Sanguines and we like fun and parties." He thought a moment and then added, "Randy and Poppa and Uncle Chuck are Melancholies." As he said this he leaned over to me and whispered, "Let's not tell them."

What a perfect Sanguine request! Even though I had been positive about each type, Jonathan knew in his spirit that what he was, was the right thing to be—and it was better not to let those other people hear the bad news!

Recently at six, Jonathan said to me without being prompted, "I'm not Sanguine anymore, Grammie. I've calmed down a lot."

Children catch on so quickly with such open minds that we should teach them to understand themselves as early as possible. I have prepared a sample chart you could duplicate as a teaching tool for little children. The original terms given the personalities 2,000 years ago were:

Sanguine   *Choleric*   *Melancholy*   *Phlegmatic*

In this book we will use simultaneously:

Popular   *Powerful*   *Perfect*   *Peaceful*

For little ones I have used colors:

Yellow	*Red*	*Blue*	*Green*
(like the sun)	(like a fire)	(like the ocean)	(like grass)

Children's Chart

Popular Sanguine	Powerful Choleric
Bright	Hot
YELLOW	RED
Like the Sun	Like a Fire
Talker	Leader
Peaceful Phlegmatic	Perfect Melancholy
Cool	Deep
GREEN	BLUE
Like the Grass	Like the Ocean
Follower	Thinker

You could take construction paper of these colors and make the four squares as a visual aid. I have found that using the squares is better positionally than columns, because we can see the opposite personalities more clearly. The bright yellow sun is opposite from the deep blue ocean. The hot red fire is opposite from the cool green grass. The talker is different from the thinker, the leader from the follower.

As you make up a chart you can teach children, teens, and adults from the same visual. Encourage others to talk about how they really feel about themselves, not how they think they ought to be. Help the children to begin to see themselves as part of a group, to identify themselves as more than a little body. Show them why they get along with certain people better than others. Teach them that God made all kinds of people and our purpose is to love them and accept them as they are and not try to make them over to be like us. It is never too soon to learn the truth that God accepts us as we are. He doesn't want us to become little cookie-cutter children all saying and doing the same things.

What a service you will be doing for children and adults alike when you can give them a tool to open up new understanding and acceptance.

"Wherefore accept one another just as Christ also accepted us" (Romans 15:7 NASB).

One other idea that we have used to open up the teaching of personalities is to make a family page for each child and parent, such as the one on page 76. We originally did this at one of our Family Fun Nights. Encourage the children to draw and color in what they see each person to look like. Don't be surprised at their view of you. Marita once drew me with purple hair. The teacher, deep into psychology, called me and suggested I talk with Marita on the hidden significance of her seeing me with purple hair. I prepared for an analytical session and asked Marita the big question. Her simple reply was, "They didn't have any blonde crayons."

As each child fills in the faces on his page, begin to teach him about the personalities using the children's chart. Once children agree on the personality of any family member have them fill

FAMILY FACES

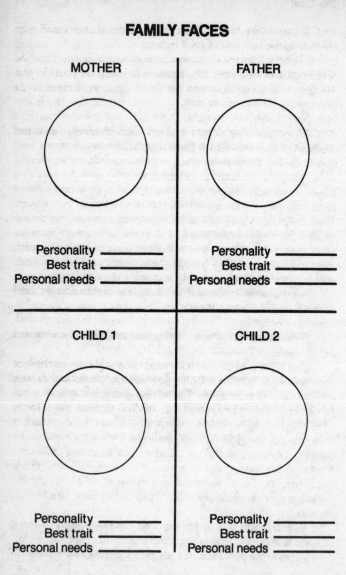

MOTHER

FATHER

Personality _____
Best trait _____
Personal needs _____

Personality _____
Best trait _____
Personal needs _____

CHILD 1

CHILD 2

Personality _____
Best trait _____
Personal needs _____

Personality _____
Best trait _____
Personal needs _____

in the personality blank under each picture. Later spend time discussing the best trait of each person:

"What I like best about daddy is _____." At this point don't get into any negatives as you want to make this study a positive experience and not have them dread these family discussions for fear of criticism.

When the time is right, move into the areas of personal emotional needs. The direction should be into *feeling* needs not *material* ones, but don't cut them down if they say, as young Fred did in one of our discussions, "I need a lightbulb in my closet." We wrote that down and got him a new bulb.

You may add other questions that fit your group such as favorite sports, books, TV shows, verses, all followed by the question "Why?" You might include: "What person would you choose to be if you could be anyone in the world?" For future ideas see the section on Creative Communication. Remember the purpose is to be open and positive, to instigate meaningful conversation, and to give the family a tool of mutual understanding and self-worth. Don't ask questions with yes or no answers. Phrase them so there are no wrong answers.

As you lead your family into wholesome discussions with some feeling you will prepare them for family Bible studies and for the family evaluations we suggest in Chapter 25.

Remember that you can bring up your children in the best house in town and send them to Christian schools, but if they have no feeling of who they are or what they might become, they can still stray from the fold when they reach their teen years. Every hour you spend face-to-face with your children is an investment that only you can make and that, ultimately, will pay dividends.

SANGUINE
—the Popular Personality
(Bright yellow like the sun)

The Extrovert	The Talker	The Optimist
Strengths		Weaknesses

BABY

Strengths	Weaknesses
Bright and wide-eyed	Screams for attention
Curious	Knows he is cute
Gurgles and coos	
Wants company	
Shows off	
Responsive	

CHILD

Strengths	Weaknesses
Daring and eager	No follow through
Innocent	Disorganized
Inventive and imaginative	Easily distracted
Cheerful	Short interest span
Enthusiastic	Emotional ups and downs
Fun-loving	Wants credit
Chatters constantly	Tells fibs
Bounces back	Forgetful
Energized by people	

TEEN

Strengths	Weaknesses
Cheerleader	Deceptive
Charms others	Creative Excuses
Gets daring	Easily led astray
Joins clubs	Craves attention
Popular	Needs peer approval
Life of the party	Con-artist
Creative	Won't study
Wants to please	Immature
Apologetic	Gossips

Emotional needs: attention, approval, affection, acceptance, presence of people and activity

Avoids: dull tasks, routines, criticism, details, lofty goals

CHOLERIC
—the Powerful Personality
(Hot red like a fire)

The Extrovert	The Leader	The Optimist
Strengths		**Weaknesses**

BABY

Adventuresome	Strong-willed
Energetic	Demanding
Outgoing	Loud
Precocious	Throws things
Born leader	Not sleepy

CHILD

Daring and eager	Manipulative
Productive worker	Temper-tantrums
Sees the goal	Constantly going
Moves quickly	Insistent
Self-sufficient	Testing
Competitive	Arguing
Assertive	Stubborn
Trustworthy	

TEEN

Aggressive	Too bossy
Competent	Controls parents
Organizes well	Knows everything
Assumes leadership	Looks down on dummies
Problem solver	Unpopular
Self-confident	May become a loner
Stimulates others	Insulting
Excels in emergencies	Judgmental
Great potential	Unrepentant
Responsible	

Emotional needs: appreciation for all achievements, opportunity for leadership, participation in family decisions, something to control: own room, garage, backyard, dog

Avoids: rest, boredom, playing games he can't win

MELANCHOLY
—the Perfect Personality
(Deep blue like the ocean)

The Introvert	The Thinker	The Pessimist
Strengths		**Weaknesses**

BABY

Serious	Looks sad
Quiet	Cries easily
Likes a schedule	Clings

CHILD

Thinks deeply	Moody
Talented	Whines
Musical	Self-conscious
Fantasizes	Too sensitive
True friend	Hears negatives
Perfectionist	Avoids criticism
Intense	Sees problems
Dutiful and responsible	Won't communicate

TEEN

Good student	Depressed and withdrawn
Creative—likes research	Inferiority complex
Organized and purposeful	Inflexible
High standards	Suspicious of people
Conscientious and on time	Critical
Neat and orderly	Negative attitude
Sensitive to others	Poor self-image
Sweet spirit	Revengeful
Thrifty	Lives through friends
	Needs approval

Emotional needs: sensitivity to deep desires, satisfaction from quality achievement, space to call his own, security and stability, separation from noisy, messy siblings, support from parents: "I believe in you."

Avoids: noise, confusion, trivial pursuits, being "jollied"

PHLEGMATIC
—*the Peaceful Personality*
(Cool green like the grass)

The Introvert	The Follower	The Pessimist
Strengths		**Weaknesses**

BABY

Strengths	Weaknesses
Easy-going	Slow
Undemanding	Shy
Happy	Indifferent
Adjustable	

CHILD

Strengths	Weaknesses
Watches others	Selfish
Easily amused	Teasing
Little trouble	Avoids work
Dependable	Fearful
Lovable	Quietly stubborn
Agreeable	Lazy
	Retreats to TV

TEEN

Strengths	Weaknesses
Pleasing personality	Quietly stubborn
Witty	Indecisive
Good listener	Unenthusiastic
Mediates problems	Too compromising
Hides emotions	Unmotivated
Leads when pushed	Sarcastic
Casual attitude	Uninvolved
	Procrastinates

Emotional needs: peace and relaxation, attention, praise, self-worth, loving motivation

Avoids: conflict, confrontation, initiative, decisions, extra work, responsibility, tension, quarrels

> You shall know the truth, and the
> truth shall make you free.
> (John 8:32)

6. Cast Costumes

All of us have worn masks at some time in our lives. As children we dressed for Halloween and went boldly door-to-door to beg for candy in a manner we would never attempt with an uncovered face. Some of us as insecure teens took roles in the school play so we could dramatically try out on stage what we didn't dare do in real life. Some of us have lived dangerously at costume balls where we became Caesar and Cleopatra or Napoleon and Josephine.

How differently we behave when we don't have to be what we assume other people expect us to be! Somehow a disguise frees us to be daring, to step out of our prescribed pattern of life.

Our aim in this chapter is not to put on a costume, but to take one off, to find out who God really intended us to be, knowing that when we discover the truth about ourselves it will set us free.

It's easy to spot those other people who are phonies, who are acting even off stage; but how about ourselves? Are we for one reason or another putting on costumes that don't fit? Are we, without understanding, wearing a mask in public?

Yes, we all wear masks at one time or another, and there's nothing wrong with some occasional role-playing. But the problem comes when we don't realize what we're doing and how our whole life is somewhat of a subconscious show.

In my twenty years of personality counseling, I have had hundreds say, "I just don't know who I am." There is some vague feeling underneath that what others see is not what's truly inside. This situation is not the same as someone who behaves differently for one afternoon because the pastor's coming or some friend who doesn't mention politics or religion for fear of offending. These behavior modifications are for a reason and a season. What we want to examine is our own natural personality and see if we are real before we try to raise genuine children.

As parents we can't teach something we don't know, and it's difficult to give our children a clear sense of worth and identity if we don't know ourselves. We can seldom lead people beyond where we have been.

Those of us who don't know who we are usually have changed our personality in the past because of some circumstances that showed we were not acceptable as we were. The little Perfect girl wants to please Popular father. Every time she goes to him with problems, he cheers her up by saying, "It's no big deal. Lighten up. You're always too serious. Why can't you be fun like your sister Suzy? See how happy she is. See how she tells stories and entertains her many friends. You'd be a lot better off if you could just try to be like Suzy."

The child, a serious and thoughtful little girl, analyzes what's been said. She wants to please her fun-loving father and be popular like Suzy, and so without knowing what she's doing to her future self-worth, she puts on a Popular mask and tries to be like Suzy. This act may please her father and may fool many people, but when I face this lady at forty trying desperately to maintain a light-hearted approach to life, swinging frequently from loud laughter to outbursts of tears, depressed at her lack of serious achievement, and totally at a loss as to who she is, I see the results of a mask put on to please a parent.

Few of the parents who are putting masks on their children have any idea of what they're doing. Without understanding the personalities, we have no practical measure by which we can judge what we're doing to each other. Some people I talk with as adults have functioned with a mask for so long that they have developed careers and hobbies to fit what they were told to be as children. I have never met a person who was comfortable with himself who was not functioning in his birth personality. God wants us to seek truth in our innermost parts, but sometimes it takes deep soul searching and time in prayer to come up with what God originally intended us to be.

One simple indicator that we are not living in truth is revealed when our Personality Profile comes out with us being half of two opposites, one-half Popular Sanguine with one-half Perfect

Melancholy, or one-half Powerful Choleric with one-half Peaceful Phlegmatic. God did not intend for us to be at war with ourselves and we weren't originally both outgoing/optimistic and talkative and also introverted/pessimistic and thoughtful. We don't start out to be strong, domineering, and decisive while also being shy, submissive, and indecisive.

If you or your family members find these contrasting results in one person, don't panic or run to a psychiatrist, but begin prayerfully to seek which of these you were as a child. So frequently I find that when people know what they're looking for and have a key to the truth, they can find the mask quickly and take it off.

I talked with one couple recently who said they were both Sanguine/Melancholy combinations. They listened to me speak on the personalities and then we met to discuss this mix-up. As we began to communicate, I could see in Joan a Sanguine twinkle when she directed her comments to Fred or me, but as she turned to Bill anger surged up followed by a slumping of her shoulders and a sigh of "it's no use."

As I asked questions I established quickly that as a child she had been Popular. She brightened right up when I put her into fun experiences she remembered clearly. "When did the fun stop?" I queried. "When my father got drunk and began to beat me. He'd scream at me, 'You never do anything right!' I tried so hard to please him, but he would hit me when I forgot to do what he wanted."

Little Joan had put on the Perfect mask: "I will try to be Perfect for him." When her father beat her anyway, she sank into the Melancholy weaknesses of withdrawal, depression, and focusing on the negatives. She'd married a man who beat her; she'd divorced him and in her search for some spiritual direction, she had started going to church where she met Bill, a traveling evangelist and singer. That should have been, "Happy Ever After Time," but Bill was extremely critical of Joan's every move and even though he didn't beat her, he abused her emotionally, causing her to put her mask of pain back on again. She didn't know who she was.

Bill wasn't much better off, even though he'd been brought up in a Christian home. As I checked his childhood, I found he'd been part of a Christian family singing team who traveled about performing for his denominational churches. Mother had been a chubby, bubbly Popular star and father had been a serious Perfect musician, arranging their music and playing the piano. Bill's two sisters were full of life and popular with the crowds. He was like his father but learned early in life that if he wished any attention from mother or the crowds he had better be cute, precious, and adorable. He put on a Popular mask when he was probably about three and still keeps it in his back pocket to clip on when he's on stage in his current singing group or at church parties where he is expected to be the charming star of the show.

In a quick analysis we can see we have a Popular child inside Joan's adult body and on top we have a Perfect mask trying desperately to be good enough to deserve Bill's love. At the same time we have a husband who swings in and out of his critical, perfectionistic nature and his Popular mask which is so much a part of his act that most people can't believe he isn't really a Sanguine, fun-loving boy. When we look at this marriage with both of them masked, is it any wonder they need help? They are a show about to close.

The exciting conclusion is that with the tool of the personalities, they were able to see their masks, take them off, and become real. It's hard to be real when you don't know what real is. They had to give each other permission to become who they were meant to be. They are in a period of adjustment facing a new world without their masks.

As you examine your own life, ask God to show you what He originally intended for you to be. Once you have a sense of your true self, begin to look at each one of your children carefully, and see if you have unconsciously made them play a role that God never intended.

Some masks, like Joan's, are initially put on for self-defense. A child who is beaten or sexually molested often changes his or her personality in the mistaken belief that it is this nature that brings on the abuse. "If only I weren't like this, he wouldn't hurt me." The most frequent mask put on for this reason is the Perfect one. "I will do everything right. Then I won't have these problems." Unless the child was born with a perfectionistic nature, playing this role leads to emotional chaos, for no matter how hard the child tries, the behavior doesn't remove the abuse.

When I talk to an adult who was abused as a child, I usually find a split personality. Way inside is a fun-loving little girl who was never allowed to grow up and have her own personality. On the surface is a hard-bitter face with an unforgiving nature. Frequently she is overweight, has unexplained illnesses and migraines, and has a dead, hurt look in her eyes. She is a compulsive perfectionist and yet she can't ever get things right. She's the result of a mask of pain put on in self-defense.

Any time I see a split between the Popular and the Perfect, as a counselor I must determine whether this is a child like the first lady who was created to be a serious, deep, thoughtful, Perfect who put on a Popular mask for approval—or whether I have before me a child destined to be the life of the party, a born Popular, who because of circumstances beyond her control has put on a Perfect mask and tried to earn acceptance.

I ask a few obvious questions: As a child, would you have had fun if given a choice? Or did you enjoy being alone and reading? What was your relationship with your father or mother? Were you abused in any way? Frequently the answers to such simple questions will establish what is the real personality and what is the mask. Once discovered and explained, the mask can be removed. For some, this is done instantly, for others there is gradual change. For those who have deep scars from abuse, a period of healing therapy is required. Most gratifying for me is the letter saying, "I didn't realize how pent up I'd been until you took off my mask. Now I'm free to be me!"

When Barbara Taylor first came to CLASS her Personality Profile indicated Sanguine/Melancholy. She was bright, bubbly, and talkative, but she was constantly striving for perfection. As we discussed her personality, she mentioned that her father had been an alcoholic when she was a child and that her parents had divorced when she was twelve. Both alcoholism and divorce equal rejection to a child and cause little ones to hide their own personality and put on a mask.

In Barbara's case she had put on the Melancholy mask of Pain and Perfectionism on top of her inborn Popular Personality. In her book, *From Rejection to Acceptance*, a book born from her self-analysis, searching prayer, and personal discoveries, Barbara tells of her healing steps in becoming real:

> There were other effects of rejection. One was my compensation with perfectionism. Since I seemed to have no one who cared enough to actively approve of me, I tried to act and think perfectly. Another symptom was that I simply felt I was not allowed to be me for twenty years during Jack's pastorates. I sometimes received rejection when introduced as "the pastor's wife," or "the evangelist's wife," or "the author's wife." Of course, people were not standing around blocking my path to being who I was, but that is how I perceived it.[4]

Gratefully Barbara has been able, with the Lord's help, to take off her mask of perfectionism and become the adorable Sanguine God intended her to be.

Are you a split between two opposite personalities like Barbara was? If so, start thinking back to your original child, see when the mask was thrust upon you, and prayerfully begin to peel it off. Find the truth and set yourself free.

Not quite as frequent as the Popular/Perfect confusion is the mix of the other two opposite personalities in one individual. Often a man will tell me he is a combination Powerful/Peaceful. I have not yet found a genuine blend of these two, although I have counseled men who tested out that way. The question again is which is real and which is the mask.

Let's take a Peaceful boy who is happy to take it easy and has little self-motivation. Put him in an alcoholic setting with a dysfunctional mother and possibly a workaholic father who seldom comes home, a drinking father, or a non-existent father. In either case, the boy looks around one day at the hopelessness of his home. Mother is tuned out, little sister is crying, father's not around, and there's nobody in charge.

A natural Powerful would have assumed control long ago, but a Peaceful avoids trouble and responsibility until there is no other choice. When life is disintegrating before his eyes, he will put on a Powerful mask for survival.

Joe recounted, "If I had not taken control, my little sister would have starved to death. I was cooking on gas burners when I was three years old and soon I was even feeding my mother. Now I see why my whole life has been bursts of energy and control, followed by periods of exhaustion. You get very tired when you're forcing yourself to be someone you really aren't. I'm going to keep motivated, but I'm going to relax the pressure and frenzy that have worn me out."

Joe was a Peaceful boy who had put on a Powerful mask to survive the pains of his childhood.

Bert had similar symptoms. He had been born with a Powerful nature and had tried to achieve far beyond his years. He had athletic ability and was on at least one team a season. Bert had a Powerful father who worked constantly and thought going to a ball game was a waste of precious time. His mother was a weary Peaceful who never quite got herself together on any given day and certainly couldn't make it to the ball field.

Nothing the boy did was noticed, and when he received all A's and one B on his report card, his father barked, "Why'd you get the B? What's the matter with you?" After years of this, the boy gave up, put his Power in the closet, and took out the mask of Peace. "What difference does it make? They don't care anyway. Why bother?" Bert's emotional needs of praise for his achievements had never been met by either parent and he had given up.

The Powerful like Bert wearing the mask of the Peaceful fluctuates between an apathetic attitude and times of intense achievement. When in a work situation where his supervisor gives praise and credit for achievement, he will pull out his natural Power and be the top producer. But at home with a carping, critical, or indifferent wife, he may do little to help. Once Bert and his wife saw why he had such highs and lows and what her criticism was doing to wipe out what little ambition he had, they both began a process of healing.

One lady I counseled who talked and walked like a Powerful showed me her Personality Profile. She came out half Powerful and half Peaceful. I asked her what her home life was like as a child. Within minutes she had described a Popular/Powerful mother and a Powerful/Perfect father. They bickered constantly, agreed on nothing, and pulled her between them. I thought she meant pulled emotionally, but she affirmed it was physical. One took her right arm and the other grabbed her left. Each one insisted she be on their side. Even though she had a strong mind of her own, she was not allowed to use it. If she defended one, the other became furious. Ultimately she gave up, quietly mediated the arguments, and tried not to care who won. This capable child put on a Peaceful mask and became apathetic toward life. She could produce in placid situations, but any time she worked amidst contentious people, she was reduced to incompetence.

Isn't it amazing what our parents have inadvertently and unintentionally done to each of us? And isn't it frightening to consider what we may have done—or may still be doing—to our children? There is a great Proverb (22:6) that says, "Train up a child in the way he should go, and when he is old he will not depart from it." If we understand each child's personality, encourage him to grow up using his maximum strengths, and help him to overcome his weaknesses, we will raise up adults who know who they are, who have not departed from their birth personality, and who are not wearing masks.

Two generalities that I have observed in those wearing masks are: 1) They have a tremendous well of suppressed anger which can erupt at anytime without logical explanation; and 2) they are frequently exhausted and often looking for some medication to pep them up.

The anger was deposited in them when they first put on their mask. An abused little girl couldn't fight back and any expressed anger was an invitation for more punishment. She learned to hide her anger and not let it show. A parent made a child be something contrary to his inborn nature showing him in his heart that he was not acceptable as he was. This feeling of rejection caused anger but because he couldn't express it openly he pushed it down inside. Much adult anger comes from childhood hurts and rejections that have never been recognized.

The exhaustion comes from the amount of energy it takes to play an unnatural role. If you've ever been in a play or a pageant and had to act a part that wasn't you (and hoped you'd say the right lines at the appropriate time), you know the pressure you were feeling. Even if you loved acting, your pulse rate increased and your adrenalin raced and when you went to get up the next morning you were exhausted. When you suppress your own natural emotions and put on a mask, you are acting twenty-four hours a day, seven days a week. No wonder you are exhausted!

Don't live another day like this with either anger or exhaustion. Trace where these feelings came from, take them out and examine them, ask the Lord to free you from these fetters of the past. Talk to a friend or your mate about these hidden feelings and incidents and ask them to help you become real.

We never function effectively when we are living a lie, even one that's subconscious. When we're wearing even an invisible mask, people can sense that we're phony.

Are you wearing a:

Popular mask of personality—for approval and applause?

Perfect mask of pain or perfectionism—to cover up childhood physical or emotional pain?

Powerful mask of control—in order to survive childhood hurts?

Peaceful mask of indifference—to keep peace and avoid confrontation?

Don't let the pains of the past prevent you from producing today. Don't force others to be what you want when it is not consistent with their nature. Be the real thing, for no one can love a phony.

Betty had heard me speak several times on the personalities but was still confused until one day when she was sitting in one of our seminars and the Lord suddenly put a spotlight on her mask. She had suffered with depression and headaches for years and had been through different kinds of counseling.

Betty wrote:

> During all this time I kept wondering who I was. I could never get the personality charts to come out right. At Long Beach it was as though I finally got the microscope I'd been trying to examine my life with into focus. A truly exciting moment!
>
> I won't take time for life stories, but this is the first week I have lived in my 58 years that I really know who I am—and it is ok.
>
> After I left the church Saturday, it was as though all the tapes from my early childhood began to run through my mental VCR. It was amazing to see my little Sanguine person being free to show herself to me.
>
> I had assumed I was Melancholy/Phlegmatic, but it was such a complete masking. (I am Phlegmatic.) It was the realization that I had all the Melancholy weaknesses, but none of the strengths that made me understand I wasn't allowed to be Sanguine.
>
> My father was Sanguine, and mother Melancholy. She depended on me for her support system and needed me to be Melancholy, too.
>
> It will take me some time to discover what all this means, but I am feeling a freedom I have never known. I am going to be able to deal with some guilt that I had been unable to release.
>
> Thank you so much for what you are doing and for helping me to understand all this.

Begin today to understand yourself as Betty has and check over each one of your children. Take off all your masks, put them away in a box, and only take them out for parties or the school play. Don't be encumbered by a costume!

Some people in taking the Personality Profile came out even across and tell me, "I'm just a little bit of everything." It sounds well-balanced but actually no one is just a little bit of everything. We are usually one with a secondary of another. I am Sanguine/

Choleric and Fred is Melancholy/Choleric. We may have a scattering of other traits, but we will be concentrated in one or two areas. When we seem to be even, we are often wearing two masks and don't realize it.

As I question a person like this I usually find they behave one way with their mother, one with their mate, one at church, one at work. They have tried so hard to be all things to all people that they have ended up nowhere with no feeling of identity.

Search your past, check with your relatives, look at your pictures, try to determine what you were meant to be. Then, make sure you are not putting the same mask on your child that was put on you.

After speaking at a leadership conference I was asked by a pastor if I thought he was wearing a mask. He said he was Sanguine/Melancholy yet he stood, walked, and looked Choleric. When I asked him about his parents he told me they were both negative and legalistic, and didn't believe in fun. They demanded perfection of him and checked on everything he did.

I asked him if he felt he had any repressed anger and he replied, "I keep it under control most of the time." Translated that means, "Yes, I have repressed anger."

Summing up our conversation, we concluded he was a Sanguine who was not allowed to have fun and a Choleric who was not permitted to ever be in control of anything. He had stuffed his anger under and put on a perfectionistic mask, trying desperately to please his parents. When he saw this, a flood of relief came over his face. "I can't believe I feel so good so quickly. I've taken off my mask. I know who I am."

Then he paused and said, "I think I've done the same thing to my daughter. She used to be fun-loving as a child, but now she's depressed a lot of the time. I'm going to go see her tonight and apologize for what I've done to her. We'll take our masks off together."

He then thanked me and told me he knew God had sent him to hear me that he might be set free.

You shall know the truth and the truth shall make you free!

His unchanging plan has always been to
adopt us into His own family. . . .
(Ephesians 1:5 TLB)

7. Cast Additions

Sometimes in a show a new part is added and a new person brought in to round out the cast. Sometimes in our families we adopt a child to bring fulfillment to our lives. Some, like Fred and I, adopt to fill in a gaping hole left by the death of other children, some because they are unable to conceive, and some because they desire to help some disadvantaged child—possibly of a different ethnic background.

Because I have an adopted child, frequently other adoptive mothers come to me with their stories. Frequently they tell me of early teenage rebellion and statements such as "You aren't my real mother and you can't tell me what to do." In my personal experience, sharing, and study I have concluded two points that may be helpful for those of you considering adoption or already having done so.

In recent years psychologists and regressive therapists have agreed that the baby knows whether or not he or she is wanted while still in the womb. Researchers have dramatic evidence and I have talked with many adoptive children who say they had an inborn feeling of rejection from as early as they can remember. Whether or not you believe this theory, it will help you to consider that babies taken away from their natural mothers do instinctively know that all is not well. Whether or not they are told about the adoption, they often grow up with feelings of insecurity, rejection, and unexplained anger. They also feel guilty for their negative reactions.

This concern does not mean we shouldn't adopt a child or that the unwanted child would be better off with an immature teen mother. I mention it only to ease the feeling of guilt so many adoptive parents have when the child rebels. So many fine Christian parents cry out to me, "Where did we go wrong?" The seed of rejection was already there and you could have been perfect parents and yet have raised a child who rebelled and turned hostile.

A second comfort is that the anger they direct toward you is not really yours to bear. As children begin to understand how babies are conceived and born, the day comes when suddenly they realize why they were given up for adoption. Several emotions follow this revelation: rejection, emptiness, rootlessness, insecurity, resentment, and anger. All these feelings would be directed against the birth mother except that she is not available; but just because she's not present doesn't mean that the feelings don't exist. They have to be placed somewhere and the adoptive mother usually bears the brunt of the anger.

Realizing that the anger is misplaced may not prevent it from happening, but it will at least let you know that you are only the stand-in. I would hope you will be able to "take it" without reacting in anger yourself. Let the child know you understand how he or she feels and encourage the child to express whatever is bubbling up in his emotions. Don't reprimand the child for his feelings, but realize that he is going through a double love-hate relationship that is more than he can comfortably handle.

Even though the birth mother may have wanted to keep him, he feels rejected and unwanted. At the same time he now knows there was another mother who gave birth to him and even though he can't picture her, he feels a new type of love for this absent person. As these thoughts are tumbling through his mind, he has the simultaneous contrast of feelings for you. He loves you as his mother and yet suddenly he's angry at you. Perhaps if you hadn't taken him, his "real mother" would have kept him. When you consider this double set of emotional problems the child is going through, probably at the same time that his own sexuality is a new preoccupation, you can begin to understand his confusing emotions.

You may not be able to prevent this self-doubt and questioning, but you can be prepared for it, not overreact, and let him tell you what's on his heart without rebuke.

We told our son he was adopted long before he understood what it meant. I shared that he was special and that God chose him for us over all the other little boys in the world. We loved him dearly, and his two sisters, having lost two brothers, absolutely doted on him. In retrospect, I can see no way we could have done much better with him to make him feel loved. Yet when he was in his teens and the realization of his origin hit him, he came into our bedroom late in the evening and said, "I have something to say to you two." He had always had a gentle spirit but that night there was a tension and anger that we had not heard before. "I am not your flesh and blood. I do not have your drive and ambition. I am not as fast and as smart as Marita and Lauren and I never will be. The sooner you two get that into your heads the better off we'll all be."

Gratefully, Fred and I kept quiet, listened, and didn't respond defensively. When he had said his piece, we both thanked him warmly and told him we loved him. Once later he asked me if I knew anything about his mother. When I told him the description of her looks that were just like his—brown curly hair, big brown eyes, turned up nose, and dimple in the chin—tears came to his eyes.

During his junior year in high school, he had a friend who looked so much like him that people thought they were brothers. This other boy got a girl pregnant and her family insisted they get married. The baby had big brown eyes and brown curly hair and young Fred became attached to this tiny boy. He'd visit him and tell me what the baby was doing and I could tell he was seeing himself in his friend's baby. One day he came home upset. His friend was leaving his young wife and had no place to go. His father had remarried and didn't want him around and the mother-in-law was furious at him every time she looked his way. Fred wanted to know, could we take his friend in? Although I had no desire for another teenage boy, I could tell this whole experience was very draining for young Fred. So I let the boy move in.

This time was a growing experience for all of us, as the boy had no one to turn to for help. He would ask Fred questions. Fred would then come to us for answers for his friend, and we would discuss all sides of the issue. Then he would go back and counsel him. By answering the boy's questions second hand we were able to talk about situations, morals and responsibilities that we might never have been able to discuss otherwise. When the boy decided to divorce the girl and go on his way in life unencumbered by family responsibilities, Fred was heart broken and he said to me, "How can he leave that little baby without a father?" I know what Fred was really saying and I also know that he had grown up through this experience. He could see how these "accidents" happened and how many lives are affected by thoughtless, undisciplined behavior.

At that time I asked our son if he wanted to search for his birth mother and he replied, "You're the only mother I've ever known and I don't want to find another one." Later, when I was writing *Your Personality Tree*, tracing back family strengths and weaknesses, he commented, "I guess I don't really fit into this family tree, do I?"

I felt sorry for him as I had to admit that he didn't inherit any traits from us directly. He looked suddenly lost and lonely. Now that he is twenty-four and will probably get married within a few years, he's talking about finding his mother. Knowing how difficult it is to think of having a family when you're not sure of your own roots, we've given him all the information we have. He knows the name of the agency in Connecticut through which we adopted him when he was three months old. If he cares to pursue his quest, he knows he has our blessing.

When people ask my advice, I share that I think the child should not be encouraged to find his birth mother until he's over eighteen—and then only if he wants to search on his own. I feel that the adoptive parents should be cooperative but should not be the initiators. This way if the outcome is an unpleasant one or the perceived rejection is repeated, the responsibility is not on the parents' shoulders.

In July 1987, my husband and I conducted a cruise to Alaska. Among the group of thirty couples, there were six who were adoptive parents. We were surprised to find each other and we shared our experiences. We all agreed that our adoptive children had an above average need for affection and assurance that they were loved and accepted. These children did seem to manifest the emotional responses to rejection; they had at some point lashed out at us in unexplained anger. Adopting a child, we all concluded, was not as simple as taking in a precious little baby and helping him grow up.

The results for us have been positive and the rewards even beyond that of our girls. Because they were our flesh and blood, we expected them to be exceptional. Then we lost our two boys and learned that we were fallible human beings who produced imperfect sons. Beyond that, God gave us our beautiful adopted son and we marvel at how he has matured into a responsible adult and businessman.

In a Dear Abby column on adoption, a mother wrote in with some excellent suggestions. She had two children and then adopted two more, one from Korea and one from India. Her comments are representative of many I have heard:

1. Please don't tell my children how lucky they are, as if they were poor little waifs in need of a handout. My husband and I are just as fortunate to have these wonderful children as they are to have us, and your attitude is patronizing. Anyway, a biological child owes his parents even more—he owes them his life! . . .

2. Please give equal attention to our two biological children. All four will thank you—but don't spoil it by asking if they, too, are adopted. After all, it really is none of your business. And yes, Virginia, many people without fertility problems have chosen to adopt for other reasons.

3. Please don't tell us about your cousin, neighbor or other acquaintances who have adopted. We're really tired of being stopped on the street to hear these tales, especially the ones that end with the woman becoming pregnant and having a baby of "her own" after all.

4. Please spare us your speculations about what kind of villain their "real mother" must have been to give up such "cute" children. It takes a courageous and unselfish woman to give up a child she cannot care for, and it takes precious little character to get an abortion instead.[5]

The most famous adoptive child in the nation today is Michael Reagan who has written a book, *On the Outside Looking*

In. In it he tells of being molested by a camp counselor, a trau-matic experience he had never told anyone before. This, added to the innate rejection an adopted child often feels, caused him to be defensive and angry, thin-skinned and resentful, self-loathing and insecure. During a time of introspection he decided to seek out his birth mother. In September 1987, Michael applied for his California adoption papers and through a series of circumstances he found his half-brother, Barry Lange. Through him he learned that his mother, Irene, a part-time actress, had died in 1985 but that she had followed his progress from the day he was born on 18 March 1945 and adopted by Ronald Reagan and Jane Wyman.

In a *People Magazine* article, Margot Dougherty wrote, "Suddenly it became clear to Michael that a woman he had never known had been tracing his steps when he was continuously shuttling from school to school. For the first time in his life, he felt that this natural mother was not uncaring and, like Jane, had actually loved him in full measure. 'It was the most wonderful feeling in the world when I found out she knew all along who I was,' he says. And that this mother had kept track of this child."

For the first time Michael realized that his birth mother did love him and since this discovery, he has become willing to look at his life realistically. He has undergone treatment at a Santa Monica center for molested children, and he has been able to explain and release his suppressed anger and become free from his guilt and defensiveness.

As adoptive parents, when we are aware of the emotional burdens our children carry, we owe it to them to be understand-ing, to talk openly, and to listen without becoming defensive. We should entertain the possibility of outside counseling where the child can more freely vent his feelings without fear of reprisal.

We all need to be rid of the residual pains of our past, but nothing much happens until we face the facts, pray for direction, seek godly counsel, and desire to change.

Part III

THE DIRECTORS

How can I except some man
should guide me?
(Acts 8:31)

Let us walk by the same rule,
let us mind the same thing.
(Philippians 3:16)

III

The Directors

If we were to consider a Broadway show, a business in Boston, or a football team in Texas, we wouldn't dream of functioning without an appointed leader. A play would never get to opening night if it had not been carefully directed, if the cast did not know their positions, and if everyone didn't have the same firm purpose in view. There is no business that happily functions without guidelines or supervision, that succeeds when no one cares, or that makes a profit when no one is keeping the books. There could never be a winning team without a coach, a game played with no consistent rules, or a football team where every player was a quarterback.

We are all too bright even to consider such lack of management and yet many of us have families with no unified sense of purpose, no game plan, and no coach. Some of us live in a way that would bankrupt a business and that would baffle a board of directors. Some of our household dramas are being played on cluttered stages, by actors who have never read the script, with absentee directors who allow the cast to come and go at will, while ad-libbing their way through life.

Why is it we will study, work, and practice on so many pursuits and yet let our family run on its own? We take no basic training and we assume that by nature we will happen to be godly parents. If this miracle happened more than infrequently, we would not have the abundance of family problems we face today. No business, play, or team could win without a leader. No family drama can make it to the last act without a director. God gave parents authority over their children, not so they could exercise tyrannical control, but so they could guide, coach, and instruct their children from their cumulative experience and spiritual wisdom.

> "Two souls with but a single thought,
> two hearts that beat as one."

8. Unity of Direction

Once we recognize that God has called us to be the human directors of our production and He has chosen the cast, our job is to have unity in our instructions. It is obvious that no show could make it through the first rehearsal if there were two directors each giving his or her own creative suggestions.

"This is going to be a comedy and we're all going to wear colorful costumes."

"No, this is going to be a drama and we're all going to dress in symbolic black."

The cast would be so confused that there would be a stalemate, a defection, or an insurrection. Without unity of purpose little can be accomplished in any group activity. Yet I find in families, the most important unit in the history of mankind, that the cast functions daily under conflicting information. Mother says one thing and Dad another. The little ones don't have to be very old before they assess which director to go to or avoid. Although the Bible stresses unity, few Christian parents spend any conscious time discussing and agreeing upon general household procedures. They hear verses and sermons, nod in assent, and that is the end of their unity. The Bible tells us that when we get married "a man must leave his father and mother and so perfectly unite himself to his wife that the two shall become one" (Genesis 2:24 Williams).

As we understand the different personalities we can see that this doesn't happen by chance. By the law of averages there's no way that two people (because they made some marriage vows) suddenly think with one mind in unity. Since we usually marry opposites we don't think alike at all. The Popular wife wants to party and go to a social church. Her Perfect husband can't stand wasting time at parties with trivial people who have nothing of value to say. And he prefers a church where the pastor is deep, professorial, and traces each word back to the Greek. The Powerful man aims to work, achieve, and build and he wants to go to a church where he can take control and get the dummies moving. His Peaceful wife shudders in fear that he will stir up trouble and cause controversy. She prefers a church that is restful and demands no more of your effort than an hour on Sunday.

When you marry any of these combinations to each other you have opposite opinions on everything including going to church. Paul pleaded with the people in Corinth who couldn't seem to come to any meeting of the minds, "But I urge and entreat you, brethren, by the name of our Lord Jesus Christ, that all of you be in perfect harmony, and full agreement in what you say, and that there be no dissensions or factions or divisions among you; but that you be perfectly united in your common understanding and in your opinions and judgments" (1 Corinthians 1:10 AMP).

God wants us to have harmony, agreement, and unity, but this bliss does not drop down from heaven, we have to work at it. In the Old Testament newly married couples took a year off to get to know each other and establish unity before they had children. Today many couples get married, both work each day, and they arrive home too exhausted to have meaningful conversations or make long-range, harmonious plans. Many couples have no framework of reference such as the four personality types and some feel that if they're both Christians everything will turn out all right. If that were true we would have no problem Christian marriages or no mixed up Christian teens (and I would have no work!). But since I have people standing in line at every conference desperate for help in their marriages and overwhelmed with their children's problems, I know there is a need.

"So let us then definitely aim for and eagerly pursue what make for harmony and for mutual up-building (edification and development) of one another" (Romans 14:19 AMP).

Understand Our Differences

How do we pursue unity? First, let's start with our differences because our aim is not to obliterate our own personalities but to understand our differences and accept the other person as he or she is, not try to change each other. I teach this to you not as an academic exercise but from the heart of a mother and a wife of thirty-five years who has lived it both ways. For fifteen years of our marriage Fred did his best to shape me up. After a while my resistance to constant training became so strong that I worked at quiet sabotage. Since open rebellion didn't go over well with Fred, I just plotted to undermine what he planned so Perfectly. I became the Popular mother, the fun one. "Come to me and you will live abundantly."

When Fred was on business trips I would say, "The ogre's gone, now we can have a good time. We can all stay up late, eat when we feel like it, and not bother checking off our work charts." We would live it up and have what we called "a high old time."

The night before Fred returned I'd line the children up at the charts, check off the whole week's work, and let them know the fun was about over. The minute Fred arrived he would go immediately to the charts to make sure we had been functioning properly while he was away. We would all beam proudly and try to look like dutiful angels as he observed our obedience.

I look back on this act now and am appalled at how Fred and I were running this show with two sets of directions, not even realizing what we were doing or how harmful it was to the children to live with such parental instability. When we became committed believers we didn't change overnight, but the Lord began to peel back our self-protective layers and we saw that we were leading the same army in two different directions. As soon as we saw the need for unified instructions, we began searching God's Word for family verses. Whatever we learned we started teaching others. I look back in wonder at how God used us to train others when we had received no training ourselves. We had taken no courses, seen no films, and read no books on marriage or family, but we sat down with our Bibles and one concordance and in 1968 we wrote our first course called "Harmony in the Home."

We taught scriptural truth laced with our personal examples and found "how good and how pleasant it is for brethren to dwell together in unity" (Psalm 133:1).

As we taught, we found it was difficult to help people of different personalities have unity when they didn't know why they disagreed. Thus on our second time through our "Harmony" course we added the personalities as a measuring stick— and that was when the course began to blossom. Even though the couples wanted to work on their children, we found the children didn't improve until the parents changed. We had to put first problems first.

So let's start with the two of you who probably have quite different personalities. We find that many well-meaning Christian couples don't know how to talk about their differences because they don't know where to start—and each one becomes defensive when the other one mentions anything wrong with the other. This tension shuts down communication and when there is no verbal exchange, there soon is no emotional relationship. Either the two are in constant conflict or one tunes out and lets the other run the show, stepping in only with criticism when things go wrong. I find so many Christian homes where there is little agreement on anything and, frankly, I don't know how as many stay together as they do, considering they live in conflict and see no hope of restoration.

There is hope. We changed and so can you. Once you begin to see that you each have weaknesses with which you came into marriage, that you are responsible for your own faults not your partner's, you have made the big first step. I find many marriages change just on the acknowledgment that each partner has weak-nesses and is going to be mature enough to do something about them, instead of nagging the other. Once the marriage partners have a checked-off list of faults before them, they can see where they need to improve and get on with the changes.

"If we confess our sins, he is faithful and just to forgive us our sins, and to cleanse us from all unrighteousness" (1 John 1:9). This is a popular Christian verse for other people. It only be-comes applicable to us individually when we are conscious of our failures and have them written out before us. Instead of wasting energy blaming each other for the family crises, we can lay our sins before the Lord and know He will give us the power to change. The Amplified version puts it this way: "If we [freely] admit that we have sinned and confess our sins, He is faithful and just [true to His own nature and promises] and will forgive our sins (dismiss our lawlessness) and continuously cleanse us from all unrighteousness—everything not in conformity to His will in purpose, thought and action."

Analyze Your Family

We know it is God's will that we manage our families well for He tells us so. In speaking of people eligible for Christian leadership, Paul states clearly, "He must manage his own family well and see that his children obey him with proper respect. If anyone does not know how to manage his own family, how can he take care of God's church?" (1 Timothy 3:4–5 NIV). That's a good question.

Let's assume now that you, as a couple, have spent some prayerful time looking at your own areas of weakness and then discussing your different opinions in a positive way. If you have not accomplished this first step, the next one will be overwhelming.

Look at your personality differences and expand this over-view to the rest of the family. Look back at your pages of Family Faces. What different personalities are living under your roof? Can you see that if you don't start with yourself that looking at all the rest will be too much to handle? Mathematically, there are endless possibilities of combinations. Helen wrote me to say she was a strong Choleric with a Peaceful/Phlegmatic husband. They had four children, one of each personality. They had never known why they got these children, no two of whom were alike. "Before we studied *Your Personality Tree*, we thought we were all misfits. I came across as bossy and my husband appeared henpecked. He didn't seem to care about anything and I was beating my head against a wall trying to tone down my Choleric child who was telling everyone, including my husband, what to do, trying to motivate my Phlegmatic girl who liked sitting around with her father watching TV, trying to get my Sanguine serious about life and on with her homework, and trying to cheer up my Melancholy son who couldn't stand the confusion and was constantly locked in his room. When I read your book the chaos of our home life suddenly came into a clear focus and I could see what I was dealing with. Suddenly the whole sad scene became funny. Once I stopped laughing, I called a family meeting and began to teach your material. Our show has gone from being a tragedy to becoming a comedy. Naturally, I'm still the director, but at least I see hope that we'll make it to the last act!"

How about you? Are the directors of your show in harmony or are you all doing your own thing? Be willing to spend some time in positive analysis of your cast so that you may all be heading in the same direction before the curtain falls.

9. Normal Families

Thomas Deshler, a therapist/researcher at Cedars-Sinai Medical Center in Los Angeles, advertised for some "normal" families who would like to receive a free "check-up on their mental health." Although his project was widely publicized, he received only thirty calls and found only fifteen families who were willing to spend two hours with him in simple introspection.

Deshler's definition of "normal" was a family with a mother and father and two or more teenagers who have not been in therapy, in the hospital, or in legal trouble in the last three years. This was hardly a narrow definition of "normal," and yet even with diligent searching, he could find only fifteen families who fit his description.

The purpose of Deshler's project was to find out what makes a normal family function, realizing that most research is done on dysfunctional units and that therapists have largely ignored the healthy American family. Even though Deshler's analysis was completed on only fifteen families, some significant conclusions were made.

The one most important point was that in healthy families there is no power struggle going on. "It's fairly clear who's in charge, no matter who. My guess is a healthy family has a clear leadership and leadership is invested in one or both adults."[1] Deshler states this is in contrast to families in trouble where there may be no authority at all or where it may rest in the hands of the children. Biblically speaking, we all know that there is to be loving control by the parents, not indifference or tyranny. Yet as I talk with troubled Christian families, I often see either of two extremes.

One, the parents are either too busy or too insecure themselves to exert any effective influence, or two, they are so determined their children will not get out of control that they institute a dictatorship where family give-and-take is nonexistent. The first produces teens with no sense of discipline or moral standards, feeling the world owes them a living. The latter warps any creativity, stifles initiative, and leads to either rebellion or unhealthy dependence on the parent.

Deshler was looking for families who were "neither so fragmented that each member is going his own way, nor so enmeshed, glued together, that everyone thinks the same way."[2]

His second major point was that healthy families were able to resolve conflict by discussion and compromise, where troubled families couldn't come to any mutual agreement no matter how long they took in the attempt. They would become hostile, give up on any mutual consensus, or give in to the most verbal or abusive member.

Using Deshler's terms, would you consider your family to be normal?
1. A mother and father _____
2. Two or more teenagers _____
3. Who (in the last three years) have not been
    In therapy _____
    In the hospital _____
    In legal trouble _____

If you had been offered a free family mental health checkup, would you have been interested? If not, would your reason have been

There must be a catch to it _____
My mate would never go _____
We don't need help _____
I wouldn't want anyone to think we needed help _____
I wouldn't want to be questioned on my feelings _____
We don't have the time _____
No one would change anyway _____
What difference would it make? _____

Using the two signs of a normal family, would you fit the pattern?

There is no power struggle in our home _____
We resolve conflict by compromise _____

10. Family Meetings

When Fred and I consciously decided to improve our family relationships to end our parental power struggle and to begin to compromise, we started family meetings. In the beginning the children were apprehensive and wondered if these meetings would become training sessions. Since we had never sought out their opinions before, they couldn't believe that we were actually asking them to share in setting family policy.

The purpose of a family meeting is to let the children know that their opinions count and to keep the lines of communication open.

To achieve our purpose we first had to establish that these meetings were for exchange of ideas, not for a lecture from the parents. Years later they told us that they had not believed it was possible for us to keep quiet throughout an entire evening and not lecture! Their comment on me has always been, "Where two or three are gathered together, mother will give a seminar."

It wasn't easy to listen when I had so much to say, but both Fred and I agreed that we would help each other keep quiet. The first time we had a meeting everyone was cautious with comments, but as we continued and did affirm the children's opinions, they began to talk more openly.

Fred and I set some rules for ourselves that might help you as you begin to communicate in family meetings:

1. Make these meetings a positive time that the children will look forward to attending.

2. Be sure to listen to what the others have to say.

3. Do not interrupt no matter what your opinion is or how brilliant your thought.

4. Do not use the time to lecture or threaten.

5. Don't hold what they say against them and throw it back at them later.

6. Don't reprimand family members in front of each other.

7. Have private meetings later for discipline problems or personal questions.

8. Don't schedule meetings during a favorite TV show or while friends are waiting outside.

9. No matter what the children say, don't comment, "That is ridiculous"; "What a stupid idea"; "Will you ever grow up?"; "I can't believe a child of mine would ever say such a thing!"

10. Encourage them to express real feelings and not just what they think you want to hear.

11. Family Objectives

As we made plans for our first family meeting, Fred and I sat down seriously and began to map out our long-range objectives.

Looking back we can now see the value in our goal-planning and in our giving ourselves a measuring stick by which to judge our performance as directors.

We first came up with a definition of what our desires should be for a family. So often we don't realize we need a guideline, but when we have none, there's nothing by which we can check our decisions. The following statement of purpose has helped us, and many others, to focus on a family plan:

> Our desire is to bring up well-adjusted children who will be able to function responsibly without us.
> Our goal is not to reign forever but to abdicate gracefully at the right time.

With these statements in mind we could measure whether or not a certain request from one of the children fit our family plan. Would the request be something that would help them to adjust better to life and to people? Would it be an activity that would increase their sense of responsibility? Would it help them to grow up? If the answers were positive, we would encourage them to participate.

We always kept in mind that our job was to prepare them to get along without us, not bind them forever to our sides. A friend of ours with six children had an "Eighteen and Out" rule that worked well with his family as they all knew from childhood that they were not going to sit around and let their parents support them.

Our theory was "you may live at home until you get married as long as you go to school or work, and as long as you contribute in some positive way to the household." Lauren lived at home while attending California State University, San Bernardino. She also worked in our restaurant, helped with the housework, and kept reasonable hours as we had agreed. We allowed her to have friends in our home, but it was up to her to see that they adhered to the family rules. Lauren lived with us until she was married at twenty, and we can honestly say that neither she nor her friends ever gave us any trouble. One rule was that everyone in our home came down to breakfast when Fred played the chimes each morning. We were never sure how many would appear. Young people who never got up for breakfast at their own homes (assuming they had it served to them), or warmed up a frosted raspberry Poptart, cheerfully arrived at our table without coaxing.

Marita lived with us until she married at twenty-four. The day she was eighteen she gave Fred and me a personal declaration of independence. She and her friends had discussed that they were now "of age" and no longer had to do anything their parents requested. Coming to breakfast had always been an important family time of togetherness and Marita chose to rebel on that point along with a few others. She would no longer abide by our basic rules unless she "felt like it." Having had such an easy time with Lauren, we were unprepared for this unexpected decree from Marita. For once I didn't know what to say, but I didn't need to, for Fred took charge. Using our agreement principle—when attacked, find something you can agree with as a starter—he acknowledged she did have all these rights that she and her friends had outlined for their parents' approval. She gave a satisfied smile until he added, "but that is only when you live outside of our home. If you wish to live here, you will abide by the rules and be at breakfast in the morning."

This statement was followed by heated questions such as "Would you pay for me to rent a place?"

"Absolutely not."

Several times I was ready to give in to a few things, but Fred held lovingly firm. By the time Marita went crying to her room, declaring that we didn't understand, I was sure we'd lost her for good. All night I waited for the sound of the squeaky front door hinge. When I didn't hear it, I thought she might have gone out the window. She'd done that before, but when the breakfast chimes sounded in the morning, Marita appeared as bouncy and happy as ever.

We didn't discuss that situation for several years and when we did, she shrugged and said, "It was worth giving it a try."

When Fred, Jr., turned eighteen, we were ready for him. We had looked up "the rules" ourselves and approached him by stating that legally we no longer had to support him. If he wished to stay with us, we would allow him to keep his room and not pay room and board as long as he was in college. If he chose not to stay in school, he would have to leave or contribute to the household expenses.

For the last few years he has taken over the expense and care of our yard as his price for room and board. It is his responsibility to see that the lawn is mowed and he employs a boy to do this. He waters the many plants I have and puts new flowers in with each changing season.

When he wanted a dog, he paid to fence in the backyard. When he noticed the front door needed staining, he bought the materials and did it. When he didn't like the plain shelves in the kitchen cabinets, he bought linoleum tiles, cut them to fit, and lined every shelf. All these things are his choice because he feels responsible to do all he can for me since I am on the road so much of the time.

As a parent my job has been to train him to be self-sufficient, to show him how much work it is to maintain a home, to teach all the children growing up that housework is a shared obligation not a sole project for Mother, and then, most important of all, praise each one for what they've done, especially if it was beyond what they were assigned.

By following this plan, I have been able to raise children who are responsible adults who can get along without me.

12. Family Meeting Plans

Start with Prayer

The first thing we did at our family meetings was to pray for each of us as a unit and for our specific personal needs. We tried to avoid lengthy and lofty prayers, but encouraged each one to say what was on his mind, not what would sound religious. Starting with prayer gave a feeling of harmony and the Lord's blessing on our time together.

We often shared a verse and rotated whose turn it was to find some scripture that was meaningful. We were more interested in the children being involved than in our giving deep teachings.

Find a Comfortable Spot

To make the family meeting special, it should be somewhere a little different from the regular gathering spot, if there is an alternative place. We found that bringing the children into our bedroom, or our study, or the back patio instead of sitting around the family room added an air of excitement and awe. Sometimes we let them choose where they'd like to meet, but the main emphasis was on being comfortable and casual and not having a "classroom" atmosphere. Often we would all get into our pajamas first so that we would be really relaxed.

Have a Simple Agenda

After our prayer and verse study, Fred would bring up our major topic for discussion. This varied from vacation plans, creative activities, weekend projects, pajama parties, birthday celebrations to more serious topics such as bedtime hours, TV rules, allowances, dating regulations, setting standards. Starting with the youngest child, we had each one give his or her opinion of the subject at hand. When they'd all said what they thought, Fred and I would add our ideas and ultimately agree on a plan.

For example, on having their friends in for dinner, we all agreed that the child had to ask my permission first, and they should not ask in front of the guest. I needed to have the option to say no. If a child asked in front of the friend, I would automatically say no. Each child tested me once, and I remember when Fred in first grade asked if Mike could stay for dinner. Mike was an adorable Sanguine with blond curly hair and big blue eyes. I was happy to have him around, but I had to honor our agreement. I looked at him and said, "Mike, you are a good little boy and I'd love to have you stay, but our family rule is that Freddie has to ask me privately. Since he didn't, I have to say no."

As they walked out of the room, Freddie muttered, "I didn't think she'd do that to you." He never asked in front of anyone again. If we don't show our children we mean business when they're young, they'll be hopeless by the time they're teens.

13. Family Meeting Suggestions

As I have stressed the value of a time when the family can get together to let the children have an opportunity to speak, many mothers have added their ideas. Betty Barnett and her husband Greg wrote of their family time.

Our nightly Family Times around the dinner table began when the baby was still in a high chair and have continued until today when the children return home for a visit. These times lasted anywhere from five to thirty-five minutes and every so often included a trip for a present-buying spree or ice cream cones at Thrifty's Drug Store. If Dad was home, he planned these—if not he assigned Mom or one of the children to be responsible for coming up with a Family Time idea. Biblical issues were raised as well as news items or perhaps the reading of a family book such as *Chitty Chitty Bang Bang* in nightly installments. The question of the evening might be "Share one thing God is teaching you right now and one area you see progress in" or "What is one thing you like about every other person at the table and one area you'd like to see improvement in?" Guests were included and one night a thirteen-year-old girlfriend of one of the children took part in answering the question, "How is God like an orange?" Her excellent answer, "Oranges heal scurvy and God heals us!" These sharing times gave a "safe" atmosphere where no answer was wrong and a twelve-year-old could safely bring up negative feelings against parents. It fostered open communication which is what God encourages each of us to have as His children. Spiritual questions and doubts could be discussed and answered. The children's friends accepted Christ and grew spiritually during these family times.

Our dear friends Bob and Emilie Barnes have raised two outstanding young people. Recently, at Emilie's fiftieth birthday party, Jennie, a young mother of three and the wife of a dentist, and Brad, a handsome business executive, both stood up to give testimony to their parents and how well they had brought them up. Over the years I have observed their home life and know that Bob and Emilie were always available to listen to what their children had to say and to attend their various events.

As Brad pointed out, his parents put him, and Jennie, on top priority. They supported him in Little League, volleyball, Pop Warner football, and swimming meets. They visited teachers and always showed up for the high school open houses that few parents cared to attend.

One night when Jennie was in high school and wanted to go to a questionable party, Bob said she could attend but he would go with her and meet the parents. When he and Jennie arrived the party was already rowdy, but Bob went in to find the parents. While he was searching through the crowd, Jennie came over to him and told him he could forget it, she didn't want to stay. She later thanked him for being with her.

Bob put in writing one of the positive ideas he and Emilie used to promote open family relationships.

> Whenever any member of the family had a problem relating to our family relationships we could call a "Family Conference" with the other members in attendance. No holds were barred: use of car, allowance, dating, church, parents, brother, sister, friends, etc. Through this we were able to keep on the table how we felt about other people in the family. A family member could call a conference as often as needed. We scheduled this meeting according to our various time schedules. Many times we scheduled this conference on Friday evening over hamburgers at a local restaurant. This format really worked for our family to keep the lines of communication open.

Norm and Bobbie Evans, Christian speakers on marriage relationships, had fun with their family. Bobbie wrote me,

We tried to plan special evenings at home for the family. Periodically, it would be "Your Night." The family member selected would sit at the head of the table, eat on a special place setting of very different dishes, would be the center of the dinner time conversation, and would choose the menu for the evening, as well as how the duration of the evening was to be spent. We remember one evening in particular when Deana, who was about thirteen, chose Mexican food and cherry pie for the menu (Ugh!) and then planned a game of hide-and-seek for the rest of the evening. We live in an A-frame and discovered that hiding places were few and far between—even with the lights out. Her dad, who is 6'5" and 230 lbs., had the hardest time "hiding" of all of us! It is an evening all of us remember . . . and family memories were a priority. We find you have to plan to make them!

In the September issue of *Learning* '86, Nancy Cornell wrote an article, "Encouraging Responsibility—a discipline plan that works." While there is no perfect program that fits every child, the theory discussed in the article, based on William Glasser's approach to discipline, contained some ideas I thought we could apply to our home instructions.

Traditional discipline systems, which are based on threats and punishments, make *adults* responsible for kids' behavior. Reality therapy teaches children to be responsible for themselves and their own behavior. At its heart is the notion that children must learn to recognize behavior that hurts themselves or others, then make specific plans to solve their behavior problems.[3]

In practical use the teachers work on the premise that school should be a positive place with reasonable rules and they have class meetings each day if possible. Principal Phoebe Barash of Lincoln, Vermont, has been excited over the results of six years of the Glasser approach:

Class meetings are an essential part of reality therapy. Children frequently misbehave to get attention. They act up a lot less when they know that every day, in class meeting, they'll be able to talk and that the teacher and the rest of the class will listen.[4]

The simple school rules are posted and when one is broken the student is asked four questions used by the teachers, cooks, playground aides, and bus drivers:

1. What are you doing?
2. Is it helping you?
3. Is it against the rules?
4. What will you do to change that?[5]

After answering these questions the student is asked to write a course of action that will help him not to repeat his mistake. The teacher gives the child a check-back time when he is due to present his plan. To do this the child has to think about what he did and evaluate whom it is hurting. He then has to work out his own plan of behavior on paper. Teachers found that frequently the children had no idea how to think logically about any problem and that choosing a logical and better pattern of behavior was a totally new concept.

As I studied over this approach for class meetings and individual accountability, I wondered whether many of us parents would take the time to meet with our children and establish family rules. If we did, would we be able to handle disobedience rationally and call for a written plan for changed behavior? If we asked for it, would we remember to set and meet a check-back time? Would we in fact follow through? One of the hardest things about being a parent is getting up out of the chair and checking to see if the chore was completed on time.

Without consistency on the part of the parent, no discipline program will work. We could read every child-raising book in the world, but if we didn't follow through on what we said we'd do, the system just wouldn't work. If you mean business with your children, you'll meet to set the basic rules, you'll give clear instructions, you'll observe behavior patterns, you'll ask for written plans for improvement, you'll establish a check-back time and be there, and you'll show the children in a family meeting that good behavior blesses the whole family and that disobedience hurts everyone.

14. Family TV Rules

Television has often been referred to as the great national baby-sitter and it surely does provide a service not available when I was a child. Because there are many educational programs, newscasts, and family shows, we can be grateful that such a broad spectrum of learning and entertainment is available to us without leaving our own living room. As with any positive activity, however, too much of even a good thing can become a negative pattern.

As parents we and our children must establish guidelines for how much television is acceptable. During our family meetings we created our own TV rules and included each child's opinion.

No Television During Meals

Because our breakfasts and dinners were the focal points of our family day, we wanted no interference in our conversation. This rule was agreed upon and accepted as fact. The minute the meal was announced, everyone was to come to the table, no matter what they were doing.

Many of the children who visited in our home were amazed at the conversation that took place at our dinner table. When I asked them, "What's it like at your house?" their usual reply was, "Oh, we all watch TV." The family of one of the boys Marita dated had all of the living room furniture facing the TV. After her first meal there, Marita came home amazed. She said, "Mom, they don't talk to each other. We all sat and watched TV while eating dinner off of TV trays."

Fred, Jr., has been surprised at the same thing with the girls he's dated. He never wants to go to their homes because the family is so dull.

Balance TV with Reading

With our daughters, watching TV was not a problem, but with Fred, Jr., we found that as a child he would sit in front of the set forever if not supervised. We established a rule with him that he could watch as many hours of TV as he spent reading books. If he read for an hour, he could watch for an hour. The only time this rule didn't apply was when we all watched a program as a family—or when he was assigned a program as homework. This rule caused him to read more and watch less.

Get Approval on Subject Matter

If a program was anything beyond the preapproved list of accepted shows, the child had to check it out with one of us. Because they knew our standards, they seldom asked to view something of which we would not approve.

Lauren has carried this plan over with her children and I was amazed to find that ten-year-old Randy knew the rating system for movies. He had checked them out in the paper and told me, "There's not one G (General Audience) movie in town. It's got so there's not a decent thing for kids to look at any more." What a sad truth and yet how grateful I am that he accepted the grim fact that there was nothing for him to consider.

Homework Must Be Done First

Until the homework was done we didn't permit anyone to watch a program whether or not we were there to check.

My friend Marilyn was a high school counselor for several years. When students consistently failed to hand in homework, she routinely asked how many hours they spent watching TV. She often discovered the students were trying to do their homework in the same room where the rest of the family was watching TV. When she would suggest to the parents that the TV remain off until all homework was done, the parents often responded, "But what am I supposed to do while I'm waiting for them to finish their homework?"

Give a Review

After watching a show the children were to sum it up for us and tell us what it was about, what point it made, and how it applied to them. Bob Anderson, counselor and teacher in Fort Wayne, explained that his family would watch a program together and then turn it off and discuss it. Each one would give his opinion of the theme, the characters, and the acting ability. With him leading the discussion, the children were able to learn how to evaluate the merits of a show and how to be discerning in their selections.

Allow Television Only As a Last Resort

We have all read facts about the children of today being more out of shape than any previous generation. Most of them come home from school and head straight for the refrigerator and then the TV. They eat snacks with high calories and low nourishment and avoid exercise, both physical and mental, while watching TV.

Following the suggestions of doing homework first and balancing TV with reading will help cut down on television time, but the underlying message that must be presented is that TV watching is a last resort. Other activities need to be offered to fill the time that would be spent in front of the TV. Find a sports event of interest to your children and sign them up for a team. Today these physical outdoor activities are not limited just to boys. They help build team spirit, physical health, and they are not done in front of a TV. If your child is not athletically inclined or if after sports still has too much time on his or her hands, offer lessons such as piano, violin, art, or dance. Most of the YM- or YWCAs across the country offer many options for such activities at a very reasonable cost. Another choice might be to enroll your older children in a reading program at the local library where they receive points and prizes for the number of books read. Be alert; there are many options available that put your children's mental and physical growth first and make TV a last choice.

Marita, a non-TV watcher, writes here about two neighborhood girls, Eve, 10, and Amy, 12.

These girls are vidiots! All they want to do is watch TV. When they come to visit at my house they bring videotapes with them since they know my TV is only hooked up to the VCR. They are both overweight and lack the social skills needed to make new friends in a strange place. They are new in our neighborhood and although there are children everywhere, they seem to have no real friends. Their Phlegmatic/Sanguine mother is newly divorced and is struggling to keep her head above water so I guess it is easier to let the TV babysit while she nurses her wounds.

Chuck and I have no children and we wanted to do something to help this overwhelmed mother. We started having Eve and Amy over a few afternoons a month and let them both spend the night from time to time. That was when my husband declared them to be vidiots.

Together we decided that we were going to make a difference in their lives. We knew it was not our place to change their mother, but we could encourage the girls in the social skills they were lacking.

On their next visit they arrived as usual with their bag of videotapes, but none of them ever got watched. We all went to the pool and played together. Amy and Eve met some of the other kids and wanted to stay and play all day. At dinner Chuck decided to teach them culture, so he put Vivaldi's "Four Seasons" on the stereo. I cooked low calorie, healthy foods and served fresh fruit for dessert. At first they fussed at some of the foods that weren't hot dogs or spaghetti, but now as they've come back, they have learned that they are expected to cheerfully have at least three bites of everything.

After dinner we work on a puzzle or play a board game and at bedtime I've started reading them a multi-chaptered children's book, one chapter each night they are there. (OK, sometimes I read two if they've been really good.)

The last few visits the girls haven't brought the videotapes and don't seem to notice their absence. Their time with us is filled with other activities. I was afraid they'd think a story at bedtime was dumb, but they look forward to it and are eager to be good so they can hear more. Last week they reported to us that they were now on a girls' softball team. They have made new friends in the area and are learning the social skills that will help them get along in life. Most importantly, they have learned that there is life after TV!

15. Home Responsibilities

To raise children who can get along without us, we need to train them in the area of home responsibilities. They must learn at a very young age that there is no great housekeeping angel who swoops down and does dishes. There are no nocturnal elves who scamper through the house wielding feather dusters. We are those elves and angels and we must do the work. It is always easier for mother angel to do it all herself, but the time spent in training the troops will be well worth the trouble in the long run.

If you institute family meetings, these times would be appropriate to review basic responsibilities. As with financial matters, the children need to know what it takes to keep the home together. Since our minds can retain information better if it's logical, let's start with a list of chores beginning with the yard and working inward through the front door, foyer, living room, kitchen, family room, bedrooms, bathrooms, and patio. As you mention each room, ask for jobs that need to be done in that area and list them. You may be surprised that some of the children will come up with improvements you hadn't thought of. Once you have constructed a list of duties, go back over them and see how often each one has to be done: beds each morning, dishes three times a day, lawn once a week, bedroom every Saturday. By the time you complete the household needs, the children will see, perhaps for the first time, what it takes to keep the house in decent shape. That is step one. The next procedure involves a creative way to see that the needs are met and by whom. These things won't get done by chance and will only be maintained by praise.

As we were raising our children, we used our family meetings to discuss the duties and then Perfect Parent Fred made a chart. Although I had bucked some of his organization in the past, I could see the merits of listing the duties and having the children check them off.

The Family Work Chart is a copy of the one we used for years.

To get performance from the little stars in your home show,

FAMILY WORK CHART

		DAD	MOM			
SUNDAY						
MONDAY						
TUESDAY						
WEDNESDAY						
THURSDAY						
FRIDAY						
SATURDAY						

you have to make the instructions clear and not leave them to chance. You must also have the expected duties posted ahead of time so that the children won't find out on Saturday morning that you expect them to paint the kitchen or wash and wax the van.

I have found from my own experience and from talking to teens that they don't mind doing some work if they know ahead of time and don't get surprised at the last minute. Our Family Work Chart had the children's names and also Fred and I were listed. We wanted to make sure that the children didn't think this was a slave labor camp but a division of responsibility. If I noticed something broken, I would write it in Fred's column and if the children had a need they could write a request in mine. The children rarely did this but they had permission to ask for our help.

We started our chart with Saturday because that was our big work day at home and we left a big space for me to fill in. On Thursday evening I wrote out the duties for Saturday and some for the following week. In the box at the bottom of each day, I wrote in activity reminders: piano lessons, orthodontist appointments, birthday parties, etc. All of this was posted on the refrigerator door on Friday morning. Even though it took time on Thursday, the blessings for the week were well worth the effort.

Our rule, agreed upon at the family meeting, was that you could do your chores any time from Friday on, but you couldn't leave the house on Saturday until they were completed, inspected, and crossed off. This led to midnight cleaning binges and early morning vacuuming, but I always let them know I didn't care when they did the work or even who did it. If they wished to trade off, import friends, or hire a cleaning lady, I didn't mind as long as they got the job done.

I often tell the story of waking up around midnight and hearing voices in Marita's bathroom. I got up and went in to find a little blonde girl scrubbing the toilet. When I asked her what she was doing there, she replied that they were all going to the beach early the next day and Marita couldn't go with them until her chores were done and so they'd come over to help her. "They" were three of Marita's friends all in their early teens who had sneaked out of their own homes to come over and clean mine. Only a Popular Sanguine like Marita could inspire her friends to run away from home in the night in order to clean someone else's toilet!

At one point a newspaper reporter came to our home to interview me on our "Harmony in the Home" class. I knew Freddie would come home while she was there and I thought of warning him to be sure and behave well. Then I realized he might walk in and say something like "Are you the lady I'm supposed to behave for?" I decided that I'd trained him enough and I'd take my chances.

When he came home from fifth grade that day, he walked into the family room and I introduced him to the reporter. He greeted her pleasantly, left the room, and returned within a few minutes holding a dry mop, a dish towel, a rubber band, and a can of Endust. The reporter asked him what he was going to do and he answered her as if I'd rehearsed him. "Each day when I come home from school I check the work chart to see what I am expected to do. Today I'm to mop the foyer floor so I have my mop which I will cover with this clean towel held on by this rubber band. I will spray the towel with Endust and then mop up the floor."

The reporter was amazed and said, "I never saw a child before who did his chores without anyone having to remind him."

I can't guarantee that if you organize your household responsibilities and put up a chart each Thursday your children will keep cleaning cheerfully, but I can assume that if you don't come up with some form of disciplined duties, your children won't devise it on their own.

Remember that training up each child in the way he should go is not just to make your work load easier, but to prepare him to become a responsible adult who will be able to get along without you.

Remember also to follow up on your assignments and make sure that they were done on the right day. Be sure to praise them as frequently as possible and let them know verbally how you appreciate their responsible behavior.

A lady in Florida wrote me this suggestion:

We have two children who used to quarrel over whose turn it was to feed the pets, take out trash, sit in the front seat of the car, etc. To eliminate this, we "gave" three days a week to each child. On those days they automatically assume all responsibilities that have been given them, depending upon their ages. They also get all privileges. Thus, on Monday, Wednesday, Friday one girl feeds the pets, sets the table, washes dishes, gets to sit in the front seat of the car, gets to choose what to listen to on the car radio, gets to choose TV programs, etc.; and on Tuesday, Thursday, Saturday the other one gets her turn. They seem to feel this to be very fair and we've had no problems with quarrels over who does more work or has more preferential treatment.

Occasionally someone will ask me what jobs little children can do. I started mine on emptying wastebaskets. If anything broke it didn't matter for it was trash anyway. I had them collect the baskets one at a time and empty them into a large container in the kitchen. When they got older they took them to the garage and became responsible for getting the trash cans to the curb on the appropriate days.

Another early job that was harmless and useful was gathering laundry from each bedroom. To have a child do this you must have established a place to put the laundry and train each child to deposit his clothes as he takes them off. If you have set up the system, a two-year-old can go and collect the clothes on the days you are going to wash. Freddie loved this duty and he would sit and play in the dirty wash. Again it didn't matter if he dragged the items across the floor as they were dirty anyway. Soon he began to sort whites from colors and sheets and towels from clothes. Then I let him get up on a stool and watch the water pour into the washer. He learned to add the soap and later to transfer clothes from the washer to the dryer. By the time he was a teen he was doing all his own laundry and still is.

In her book on household organization, *More Hours in My Day*, Emilie Barnes has a chapter "Jobs children can do" divided into the different age abilities. If you haven't read that book and her *Survival for Busy Women*, you must get these so you can have more hours and most of all survive!

Emilie has gathered other helpful items to make a mother's job easier and the children more willing to work. One is a simple "Chore Chart" for little ones with pictures of clothes, toys, bed, teeth, bath so that even a child who can't read can check off his chart. If you use a water-based pen (one is included) you can wipe the chart clean each week and start again.

The "Child Organizer" is a large pad of bright yellow pages divided into types of jobs with a place to check each day when the task is completed. The categories are: Clean Room, Self-Care, School, and Family. There are blank spaces for extra chores and even a box for the amount of allowance earned for extra chores. There is a reminder in the School section to bring lunch money, notes for teacher, and overdue books. Under Family it asks, "Did I treat my family with love and respect?"

Another large pad by the same "Character Builders for Kids" is called "Note to My Teacher." I wish this had been around when I was raising my children as it would have saved much time finding paper at the last minute to write an excuse. This one says:

Dear Teacher,
    Please excuse _____ on
_____ due to:
    ____ Doctor's appointment
    ____ Dentist/Orthodontist
    ____ Family emergency
    ____ Illness
    ____ Missed my bus
    ____ Overslept (oops)
    ____ Other
Comments:
_____
_____
_____
_____

Parent's Signature   Date

Emilie also has available Reward Coupon packets containing little cards saying "Your reward: _____ because you are so special, thank you for a job well done." Emilie teaches mothers to give these out to children when they have done an extra job and deserve a reward. The reward could be anything you wish to give or older children could save them up. For example, ten coupons could be worth a trip to the park or some special treat.

Another adorable reward idea is a packet of stickers with a little teddy bear saying, "I was caught being good!" Emilie uses them for her grandchildren and when they do something nice for her, she gives them a sticker to put on their clothes or sometimes a bare arm. She told me that when they come into her house they start looking for things to do and begging for jobs so they will get a sticker.

All these ideas are tools to help you train up your children to become responsible. If you don't find these in your local Christian bookstore, write to *More Hours in My Day, 2838 Rumsey Road, Riverside, CA 92506.*

Part IV

THE PLOT

> Let all things be done decently
> and in order.
> (1 Corinthians 14:40)

IV

The Plot

Is there some plan for your family or do you just take each day as it comes and hope to live through it? Any successful drama has a plot, a beginning, some conflict, a climax, and a conclusion. The author has the plot on paper and the director carries it out on stage. No director would set a group in front of an audience without any script and tell them to say what comes to their minds. This would be sheer folly and yet that is often how our household functions, somewhat freestyle.

The successful families I have observed over the last twenty years have been ones where the parents had a goal in mind. Not a dictatorial goal such as the first one will be a doctor, the second a teacher, and so on, but some family aims for progress. My brother Jim, a career chaplain in the Air Force, and his wife Katie set a goal that their children would study in a foreign country at some point in their education. They talked abut this aim from the time the children were little as an accepted fact, not just a possibility. As I have seen their six children grow up, study hard, win scholarships, spend time abroad, and learn to speak languages fluently, I have been steadily impressed.

Cherie spent time at the University of London, has a Master's Degree in Counseling and is a Vocational Rehabilitation Counselor.

Laurie studied in Paris, taught English and French to Zairean natives while in the Peace Corps, has a Master of Divinity degree from Chicago Theological Seminary, and is an ordained minister in Grand Rapids, Michigan.

Lisa has a Master's in Exercise Physiology, is Director of Education at the Akron City Hospital, writes their programs of instruction and speaks all over the country to business and hospital groups on physical fitness.

Cindy, a Phi Beta Kappa and *Time* magazine honoree as one of the 100 outstanding college juniors in the country, was a foreign exchange student to Israel, spent her junior year at Kalamazoo College in Hong Kong, speaks fluent Hebrew and Mandarin Chinese, and just received a scholarship to Vanderbilt School of Divinity.

Michelle, who became interested in the Japanese language when the family spent two years in Japan in the Air Force, is majoring in Japanese studies, speaks Japanese, and plans to work for a Japanese company.

Jimmy, the last child and only son, is still in high school but already shows outstanding promise as a highly respected student and nominee for Boy's State.

When I talked with Katie about her outstanding family achievements, she said, "Wherever you place your values will determine what your children will see as important. Too many families have no goals of challenge and excitement and they have repeat cycles of dullness from one generation to the next."

Surely there has been no cycle of dullness in their home, for besides their academic achievements they have kept a high level of wit and humor, making an evening with them better than "The Cosby Show."

As I've observed their family goals and harmony, I've been delighted to find six young people in today's world who are not strange or square, who are not into drugs, alcohol, or smoking, and who have positive outgoing personalities. They are super achievers and are still active in church. Do you think this is an accident? Were they born under lucky stars? Or were Jim and Katie's dedicated efforts and goals rewarded in an exceptional series of results?

There's an old saying, "If you don't know where you're

going, any road will get you there." Is your family on any old road going any old way? Or do you have a plan of action? I didn't make it a family plan that my children would study in foreign lands and none of them did. Jim and Katie had that goal and their children went around the world. Do you think the parents' planning and expectations had anything to do with it?

Wherever you are right now, start with some long-range desires for your family. One lady told me she and her husband had made a list of the books they wanted their children to read before they were eighteen. The list was posted in their den for years and it was an accepted fact that you would read these books and check them off each time you completed one. One family made a goal of visiting ten national parks before the first child left home and they were on their way to achieving this. Some set goals to memorize portions of the Bible and then sit down with the children and help them do so.

We tend to reproduce after our own kind and although we don't automatically raise little clones of ourselves, what we show as normal in our homes is what our children will probably accept.

My brother Ron has one daughter, Melanie. From the time she was little he took her with him to the radio station so that she could see what he did. When he would be the celebrity to draw crowds to a new restaurant or hotel in Dallas, Melanie was with him. He never told her she had to go into radio work, but when she attended Southern Methodist University she was a natural for their radio programs and became manager of their SMU network. She is now in Denver in the promotion department of a large radio station.

Once Fred and I found out what a blessing it was to know and use the four personalities, we determined to ground our children in these concepts so that by the time they were married they would fully understand the differences in their natures.

When we had couples' studies in our home, our three children greeted people at the door, and sat right in the front row. Church attendance was an accepted part of the week and because we didn't "sleep in" or choose not to go, neither did they.

When I was in theatre work, my children all learned how to

be on stage. When I was president of organizations, they found out how to lead meetings.

When we were in the restaurant business, our girls waitressed and Lauren earned her college expenses by her tips.

I never told either girl that she had to be like me (be a Christian speaker, or write a book), but they saw me speaking and writing and they have each become Christian speakers and have each written a book that's been published. My children were more likely to think of writing a book than young people brought up in homes where creative writing was not a visible occupation.

Be sure in raising your children that you let them see what you do and that you show them the pros and cons of your life's work. Do not constantly degrade your profession and tell them they should never do this because they may well end up doing it anyway but begrudgingly. Many young people I talk with have never visited their father or mother's workplace and have little concept of the energy or talent it takes to produce the family income. Involve your children in what you are doing, discuss what training it takes to enter into different professions, and help them plan their education with some specific goals in mind.

In the Gallup Survey, "Roots of Success," the researchers concluded, "High achievers' parents felt that their children knew what career they would one day pursue before the parents themselves were aware of the child's leanings. About twenty percent of successful-group mothers thought that even when their children were under twelve the children knew what field they would enter."[1]

What can you do to help your children become productive adults?

1. Don't depend on the school guidance counselor to steer your child in the right direction. Aptitude testing can give indications of your child's ability, but these standard questions cannot take your place. You know your child's talents and gifts. By now you should have a handle on his personality and know his strengths and weaknesses. Don't let someone else choose his future.

2. Spend time discussing each child's personality. I constantly meet adults who are in the wrong profession because a parent or counselor pushed them without regard to their personality potential. One Sanguine accountant told me he quit his job after hearing me speak because it was the first time he could understand why he hated what he was doing. He went into the travel business and loves being with people day and night. The Popular Sanguine will never be happy with routine work away from people. These people live for excitement, spontaneity, and response from an audience.

The Powerful Choleric will chafe under circumstances where he has no control or even the possibility of promotion somewhere down the line. He will be happiest in his own business or at least in a position where he can see steps of advancement.

The Perfect Melancholy doesn't do well in a place where dealing with people is the main objective, but he will thrive where academic, scholarly, artistic, musical, cultural, detailed, or numerical skills are needed.

The Peaceful Phlegmatic (especially if his secondary personality is Sanguine) should not be in business for himself as he is most apt to be undisciplined, indecisive, procrastinating, and poor with money. He will function best in structured situations where the steps of progress are laid out and monitored, and where balance, objectivity, and managerial skills are desirable.

Go over your children's personalities and have them list occupations that would be naturals for them. Have them tell you why they would be successful in certain occupations and not in others. Get them thinking early in life about their future careers.

3. Arrange for them to talk with people in different professions. Reading about a variety of jobs is helpful, but conversing with those already in the field is better. When Marita was in high school I sent her for a week to my brother Ron to work and observe the radio business. When she saw what it entailed and how little glamour there was to being up at 4:30 in the morning, she lost interest. Seeing (and working!) is believing.

Throughout our children's lives we have entertained in our home a whole series of Christian speakers, authors, pastors, and missionaries from this country and abroad. We always included the children in the conversation and encouraged them to ask questions. Giving to missions is only a matter of money until you meet a missionary and find out what they really do.

4. Listen to your children's ideas and don't say, "That's a stupid idea, you'll never make any money that way." In the last year, as I have been doing a message called "Silver Boxes" encouraging all of us to encourage everyone else, I have told how my father could have been a great writer if he'd been encouraged. I mention that Fred's mother wanted to be an opera singer but her parents told her she didn't have enough talent. As I tell these stories, people begin to cry and later come up to tell me of the dreams they once had that their parents ridiculed. So many of them never became what they could have been because they were discouraged by people whose opinions they respected.

Don't be a wet blanket on your child's dreams. Let him explore possibilities. When Randy was little he told me he would be a speaker like me. Later he said he wanted to be a fireman. I asked, "Didn't you say you wanted to be a speaker?" Quickly he recouped, "I'll speak on fires." Now at ten he wants to be a doctor. With his Melancholy personality and exceptional ability in science, he may be heading for his future choice.

At six Jonathan has told me he's going to be a builder. As we took a walk through his neighborhood where several new houses are being built, he showed me many structural details that he had learned from his parents on previous tours. "Do you see how those front windows aren't even, Grammie? When I build houses I'm going to measure the windows." Since Jonathan is Sanguine, he will probably not measure anything, but I encouraged him in becoming a builder since that's where his thinking is today.

Listen to their dreams, let them imagine what they might be, and don't discourage their ideas no matter how ridiculous they might sound to you.

5. Help them choose the right courses to prepare them for future possibilities. With our hectic schedules today and with many working mothers, it's much easier to let our children take what they want in high school than to go over the lists and discuss what they would need for certain colleges or occupations; yet the neglect of family participation in course selection can have a negative result. How sad it would be for your child to want to go to a certain college or vocational school only to find he is missing a key course for admission.

Don't leave the choices up to the high school whose job it is to get the right number of students into rooms staffed by the available teachers. Surely, I don't mean school counselors have no value, but always remember that the child is yours, not theirs.

6. Seek God's will in their future. Taking human steps is important, but as Christian believers we must train our children to seek God's will in all of life's choices. If you have had a vital family prayer life this step will be automatic but if you have all been closet Christians, if you have a nonbelieving spouse, or if you are a single parent whose time has been consumed in a daily struggle for existence, you will need to begin with the teaching that God cares about every part of our lives.

Read the chapter on family prayer time and start with some simple requests. Lay choices out before the Lord and ask Him to open or shut doors to aid in our direction. Even if your children or mate should scoff at your supplications, continue in faith and let God convict them. Pray for each person and each question and watch for results. Even defensive children find it difficult to rebel against a mother or father who they know is praying for them.

As with every step of parenting—planning ahead with your children, setting goals, discussing personality traits, visiting schools and businesses, teaching them to bring their questions before the Lord—all these things take time. We all have too much to do, but when it's all said and done the size of your house, the quality of your carpet, and the dignity of your position will be nothing if you've somehow lost your child to the lures of the world.

Raising children is not just tossing out seeds and sprinkling them now and then; it is a lifetime of dedication from parents who are more concerned with their families' physical, emotional, and spiritual growth than they are with their own personal pursuits of career, social status, reputation, sports, or beautiful bodies.

When your children leave to cleave, what they know about family life will be what they've learned from you. Will you be pleased with the results?

Part V

THE SETTING

Cheerfully share your home with
those who need a meal or a place
to stay for the night.
(1 Peter 4:9 TLB)

V

The Setting

In any drama the setting provides the backdrop for the action. When the curtain goes up, what you see at first, before a line is spoken, is the atmosphere created by the set. The first real drama I ever saw was *The Barretts of Wimpole Street*, starring Katherine Cornell. Our high school English class traveled to Boston to learn of the life of Elizabeth Barrett Browning, her love, and her poetry. I will never forget when the curtain opened and there was a Victorian living room with a deep red velvet loveseat, fringed lampshades, and gold framed ancestors on the walls covered with brocaded paper. To that point in my life I had never seen such an ornate setting and I was transported warmly into the Barrett home as a family member before I'd even met them.

Later, when I was directing musicals, I would get most excited over the possible set we could build to provide the initial impression we were after.

For *Guys and Dolls* we opened with the streets of New York, crowds rushing by, little Lauren twirling a hula hoop in the middle of a group of children. We wanted to portray a street scene that was busy, fun, and full of excitement. For *Oklahoma* we built the front porch of an old farm house complete with rocking chairs and had a backdrop painted with fields of corn "as high as an elephant's eye."

When I married and had my first opportunity to decorate my own set, I fluffed up our bedroom with pink embroidered organdy. In retrospect I had always wanted a real girl's room as a child. Jammed into the cramped quarters behind the store where we had neither bedspreads nor drapes, I had longed for a Shirley Temple type of room.

How Fred handled a bedroom full of pink ruffles and taffeta drapes, I can't now imagine—but this room became the setting for my childhood dreams. Later I modified my bows and lace approach and when I went through my "stage phase" I decorated our Connecticut living room with a mural of court jesters acting out different scenes and even decorated my Christmas tree with heads of little masked jesters. As I look back over my homes, I see how important my setting has always been and how easy it would have been for anyone to see where my attention was focused at the time.

By the time we moved to California and I was assigned to live in Bungalow One and make that old motel a home, I had to learn that size and glamor were not terribly important. With eight of us living in five rooms and a porch, I had to rethink the purpose of home decorating and realize that cozy comfort had to be my new objective.

After two years in Bungalow One, we built a large home where each child could once more have his or her own room. We let each one choose a theme and decorated each room in a nationality of our family background. It probably will cost no more money to decorate with some unity of purpose and some exciting color than it does to paint the whole house white. Our bedroom was done in English style with brocade paper and Wedgewood pieces as accents. The study was Scotch with plaid carpeting and Fred's room was German with a striped awning and brick carpeting. Marita's was Swedish with built-in beds and ruffled curtains that dropped down to hide her away. Lauren chose Early American with a canopy bed.

We all had a part in decorating that home in the foothills of the San Bernardino Mountains and it was in that home that we had the most fun we'd ever had as a family—and where I went through what is now referred to as "Mother's Hostess on the Hill Era."

In looking back on this time, I realize how important it was to set a stage for my children where they could be comfortable, could bring in all their friends, and could learn to design and keep their own rooms in order. It was in this home that we had women's Bible studies, couples' marriage classes of almost 100 people each Friday night, monthly open house Saturday Suppers, and teen studies with guest speakers. Our home became a welcoming spot for friends and strangers and we entertained many angels unaware.

How about your home? Have you done more than move in? Do you realize the value of setting a pleasant, warm, relaxing backdrop for your family drama? Do you comprehend the value of having your children want to be home? Are you building a foundation that will provide security for your family structure and an example for their future homes?

Our aim is to provide a loving atmosphere, a colorful backdrop for our cast of characters to enjoy, a setting of compassion and comfort, of love and laughter.

Here are some ideas that you can build into your stage to make your setting an exciting place to be.

16. Personal Not Perfect

While I have always designed the type of home that could be a show place, Fred and I had to learn to give up some perfectionism in exchange for personalization—little touches like Freddie's scribble painting hanging on the refrigerator door and Marita's clay pinch pot proudly placed on the coffee table. I had to hold myself back from correction when the napkins they chose in setting the table were not the "best choice." And I had to allow Sanguine Marita the freedom to rearrange her furniture every other week.

Our children do follow our pattern of living and Marita and Lauren's homes look like showplaces, but they are more personal than perfect. Marita's dining room walls are filled with framed memorabilia of different trips. Above the fireplace is a huge photo of Marita and Chuck on their first anniversary, and the stairway proudly displays brightly framed pictures of their nieces and nephews, and even a portrait of their puppies.

Lauren

Lauren and Randy have done an excellent job of making their home a personal expression of each family member. Randy collects mementos and maps of famed cartographer General Charles Gordon and the fall of Khartoum. Above their sofa is a large brass plaque of Gordon and a map of the Sudan that he had drawn. At the end of the hall, under a spotlight hangs a large carved-wood portrait of General Gordon, the study is full of books on Gordon, and busts of him look down from the shelves. Lauren collects Mother and Child paintings and sculptures that are prominently placed in their bedroom and foyer.

When it came time to redecorate Randy, Jr.'s room Lauren had her own ideas of what she wanted done. Fortunately before she carried out her plans, she realized that like her, Randy, Jr. has some Choleric with his Melancholy. He needed control of something, so before ordering the wallpaper she showed it to him and was surprised by his definite opinion. He didn't want plain plaid, he wanted outerspace wall paper. Because it is his bedroom, Lauren allowed him to choose the setting he would like to live in. Randy's room has navy blue wallpaper with white stars and multi-colored planets all over it. He has framed prints of the planets and solar system hanging on the walls. On his dresser are models of rockets and hanging from the ceiling is a large space shuttle. Randy loves his room. Yes, it looks small with all the darkness of the midnight sky spotted with occasional planets and stars. But he is the envy of all of his friends.

When Sanguine Jonathan outgrew his crib, I took him out on a fun-filled excursion to buy a new bed. He bounced on all kinds of different mattresses and finally selected a bunk type bed with drawers built in under one side and a secret hiding place behind them. Jonathan was so excited about *his* beds that the day the beds arrived he ran all over the house and the neighborhood to let everyone know *his* new beds were home.

We need to communicate to our family members that their desires are more important than impressing our friends with a perfect house. Last week I was speaking on parenting in Texas. I mentioned the idea of decorating our home for our family, not our friends. I asked the audience, "Why do we want our houses to be perfect? Whom do we decorate for?" They sheepishly answered "our friends." Are you guilty of that? We need to realize that our friends will come and go, we'll move on or they'll move on, but our families are with us forever. Our aim needs to be to create a setting where our family is comfortable, a place where they'll want to be. A lady came up to me after the seminar and said, "My husband says my house is so perfect he doesn't dare sit down. I'm going home and mess it up a little so my family can relax."

17. Medley Not Monotony

Another aspect of setting the stage is variety, keeping life interesting. It is easy for day-to-day routines to become boring, not only for us but for our children. One of the ways we kept excitement in our home was through hospitality. We had guests in for dinner and often for the night. Romans 12:13b commands us to "get into the habit of inviting guests home for dinner or, if they need lodging, for the night" (TLB). These guests gave our children a medley of experiences at the time and now they have many memories of the missionaries, ministers, and a multitude of others who have enhanced our lives. I remember the black evangelist Ernie Wilson from Philadelphia. He stayed at our home several times during his Southern California visits, and he became little Freddie's favorite. Freddie loved his cologne and he would crawl up in Ernie's lap and listen to his stories about how he was a prizefighter before he met the Lord.

The first time little Freddie realized that there was really a world beyond San Bernardino was the day a visiting missionary nurse from Zaire came home after church for lunch. Freddie got out his globe and carried it to the table so she could show him where she worked. He was wide-eyed as she told him what children his age did on the other side of the world.

Then came Brenda and Richard. Brenda was on staff with Campus Crusade and she went to our church. She had just come back from raising support and was looking for a place to stay. Fred and I were going to New York to speak and were planning to be gone for a week. We had made plans for someone else to stay with Freddie while we were gone, but those plans had just fallen through. So we invited Brenda to stay with us until she found a place. Freddie was twelve and didn't really need "baby sitting" but since Marita worked all night, we wanted someone there. Brenda moved in for a week and stayed six years.

Marita loves to tell the story about Richard.

I was at work in a coffee shop one evening when my mother stopped in. She loudly announced, "I've found a nice boy to move in with you!" Once she'd gotten the attention of me and all of my customers, she explained with a laugh that someone had called and asked if she could house a new young Campus Crusade staff member until he found a place to live. Since she and my dad were leaving town the next morning, she had told them that Richard could come by after work and if Brenda and I liked him, he could stay. It sounded like fun to me and the next day when the doorbell rang, Brenda and I were like giggling school girls. There stood tall, handsome, tan, curly-haired Richard. We soon decided Richard could stay. He moved into the guest room behind the house, Brenda lived in the room Lauren had vacated, I was in my room, and Freddie was in his. We had some great times together. One night we put Vaseline all over Richard's toilet seat. When he came out of the bathroom we were waiting around the corner with shaving cream cans. The four of us had a great fight until Dad came out and with one glance put an end to the whole mess. Richard stayed with us for six months and Brenda was with us for two years in that house, two years in the next one and another two years in the next one. She'd probably still be there if she hadn't gotten married.

Brenda and I shared a room in the last two houses. We became best friends. In one house our bedroom was on the second floor right over the front door. When either of us came home from a date, the other would wait a few minutes, go to the window, and holler out, "It's getting late; you have to go to work early in the morning." We knew if we wanted to come in, this gave us a good excuse but if we wanted to stay out we would say, "Ignore her, she always does that." Brenda always came in. She is now married and today Ken, Brenda, Michael, and Heidi are very much a part of our family lives.

Fred and I encouraged our children to bring their friends home with them. There they were able to see these friends in our circle and evaluate how well they fit in with the family. Some never came again, but many of their friends responded to the warm, encouraging environment so well that they kept coming back. Many of them, like Brenda and Richard, stayed for days, weeks, months, and even years.

When Lauren was in high school, she and several friends worked in our family restaurant. Many of them had emotional needs that were not being met in their own homes. They began to come over after school or after work and some ended up spending the night and often the week.

Lauren's friend, Jan Frank—the author of *The Door of Hope*—was with us so many mornings that she became a part of our family. She is still a frequent guest at our family gatherings and holidays. Her two adorable girls, Heather and Kellie, call me Grammie Florence. I was always happy to have Lauren under our roof where I could see her. If that included her friends, it was fine with us.

One day Marita came home with one of the girls she waitressed with and asked if it would be OK if Lorraine moved in with her. Lorraine's mother had just kicked her out of the house and she had nowhere to go. She stayed in Marita's extra bed until things got better at home and she could go back. While she was there she functioned as part of the family and saw Christian love she never knew in her own home.

Inviting guests "home for dinner, or if they need lodging for the night" has enriched our life experiences. We have had a medley of different lives crisscross with ours and our home life has never been monotonous.

Sue Gregg, the author of *Eat Right!*, shared this story about their house guests and their effect on the children:

> Our first house guest was Bart from Switzerland the first year of our marriage during Christmas vacation. We found such joy in sharing our lives and home in this way that it has just become a normal part of our lifestyle. Since then thirty-two people have lived with us anywhere from three weeks to two years.

Like Rich and Sue Gregg, Lauren and her husband Randy have opened their home to young men from different countries. Christoph came from Germany for the summer. They had such a wonderful time together that he came back the next year for his senior year in high school. He taught Randy, Jr. to play tennis, played with Jonathan in the pool, and doted on Baby Bryan. The guest room was empty only a few days when Olivier came from France. Randy and Jonathan take French in school and Olivier gave them a chance to sharpen their skills. Before Olivier left to go back home, his father Charles joined them. Charles looked like Mr. Clean, but his French accent and Continental charm made fast friends of all of us.

When Fred and I were in Australia we met Thomas, a young waiter from Austria. He had attended a chef school in his native land and was working his way up in an intercontinental hotel chain. We became friends and invited him to visit us in California when he came to the states on his way back to Austria. Thomas arrived for the week of Thanksgiving, enjoyed learning about our traditional family holiday, stayed with Lauren and Randy, and even did some gourmet cooking.

This summer Lauren and Randy and the boys are going to Europe. They will stay with their friends, Christoph in Germany, Charles and Olivier in France, and Thomas in Austria.

Open your home to others, you'll be glad you did.

18. Sharing Not Silence

When we do open our home to others, it is important that we share the experience with our little ones and include them in the conversation. Don't expect them to be silent but help them join in the joy of meeting someone new. For hospitality to work it needs to be more than just something you do now and then.

I often allowed the children to choose the menu items and I took them grocery shopping so that they could learn prices and quality. I taught them all how to cook and, even though it was often harder than if I'd done it alone, I felt the long-range benefits were worth the trouble. Young Fred has brought home girl friends who literally could not boil water (and one who could only cook spaghetti, heat a jar of sauce, and make a salad). We both agreed this menu would become dull in a short time, and I suggested the girl move to Italy.

When we realize that our aim as parents is to make the children self-sufficient, able to function without us, we can see how important it is to teach them how to cook and not doom them to a life at McDonald's. For hospitality to become a way of life, we need to involve our children in the planning, the preparation, and the conversation.

19. Relatives Not Recreation

While television commercials would have us believe that weekends were made for recreation, there are some other meaningful things that can be done with our weekends and leisure time.

In today's fast-paced society and frequent moves, we often lose the sense of family so vital in our own feelings of self-worth. I visited with a man who drove us to the airport recently. He called himself a "Louisiana Red-necked Baptist" and when talking of teen problems in his church, he said, "A lot of the trouble comes from our not spending time with our relatives and understanding the sense of tradition and family values. My mother didn't have to explain why we shouldn't do things, she'd just say, 'Our family doesn't do that.' We knew there was family pride at stake and we wouldn't do anything that would bring shame on the family name."

As he said this I realized that in my childhood I had been instilled with the same attitude. I never wanted to hurt my mother or disappoint my father. "Our family doesn't do that." Could we restore some of this sense of family if we visited with the cousins, aunts and uncles, and grandparents? While cousins seldom become best friends, knowing them and the other relatives gives our children a better sense of their heritage, a sense of belonging.

In my book, *Your Personality Tree*, I suggest that you spend some time reviewing your family tree, gathering pictures and stories about the family members for several generations back, and tracing the personality traits that have been passed down from one generation to the next.

The response we have received from families who have made a family scrapbook and picture album, have analyzed the personalities of their ancestors, have visited old family homes and graveyards, and have quickened their children's interest in their roots has all been positive.

Both Lauren and Marita have gone back to Connecticut to look at our home of thirteen years; Lauren went to Fred's old English Tudor home in New York and the people living there let her in and allowed her to take pictures of where her Daddy used to live. When we took Fred, Jr. to Boston, he wanted to visit the hospital where he was born. Since he is adopted, this view of the Massachusetts General Hospital was an emotional time for him and an establishing of some touch with his beginnings. Children need to know that someone came before them—and the world will go on after they are gone.

In my home I have a family tree on the wall in the hall that Marita painted as a special present to us. We've hung pictures of Fred and me as babies on the bottom of the two main branches. Above me the branch splits and there is a picture of my mother on one side and my father on the other. The tree continues up to its top branches with my great grandmother Katherine Murphy and her husband Andrew Conrad.

Fred's branch does the same thing as far back as his great grandparents on the Oelkers' side. Recently Randy, Jr. was visiting me and asked me about the tree. As I reviewed the family with him, he quickly noticed how much his "Poppa" looked like him!

Last Thanksgiving little six-year-old Jonathan announced that he had something special to say to all of us. We quickly responded and stood at attention awaiting his words.

"No, no," he said, "I need to talk to you privately." He proceeded to divide us into groups, "Grammie, Poppa Briggs, and Uncle Chuck, you come first." We were all amazed as he told each gathering something a little different. In my group he started out by letting us know that "My mind tells me that I love you very much and that you are very important to me." He continued through both sets of grandparents, Aunt Rita and Uncle Chuck, Mommy and Daddy, and Uncle Fred. His relatives are important to him even at age six, and he felt led to tell us so.

These childhood family memories stay with us forever and Marita's favorite is of visiting my Aunt Jean.

> When I look back, I remember Dad's family and going to the Littauers in New York for holidays. But what I remember most about those is that the kids were in one room and the adults were in the other. I don't feel like I ever knew any of my aunts and uncles on Dad's side. It was different when we went to Aunt Jean's. She is Grammie Chapman's sister and when we went to her house we felt special. We all ate together and we ate what we'd picked out in Uncle Ethan's garden. Aunt Jean taught us to cook and can. She invited me to stay with her for weeks at a time and mostly she invested herself in me.
>
> When I got married I wanted Chuck to meet her. His relatives all live in Southern California and I knew them, but he knew none of mine. I talked about Aunt Jean so much that he suggested I invite her to stay with us for Christmas. I did and she came. It was the first time I'd really spent adult to adult time with her. We rekindled a relationship and we've stayed in touch by phone and mail.

You may be thinking to yourself, *That is great for you but none of my family live near us and our children never get to see their grandparents.* What can you do if the relatives all live far away? How can you keep the children in contact even under geographically distant conditions? If possible, plan special summer excursions to "go back home," to see the farm or visit the places where Mommy played. Make those trips special by preparing your children with stories and photos of you and the places you'll be visiting. And when the children are old enough let them visit other family members by themselves. These times with Grandma and Grandpa or aunts or cousins can be especially memorable if the child is the only one visiting. It could become a "rite of passage" by allowing each child to make a trip to Grammie's for their tenth birthday.

Sue Gregg shared with me what they had done with their family:

> We spent four full summers on the farm with the grandparents and several holiday vacations. We cherish the relationship our kids have enjoyed with them. They have left them with the special legacy of celebrating their 50th wedding anniversary. We have tried to attend family reunions with the children as much as possible. The sense of extended family is important. On Rich's side of the family, his great great-grandfather wrote an extensive family history tracing the Gregg family back to Samuel Gregg who came to America in 1699 at age 12. He also traced the Christian heritage of the Gregg family through the 18th and 19th centuries. In contrast, I have practically no information of my own family history. I used to beg my grandmother to tell me stories of her childhood and to write them down. I treasured any tidbits of childhood my mother would give me about herself. I hope someday to have time or make time to write down my childhood and events of life to leave for my children. I think it is important to their sense of belonging, of who they are, and helps them to understand themselves better, plus children just naturally enjoy hearing about their parents' childhoods.

Another option is to bring the extended family to you. Invite the cousins to come stay with you. Bring the grandparents to your home for the holidays or for some other special visit. Once a close relationship is established keep it up through regular cards, photos, and phone calls. Remember that in an isolated society our children need a sense of belonging.

My mother, "Grammie Chapman," lived with Lauren for three years before she died. The older boys, Randy and Jonathan, got to know "Grammie" and I was called "Other Grammie." My mother read stories to the boys and was always available in her rocking chair to hold one in her lap. Even though Bryan never knew her, he will still be able to touch base with his roots for while

Grammie was still alive, Lauren did an intimate interview with her. She set up the video camera and started asking Grammie questions about her childhood and where she grew up. At first she was nervous, but once she got going on those old tales, she forgot all about the camera and captivated us all for several hours telling stories about my father that I didn't even know. This was a rare and tender time and now we have this memorable tape that will help the great-grandchildren "know" Grammie Chapman and have a better understanding of who they are and where they came from.

Relatives help our children realize their roots, but they can also fill another important role. They can be a role model for our children. Parental love and encouragement is vital but other adults who are close to our children, who care about them, are also important to give them a balanced setting on which to form their views.

If your relatives are far away, Colleen Weeks, a Christian sex education teacher, suggests that you find some adult who is close to your children to help fill that void in their lives. This person may be their Sunday school teacher, a youth group leader, a grandmother whose family is far away, or one of your friends who is younger than you are and has no children. Our teens especially need someone they can talk to about problems or questions they may have but don't want to go to Mom or Dad about. We can help them by allowing an "aunt" or "uncle" into their lives whom we know will reinforce our standards.

When Brenda lived with us, she became this person to Marita. Brenda was only ten years older than Marita, but the two of them spent many hours talking late into the night. Brenda helped Marita work through some of her feelings just by listening and offering a sensible opinion now and then. I am most grateful that Brenda was willing to be a positive Christian example for Marita in her shaky teen years.

Remember that it is not the size of the house or the money spent on decorating the rooms that molds children's characters. It is the creativity, warmth, and excitement that your children feel when they are at home.

Marita will never forget the day when she realized how important home was to her.

I remember the day that I learned what our home meant to me. I was eighteen at that time and was waitressing from ten at night to six in the morning and then going to college until two in the afternoon. This particular spring day I drove home from school and bounded into the house anxious to tell someone what had gone on in my day. No one was in the kitchen. No one was in the family room. Fred wasn't home from school yet and Dad was at work. I went to Mom and Dad's room. It, too, was empty. I sat down in the family room by myself. I had homework to do and I knew I should go to bed to rest up for my job at night. Instead I got up and went to the mall for a while just to see people. As I roamed through the mall it hit me.

My friends had been encouraging me to move out of my parents' house and get a place of my own or better yet move in with them. They filled me in on the virtues of being able to stay out as late as I wanted, of being able to eat what I wanted with whomever I chose. They had nearly convinced me. My finances were such that I knew I could afford a new car or rent, but not both.

That day as I roamed aimlessly through the mall I felt strangely alone, and I realized that if I moved out and got my own place this is how it would be every day. No one there when I came home. No one who cared about how I was doing, in fact no one who cared if I came home at all! Then I knew why I was still living at home. For me living at home was not just rules and regulations but care and concern, love and laughter.

A few weeks later I bought my first new car. That was always my favorite. Every time I see a blue '76 Cougar with a white vinyl top and white leather interior I think back with fondness to that day that I decided to stay home. I lived there so long I'm sure my parents thought I'd never leave, but six years later I got married.

I am so grateful for the strong foundation I was given at home. I have tried to carry out that same care and concern, the love and laughter in my home. I want it to be a place my family will want to come home to. For me, "my family" is my husband Chuck, two Schnauzer pups, and a rabbit.

Many times Chuck comes home unexpectedly early. In the morning he tells me he is going to the gym after work or going to visit his mother, so I expect him home around seven. When I hear the garage door open at the usual time of 5:00 the dogs and I run out to greet him. I'll ask him, "What are you doing home so early?"

His response is usually, "Well, I was going to go out, but when the day was over there was nowhere I'd rather go than home. I like coming home." I'm glad home is where he wants to be. I'm thankful that my parents gave me a setting that was comfortable, a place where I wanted to come home to, and I am grateful that through their example I've been able to duplicate that quality in my home.

Part VI

THE BACKERS

Everyone of us shall give an
account of himself to God.
(Romans 14:12)

VI

The Backers

Before any Broadway production can get under way, someone has to provide the financing. The costs of directors, cast, theatre, rehearsals, costumes, scenery, and innumerable other expenses must be estimated and then backers must be found who are willing to invest the needed money. These backers always take a chance on whether or not the show will be a success.

As we go into marriage, unless we have a million dollars in the bank, we become our own risk-taking backers. Often if we've not been trained in financial management by our parents, we learn by a lot of trial and a few errors. Some of us were brought up in affluence and didn't need to know about handling money; some were taught the value of a dollar and keep their accounts in line.

Some who were raised with little in the way of material possessions feel they are doing their children a favor by giving them what they never had and not making them work. I hope that as we learn, we will see the necessity of showing our children the basic of financial responsibility.

One day after I was speaking on raising children and the need to have them grow up to be self-sufficient, an elegant lady came up and said, "I think I'm raising a bum."

"Tell me about him," I requested.

"Well, he's twenty-five years old and he's never had a job."

I affirmed, "I think you're right. You're raising a bum. What does he do all day?"

"He goes surfing."

"How does he get there?"

"In his Mercedes. I had to give him something to drive."

"How does he pay for the gas?"

"I gave him a credit card because he doesn't have any money."

"Where does he live?" I asked.

"At home with me. He can't afford an apartment."

I summed the whole story up. "You're telling me that your twenty-five-year-old son lives at home, you've given him a Mercedes to drive and a credit card to enjoy, he goes surfing every day, and he's never worked. Is that right?"

She nodded her head and I added, "Your son is not only a bum, but he's a smart bum. In fact he's smarter than you are, and would you adopt me?"

Why in the world would the boy be inspired to get a job when he had such a plush life? Why would any young person get down to serious business when the alternative was so pleasant?

Kim Matters wrote me, "I was brought up by a mother who did everything for me and now feels I should do the same for my children. But I know that I have been frustrated by my lack of skills, so like it or not, my children will receive from my reservoir of learned skills."

Kim told me how she had played my tapes on child-raising at home and her Sanguine fourteen-year-old son listened to the story about the twenty-five-year-old surfer. He'd made no comment at the time of listening, but later when Kim was discussing the tape with her husband, Scott spoke up and said, "I'm going to sue that lady."

Kim was stunned at his comment and asked why. He replied, "She's ruined my chances of being like the guy who surfs all day!"

20. Family Finances

For those of you who don't want to raise a bum who surfs all day, where do you start? We gave our children typical little allowances when they were young, but when they were old enough to understand money at all, Fred and I began to explain what it took to run the house. I remember sitting down with the girls and showing them the family finances. We went over the mortgage payment, taxes, gas, water, electric, telephone, food, clothes, church, entertainment, car payments, gas, insurance, and other miscellaneous expenses. We took the month's total and divided it by thirty to come up with how much it cost us a day to live in our house. We were all appalled when we saw the total. The children, for the first time, actually realized that the house and car weren't free blessings dropped down from above. This sobering thought made them realize that while the best things in life may be free, we don't have many of those. We have to work to pay the bills.

Even though Fred, Jr. was only nine when we made these explanations, he did realize for the first time that heat and air-conditioning cost money. I had come home one day to find the air-conditioning on and him wrapped up in an electric blanket in front of the blazing gas fireplace because he was cold.

Once we had assessed the family finances, we all became more conscious of shutting off the lights, heat, and air when we didn't need them and of not wasting food. I feel that most children would be cooperative in being more economical if they could see the big picture and understand the amount of money it costs to keep the family going. This knowledge also cut down the requests for extra treats at the store and other unnecessary luxuries.

21. Allowances

Another financial plan that worked well for us was figuring out how much each child needed for a year. Perfect Father Fred met with each one when they got to be twelve and went over all of their expenses including clothes, shoes, school lunches, sporting events, class trips, books and records, Sunday school, and miscellaneous items. The child was allowed to suggest any anticipated needs. When both Fred and the child felt comfortable with the estimate, Fred divided the year's cost into fifty-two weeks and came up with a week's allowance. Because each one had worked on the budget, the children felt the allowance was fair and didn't constantly gripe about their lack of money.

They knew from the beginning what their allowance covered and they had to see that they didn't spend it foolishly and have nothing left for essentials. Any purchase over $2 had to be checked with us for approval and if they ran out of money, they would have to wait until the following Friday for new funds.

Lauren, our business-minded Choleric, thrived under this arrangement and was no trouble, but when Sanguine Marita came along, learning to budget money and think ahead was not easy. She wanted to treat everyone to ice cream and she lost everything. For a while we seemed to be losing the battle and our minds as well. One week when she couldn't find her gym shoes, she told me she needed money immediately to go and buy a new pair. When I wouldn't supply dollars on demand, she explained that if she didn't have her shoes she would get a zero each day for gym class. Fred and I discussed the problem and decided that three days of zeros in gym would not be a life-shattering experience and that we had to bring some discipline into her young life. So we took a stand and refused to give her money until her regular time on Friday.

For three days she flunked gym and had to sit on the sidelines until she had her allowance and could buy the right shoes. This week of anguish taught her a much needed lesson, and she kept those shoes all through high school and had them as a souvenir until she got married.

Once I shared this story at the California Women's Retreat and two years later I met a lady at a party who approached me by saying, "I should tell you right in the beginning that I don't agree with how you've raised your children." I wondered how much she knew as she continued, "At the retreat two years ago you told about making your daughter flunk gym because you wouldn't buy her shoes, and I've been angry at you ever since. I make sure my children get everything they need and I would never humiliate them like that."

I apologized for having upset her and told her that I had felt it was the right thing to do to teach this particular child the value of a dollar. After the party the hostess asked me what we had been discussing and I explained the situation. I assumed the lady had brought up exemplary children, but the hostess told me that one was still home as an adult without a job and that the other one had run away. I don't know which one of us was right in God's eyes, but when I asked Marita recently whether her gym shoes saga had been too harsh a treatment, she laughed and replied, "It was the first time I knew you were serious about money and I said to myself, 'She means business. I'd better shape up.'"

Lauren has recently put ten-year-old Randy on a budget with $10 a week for all of his expenses. Previously he had been complaining when she wouldn't buy him everything he saw in the stores, but his new financial responsibility has changed his attitude.

On a skiing trip Randy wanted some new sunglasses. Jonathan had just bought a flashy pair with some leftover Christmas money and so Randy began to try on different styles. When he found his favorite he showed them to Lauren and said, "These are the ones I want." She replied, "That's fine, just buy them."

He looked up surprised and asked, "With my own money?"

"Of course," his mother answered.

Within seconds he had the glasses off his face and back onto the rack. He hasn't asked for sunglasses since.

One day while out to lunch with the boys, Lauren bought each one what she felt was a nutritious meal. Randy asked, "Could I have french fries?"

Lauren replied, "Of course, just go buy them."

"With my own money?"

That has become his new refrain and it has eliminated his nagging for every new thing he wants.

When his power transformer on his computer broke, he was stunned to find he had to save up money to replace it. After four weeks of sacrifice he got enough money and Lauren took him to buy it. He counted out all his money and declared to his mother, "I'm broke." Lauren explained that she was too and that was why she was working all week. For the first time he understood why she had to work a little each week to get enough money to support him.

In the past he didn't like clothes for presents, but under his present plan, he has a new appreciation for the gift of a shirt or sweater. When he opened his birthday presents and saw clothes, he said, "I'm glad. These will save me money."

Each child is different and what might appear easy with one will be more difficult with another. Understanding the personalities will help you in anticipating money problems. Our Melancholy Fred, Jr. was serious about his allowance and didn't ever spend money foolishly. Lauren handled it in her brisk, Choleric way, setting aside what she needed and enjoying the rest. Sanguine Marita would have played forever and become like the bum if we'd let her. Your Melancholy Perfect children will usually have a sense for figures at an early age and they can be taught finances quickly. The Choleric Powerfuls will want money for the authority and control it gives them and they will only overspend if the act will impress others with their maturity. The Sanguine Populars will love to buy everyone gifts and treat the crowd so that they will be even more popular. It may be difficult to get their minds down to serious business and as they get to be teens they will want everything they see. The Phlegmatic Peaceful child will have a casual attitude about money—take it or leave it. Because he is a follower he will usually abide by your rules.

Marilyn Heavilin's Phlegmatic/Sanguine son Nathan earned his monthly income from a morning paper route. He bought most of his clothes and paid his school and personal expenses with his own money. One morning he mentioned to his mom that the church youth groups would be going to their favorite ice cream store for a party on Friday. Knowing that Nate wouldn't be receiving more paper route money for about two weeks, Marilyn said, "That's fine, Nate. I'm happy to have you go, but be sure you reserve enough money this week for that event."

The day of the party Nate said, "I've run out of money; will you please give me some money so I can go to the ice cream party?"

Marilyn reminded him that the party was his responsibility and said she would not give him the money. When the youth leader stopped by to pick him up, Nate told him, "I can't go because I didn't save enough money out of my paper route money."

Nate was willing to accept Marilyn's decision, but the youth leader tried to put pressure on her.

"Can't you loan him the money? My goodness, surely you can afford the little bit he would need."

Marilyn was about to come to her own defense when Peaceful, Phlegmatic Nate said to the young man, "Leave her alone; she's doing the right thing."

Fred's brother Richard wrote us about how he handled finances with his four children.

> We stopped giving 25 cents a week about the same time we became Christians and never gave allowance or financial reward for any service around the home. The principle was that all the dollars the family had belonged to God and as good stewards we would use it together to buy what we believed God wanted each member to have. We tried to treat each member of the family on an equal basis according to their age. At an early age each child was encouraged to perform service for a neighbor (snow shoveling, garden work, etc.), being willing to accept whatever the neighbor felt the job was worth on completion, and at other times doing the work for an agreed price beforehand. Each child has thanked us for not giving them an allowance and for encouraging them to seek work outside the home, and now say this is the way they will go with their own children.

There are many opinions in child-raising books about allowances, ranging from giving the children everything they want so they won't feel deprived to giving them nothing. Developing some program in between will take creative work on your part, but the issue is not the number of dollars you dole out but the training your children receive in counting the cost. It is our job as parents to let them know that life is not a series of free lunches but years of financial responsibility. We cannot achieve our goal of raising responsible children who can get along without us if we don't show them what it costs to live.

When Marita was in high school she had an assignment to find out how much it would take per month for a teen to live alone in an apartment. The whole idea got her excited and she began to read ads in the paper for an apartment. The first blow came when she went to look at the rentals that were what she considered affordable. She was depressed as she reported to me what "pits" they all were. "The kitchens were just awful, the carpeting was cheap and sticky, and the people lurking around outside looked as if they were going to stab me." Another touch with reality came when she inquired about the rent. "They want me to sign a lease and give them an extra month's rent before I even move in!" She was dumbfounded that people wanted deposits on everything.

By the time she had finished the assignment and had added up what living the good life would cost, she had convinced herself that she was lucky to live at home.

Fred, Jr. moved into an apartment when he was twenty-one. One day when I came home I found him in the garage doing laundry. I asked him why he'd brought his dirty clothes back to me. He said in disbelief, "The washing machines at the apartments cost money. You have to put quarters in them or they won't work!" After six months of living with a hopelessly sloppy Sanguine roommate, he quit the independent life of the swinging single and moved back home never yet to leave. It was amazing how much better I looked to him and how attached he became to the washer and dryer that didn't demand quarters.

Help your children to learn early in life that it costs money to live. Don't put your family emphasis on dollars, but teach them to plan ahead. Luke 14:28 says, "But don't begin until you count the cost. For who would begin construction of a building without first getting estimates and then checking to see if he has enough money to pay the bills?" (TLB).

22. Credit Cards and Interest

Because we live in a society that seems to tell us "enjoy it today and pay for it tomorrow," we must teach our children about credit, charge cards, and interest. When each of our children reached eighteen we helped them get one charge card and monitored the payments. Somehow, seeing how much they'd charged for gas and eating out in a given month disciplined their spending.

Balancing a checkbook is an essential lesson that many parents don't have under control themselves. It's difficult to teach financial management if we as adults haven't quite got a handle on our bank balance. One Sanguine lady showed Fred at the book table how she wrote checks for the correct amount but entered it in her records rounded off to the next dollar. This way, she explained, made the adding easier and created a "surprise slush fund" at the end of each month.

Marita has finally concluded that she can't keep her check book balanced even though she has tried. So she pays someone each month to do it and tell her what the balance really is.

23. Money Isn't Love

Children don't take lessons in love; they learn what it means to be loved from their parents' actions and responses.

When my husband was a child he learned that work, money, and love went together. If you loved someone you worked hard for them and gave them money. Fred's grandparents had set the stage for this continual performance. Their parents had been German immigrants who had no money, and they had been determined that their children would make it big in the new world. Grandpa had swept streets in New York as a young boy and had worked his way up into the millinery business by extreme discipline and frugality. He and Grandma opened hat stores around New York and they both dedicated their lives to the pursuit of money, to such a degree that they had no time for their two children. Fred's mother, as a baby, slept in a box in one of the stores and by the time she was 11 she was doing all the housework, cooking the meals, and caring for her younger brother. In return for her work she was given money and gifts.

Early in life Fred's mother learned that if you worked hard you were rewarded and that equaled love. As she raised her children she followed the same pattern. Both she and her husband worked long days in her parents' millinery business. The children saw little of their parents who hired a German cook-housekeeper and a German nursemaid to run the household. They lived in a large English Tudor home and gave the children all they needed except their time and their touch.

When Fred was three years old he had heard so few words from his parents that he spoke only German (which he learned from the two maids) as his native language. One day his father turned to talk to him and found they were speaking two different languages—literally. His answer to the problem was to instruct the maids to speak more English, and to spend less time with Fred!

On Sundays when the grandparents came for dinner, the children were taught to run to greet them with a kiss and to say, "Happy to see you, Grandpa dear—or Grandma dear." If they said their pieces with conviction, they were given a quarter for a reward. If they refused, they received nothing and Fred's mother was scolded for having ungrateful and unloving children. Grandpa would go into a sulk for the afternoon and ruin everyone's day, so it became a necessity that each child say his lines properly whether he felt like it or not.

This pay-as-you-go style of love was carried on with my children. When we would visit on Sundays, the same routine was expected. One time little Lauren refused to kiss Grandpa. "His face is too prickly." He went into a rage and took back the quarter he had just handed her to love him. Lauren learned quickly that prickly or not, Grandpa was to be kissed.

Fred followed in family tradition and taught our children to say, "Happy to see you, Daddy dear" each time he came home. He instructed me in complimentary phrases I was to use for him and as long as we all said our pieces well, we could stay in his good graces.

He became a workaholic in the stolid German style and when I would complain that he was never around he would buy me a present and say, "There. That should keep you happy." Since I had grown up poor, I was very eager for possessions and accepted what he gave me in place of his time. The children and I learned to work hard and say the right lines. If we did we were rewarded. Like those little white rats in psychology experiments, we ran through our mazes and were given our prizes.

Isn't it amazing how the sins of the fathers are visited upon the children, up to the third and fourth generations! If work and money equal love for the parents, that's all they have to give their children. By nature, we can't pass on what we never received.

If our family were the only one for whom money took the place of love, this story would be an isolated case. But so frequently today both parents are working night and day to provide their children with the "right things" when what the little ones are craving are time and touch! They want parents who will hold them and show them they love them.

A young girl, Kathy, told me her parents had never had time for her and whenever she complained, they'd buy her a present. Recently after Kathy had a strong disagreement with her mother, the mother called to make amends by asking, "What do you need?" Accustomed to the routine, Kathy answered, "a nightgown." A few hours later her mother appeared at her apartment door with a present all wrapped up. When Kathy opened it she found eight nightgowns. Her mother felt if one nightgown would make Kathy happy, eight would make her ecstatic!

Kathy told me, "The next time my mother asks me what I need, I'll tell her a new dresser to put the nightgowns in." Kathy tries to keep her sense of humor, but she's never felt love from either parent and has been in years of therapy trying to find out why she is so insecure when she is attractive, intelligent, and successful.

Sherry told me her father had never given her "the time of day." As an adult she is still longing for a father's love. On her birthday he sends her a check in an all-purpose greeting card from his bank, the same card every year, signed "your father." "He doesn't even take the time to pick out a special card," Sherry cried. "He thinks because his secretary remembers the date, he can check off his list and feel he's done his duty."

A card, even with money, doesn't equal love.

While speaking to a professional group, I mentioned teenage depression and suicide. A psychiatrist came up to me afterward and told me that his fourteen-year-old daughter had attempted suicide and had, in his terms, "fried her brain." He couldn't understand how *his* child, one who had everything money could buy, would even consider taking her life.

I was amazed that he wanted my opinion and I asked if she had ever given him any clues as to what she felt was missing in her life. He answered, "Nothing that makes any sense. She just told me that she wished we lived together like a normal family." Then quickly he added, "But we're not a normal family and we can't live like one." He then told me his life story, how he rose from poverty to become a millionaire and how he had placed his daughter and her brother in one of the finest private schools in the world. "I would have been grateful if my parents had put me in such a place."

"Is she glad to be there?" I asked.

"She kept telling me she didn't like to be away from home all the time but I didn't believe her. Besides, with all the traveling we do we couldn't have the kids around to worry about."

It was obvious to me, and to the daughter, that she and her brother were in the way. She wasn't impressed with the price of tuition, she just wanted to be with her parents and to have a "normal home." Yet even in his grief he kept repeating, "I've given her everything." He still didn't understand that money doesn't buy love.

Part VII

THEME

> I have no greater joy than to hear that
> my children are walking in the truth.
>
> (3 John 4)

VII

Theme

The theme in any written work is the underlying idea, the thought that runs throughout the piece, the moral, the message, the principle. In our lives as Christian parents our theme is to glorify the Lord Jesus in our everyday actions, to show His power to transform our lives, to train our children to walk in the truth. We want to make the Christian life one of excitement, not one of legalism and negativism. We want to show the love of Christ in our homes and not save it for Sunday mornings.

Oswald Chambers says, "Faith is not a pathetic sentiment, but robust vigorous confidence built on the fact that God is holy love. The real meaning of eternal life is a life that can face anything it has to face without wavering. If we take this view, life becomes one great romance, a glorious opportunity for seeing marvelous things all the time."[1]

The only way our children will find life to be one great romance, to be a glorious opportunity, to be filled with marvelous things, is if we see it that way. For them to have a big picture of the miracles of the Christian faith we need to have painted it for them. If we spend our time nit-picking details, belaboring negatives, criticizing others, keeping score of violations, our children's view of Christianity will be narrow and negative.

When Fred and I were first teaching marriage classes in our church and little Freddie was only four, he ran up the aisle with some other children after the services one Sunday. A dear lady commented loudly, "You'd think if they were teaching others, they'd at least have control over their own child." I instantly saw why so many "preachers' kids" rebel. They are so programmed as children to be perfect to keep the parishioners happy that they are not allowed to be real. Many rebel as teens to show their parents and the church that they have minds of their own, and many leave the church wanting no part of a legalistic God who suppressed any joy they might have had as children. I didn't want that to happen to mine.

Recently the president of a seminary told me he had done a survey on the adult children of his denomination's leaders and pastors and found a startling figure; only 20 percent of these children were still "in church." Obviously, these young adults who were brought up in the church were so turned off by what they saw and lived through that they wanted no part of institutional religion when they were out on their own.

Where have we gone wrong and what can we do to raise children to see Christianity as an exciting way of life, not as a negative set of commandments to flee at the first opportunity? If they see mother as a mournful Moses stooped over from the weight of her stone tablets of legalism, they will miss the joy of the Lord.

Let's help our children see God's love pouring forth from us daily. Let them learn from God's words at our side. Let them see answers to prayer and train them to hear God's voice. Let them be in awe of the majesty of God. "Come my children, listen to me. I will teach you the fear of the Lord" (Psalm 34:11 NIV).

William Booth, founder of the Salvation Army, wrote in 1902;

"Be a holy example. Create and confirm in the hearts of your children the assurance that you yourself are what you want them to become. Practice daily the same unselfish love and righteousness that you ask from them. Without this, you will never accomplish the goals you have set your heart on.

"Don't expect your children to be any better in character and conduct than the example set before them—by you, by their own friends, or those they spend time with."

24. Family Prayer Time

Once Fred and I decided that we were going to start raising Christians instead of just children, we had to change our lifestyle. We'd never been drinkers or carousers and were actually considered quite square in our country-club set, so we didn't have moral shifts to make, just priority ones. Sunday went from being tennis tournament day to church day. Since Fred was the tennis champ and was always ready for an exciting match, his partner couldn't understand when Fred said he wouldn't play until 1:00 on Sundays. "Littauer's got religion" was the word that went around the club.

The Lord must have known how difficult it would be for us to change and grow in our old surroundings for we hardly knew the plan of salvation before God called us to California and moved us into Bungalow One. I went from being a social pace-setter to becoming a Bible student. In Connecticut each child had a separate bedroom; here they were stacked into two rooms with sets of double-decker beds. Instead of being able to go to our rooms, we all were together, almost on top of each other, all the time. What initially seemed a big step down on the ladder of life, in retrospect became a leap to new heights in our family relationships.

The first Christian move we made was to start a prayer time with our children. When Fred first mentioned that I was to have dinner ready at 5:30 and in a condition where it could be put on hold for fifteen minutes while we prayed, I said, "That's impossible!"

We had never done anything on schedule or by routine in our home before. Fred's arrival time in the evening had never been consistent and I had usually fed the children early, so this idea of scheduled togetherness seemed hopeless to me. Since his office was now in the Arrowhead Springs Hotel and we lived next door in Bungalow One, Fred determined that he would come home each night on time. The preparation was left to my creativity and control. The next question was how do you get children who have never prayed more than "Now I lay me down to sleep" to want to pray? Fred and I had to establish a purpose. Were we going to pray because it was a good Christian thing to do or because the children needed to know that God answers prayer? The latter was the obvious answer and the next question was how do you do that? How do you show children that an unseen God hears and answers them?

Fred, being the organized Melancholy, got out 3×5 cards and the first night we asked the children what people they would like to pray for. Amazingly, they got excited over choosing and we established several categories. On the top of each card Fred wrote the title such as: Family Needs, Friends, Church, Missionaries, School Friends. On the first night we set up the system and Fred prayed. The next night we chose one card, "Family Needs," and wrote down our requests. Next to these were two columns: Date Asked and Date Answered. We entered the date asked and then each one of us, including four-year-old Freddie, gave a sentence prayer for that particular family need.

Each night we would start our prayer time with requests for additional items to be placed on the cards. The children liked to come up with a new item and they began to think about prayer requests during the day so they would have something to add. After the new requests were on the cards, then one child each night chose which card he or she wanted us to pray about. By keeping them involved in the process, we were able to maintain their interest in our prayer time. We made sure we did not pray long, overwhelming thoughts but simple requests.

Some of the items the children wanted prayed about would not be worthy of including in Scripture, but they were of importance to them. Freddie brought up little nursery school requests and we never said, "That is not worth praying about," even though we may have thought it at the time.

One request was for Erica and Valerie's behavior. We wrote this on the School Friends card and when Freddie prayed that night he said, "Dear God, forgive Erica for lying and forgive Valerie for tattling, for if Valerie hadn't tattled, nobody would'a knowed that Erica lied."

As prayers were answered, we would record the date. Although God doesn't need records of our little petitions, we need to see results to teach our children that God does respond. As we saw answers, we began thanking the Lord in prayer for these blessings, and later we added the steps of confession and praise.

For us the Prayer Card system achieved our goal to teach our children that God hears and answers prayer. An unexpected benefit was the discipline I learned in having dinner ready on time and that Fred learned in making himself come home each night consistently. We did not realize how much it meant to the children to have some new stability from their parents. Another plus was that they knew dinner was waiting and, therefore, this prayer meeting wouldn't go on forever. This removed the fear of endless, pious platitudes from parents that so often keeps young people from wanting to be part of family devotions. Making the children active in the requests and in the selection of the nightly Prayer Card gave them a feeling of control and saved them from dreading our time of prayer. They were never bored and as adults they now know and use the power of prayer.

Sally, a single parent, wrote:

> When school began, we started a new schedule which has helped get our day off to a good start. I get up at 6:00, have some quiet time, get the children up at 6:30. By 7:00 everyone is to be dressed, bed made and in the kitchen for breakfast. We all sit down together and talk about our day. Then we have prayer time and pray for specific things for our day (tests, problems with friends or teachers, schedules to be met, etc.). We keep a notebook so the next day we can see what all was answered the day before. This has been a good way to show my children how God does care about their every need and how He works in our lives. Any time they want to mark off an answer, the Prayer Book is in easy reach.

Darrell Smith wrote me from Pennsylvania:

> We have devotions at an exact hour Monday through Friday. We have found it to be a very positive influence on our children. The consistent hour has helped them in their planning and in

doing things in a habitual way, even things they don't particularly like doing.

Our devotions are not long, drawn-out discourses, but short, sometimes two or three verses of Scripture, with emphasis on how we can apply the truth learned in our lives.

Our prayer time is not ritualistic with the use of the same phrases or clichés, but we express to God our sincere and deepest feelings.

Mike Wagner told me he had disciplined his four-year-old Joshua by explaining what he had done wrong and then telling him, "You, Joshua, have to learn to obey your parents when you are small so that when you become older and Jesus talks to you, you will know to listen to Him and obey Him."

It is never too early to train a child to hear God's voice. As we make prayer a part of everyday life, we show our children that prayer is a normal function like eating and not a boring religious ritual.

Betty and Greg Barnett gave me some thoughts on how they taught their children to pray.

One of the ways we encouraged our three children, even as toddlers, to have a "God Orientation" in their everyday lives was to involve them in the frequent prayer requests that came into our home. Whenever we received a prayer request via the phone or in person, we would gather everyone who was home and immediately pray about the need. The children accepted this as a part of everyday life and then when a family crisis occurred it was natural for everyone to gather in a common room and cry and pray together. When an eleven-year-old cousin drowned, God became our comfort as we gathered together in this way. Answers to prayers were treated in the same way with praises given to God.

We all know that our children grow up reflecting what they have seen in us, for we serve as daily examples. If you wish your children to pray and believe in God, make sure they see you living what you're teaching.

Jan and Don Frank have used much of their family time to instill Christian principles into their little girls' lives and to teach them Bible verses and hymns. Recently they instituted a new method of prayer for the family. They all sat on the floor and prayed that God would speak to each one of them. After a period of silence Don closed in prayer and noticed tears in Heather's eyes. He asked what was wrong and the little six-year-old child replied, "You didn't give God enough time to talk to me."

At bedtime Jan sat down with Heather on the side of her bed and prayed again that God would speak to her. They waited quietly and after a while Heather lifted her head with a smile.

"Did God speak to you?" Jan asked.

"Yes," Heather said softly.

"What did He say?"

"He said, 'I love you.'"

What a lesson for a little child to be helped by her parents to hear the voice of God and know God loves her.

When we are His, we can hear His voice.

Family Prayer Time

We have Prayer Cards for different needs: family, friends, church, school, missionaries. Each member is asked to add requests to any card and each member chooses a card to pray for at the meeting and until we meet together again. Review of answered prayer is exciting and shows the family that God does answer prayer.

FAMILY NEEDS	DATE ASKED	DATE ANSWERED
_____	_____	_____
_____	_____	_____
_____	_____	_____
_____	_____	_____
_____	_____	_____

25. Family Evaluation

On New Year's Day in 1970 Fred and I decided to try a Family Evaluation for the first time. We had three extra family members at the time: Dwayne, Fred's nephew was with us for a year, Gudrun from Germany had been with us three years, and Dee, a Campus Crusade for Christ staff member, also lived with us for several years. The eight of us celebrated New Year's by having a special family meeting. Fred made out charts for each one of us with all our names across the top and two categories to be answered: What I like about each person, and where they need improvement. We all got promptly to work and were able to be honest because no one would know who wrote what comment except Father Fred who tallied up our responses. Dee helped Freddie fill out his answers and we all passed them in.

Naturally, Perfect Parent Fred had a master chart and when he completed his entries, he read them off to us. We tried to guess who had said what about us as we each listened to comments about ourselves. This was such an eye-opening experience that I saved the chart and still have it before me as I write.

The things the children liked about me were: cooking ability, teaches lovingness to the kids, makes fondue suppers, is happy and loving, has true concern, has various talents, is able to have fun, has a loving, sweet spirit, is a good, helpful teacher, is an understanding friend, and makes home a fun place. My negatives were: shouldn't talk so much on the phone, shouldn't lecture so much, shouldn't tell us we're in a bad mood, shouldn't get upset so easily, should be better prepared earlier, should be more humble and patient. Isn't that quite a profile of a Popular/Powerful Parent!

Perfect Parent Fred dressed well, was neat and organized, had a consistent life, applied what he taught others to himself, was kind, sweet, thoughtful, considerate and loving, was understanding, fair and friendly. He needed to improve in being more pleasant to Marita's friends, in getting over bad moods, not being so serious all the time, not getting upset or moody over little things, being more joyful and fun to be with, and not being grumpy.

Although the children did not understand the personalities at the time, they evaluated us quite accurately. If you are a little uncertain about your own personality, doing an evaluation will open your eyes as to how your family sees you.

Looking at our evaluation from an eighteen-year perspective validates both the personalities and the opinions of the family.

Lauren—Powerful—does things with us when baby sitting, takes us for ice cream, has a mature attitude, is understanding and loving to all; however, she should stop complaining and not get mad.

Marita—Popular—is always cheerful, is fun to have around, is full of ideas, is agreeable, generous and willing to help; however, she's a little sarcastic, should hang up her clothes, and stop fooling around with make-up.

Gudrun—Powerful—makes nice clothes, does lots of things, talks to us, is willing to share; however, she's too bossy, gets too nervous, and should be more patient and humble.

Dee—Perfect—is full of good advice, always sweet and helpful, willing to sacrifice for others, always a friend in need; however, everyone agrees she should not have so many gloomy moods and should eat happily.

Freddie—Perfect—has a loving spirit, is sweet and lovable, tries to be helpful, has a tricky sense of humor, is fun to be with; however, he should be quicker to obey, not be so mad, not be so helpless, quit slapping girls, and stop sticking his tongue out.

Dwayne—Popular—has a joyous spirit, has a loving disposition, does what's right and has an attitude of self-improvement; however, he gets upset easily, should get into more outdoor sports, practice the piano more, stop his loud laughing, and quit trying to be the center of attention.

After you have analyzed the personality of each of your family members, do your evaluation and keep the results. Date the chart as Fred did, compare it year to year. In looking back you may be able to spot a "bad year" for one of you, a turning point in a child's life, or a consistency from childhood on.

When your children become parents, they will be thrilled that you kept a yearly record of their strengths and weaknesses.

Family Evaluation

Make out a chart similar to the sample one given here. Ask whatever questions you would like answered. Explain to the children that they should be honest in their answers and that you will not get upset no matter what they say. For children unable to read or write, have an older brother or sister ask them the questions and put down their answers. When everyone has filled out their paper, collect them and tabulate the results. If everyone says Mother needs to stop yelling at the children and Father needs to stay home more often, there has to be a message in the comments of the children. We do our evaluation each New Year's Day to set a positive tone for the new year.

Name: _____

My best quality is: _____

In the last year I have tried to improve in: _____
_____
_____

As for others:	Best Quality	Needs Improvement In
Father	_____	_____
Mother	_____	_____
Sister	_____	_____
Brother	_____	_____

MASTER CHART

		Father	Mother	Child 1	Child 2
Date	1				
_____	2				
Best	3				
Qualities	4				
	1				
Needs	2				
Improvement	3				
	4				

After the first few times, we added a self-evaluation of our best qualities and the ones we had tried to work on for improvement in the past year. Fred then would ask for positives on each person and ask if others agreed that we had improved in the area we mentioned. We kept this discussion on a positive plane so that each of us ended up the day feeling good about ourselves and determined to improve even more in the following year.

> Between the dark and the daylight
> When the night is beginning to lower,
> Comes a pause in the day's occupations
> That is known as the Children's Hour.

26. The Children's Hour

When Henry Wadsworth Longfellow wrote "The Children's Hour" in 1859, he expressed a thought that has somehow been lost in the passage of over 100 years. He talks about early evening as a time of pleasure, of playing with the children, of pausing from the day's occupation. He shares about the joy of having children.

> I hear in the chamber above me
> The patter of little feet,
> The sound of a door that is opened
> And voices soft and sweet.

As he goes on, he tells of the games they play together and of how the little ones climb all over him as if he were a castle they were invading. Is Longfellow's Children's Hour a thing of the past? Are our evenings too full of business, church meetings, phone calls, or television to have a "pause in the day's occupation that is known as the Children's Hour"? Can we possibly imagine what it's like for a child to know his parents care enough about him to put other things aside and spend some precious time with him before he goes to sleep?

No matter what personality a child is, he wants, craves, and needs a touch of love before he shuts his eyes. The Sanguine child is desperate for attention and is dying to hear you say, "You are so adorable—precious—humorous—pretty—cuddly—strong. I'm so glad to have you as my child. I'm so proud of you. I love you just the way you are. We're going to have such fun together!"

The Choleric child wants to know you noticed everything he did for you today and wants to hear, "Thank you so much for cleaning your room—for helping with the dishes—for reading to your little brother. I don't know how I could get along without you. You are so smart for your age and you know how to do so much. I'm so glad I have you for my helper."

The Melancholy child wants you to be sensitive to his inner hurts and quiet joys. He does not want to hear about how you like his clothes or how adorable and precious he is, but he does need affirming. "You are so understanding of other people—compassionate toward those who hurt—you are deep—thoughtful—artistic. I can't believe how well you read—sing—add up those columns. I'm so grateful to have a child who loves me as I love him."

The Phlegmatic child is the least complaining of all and the easiest to ignore even at bedtime, but he needs to know you remember he's there and that you feel he's worth something. Deep down inside he wishes he had the personality of his Sanguine sister, but he knows he doesn't. He wishes he could make decisions and be the leader like his Choleric brother. He wishes he could play the piano and do his homework like his Melancholy friend. He just wishes he could be someone else. He needs to hear, "I'm so glad I have you for my child. You are the only one in this whole family who doesn't complain, who does what I tell you with no fuss, who never gets upset. It's so hard for me to have the others talking and noisy all the time, trying to push me around, and pouting when things don't go their way. You are so relaxed and easy going. I wish everybody in the world was just like you."

If your child heard words similar to these whispered in his ear each night for ten years, do you think it would make a difference? When his friends would talk about their parents who don't love them or give them the time of day, what would come to your child's mind? Would he be less apt to get up for water, to go to the bathroom, to reappear if he felt secure in his parents' love?

If this sounds like the right approach to the Children's Hour, why don't we all do it? Why do so many children go to bed lonely, feeling unloved? Why do so many get up and down a dozen times or cry at the thought of bed? Could it be that they don't get enough attention according to their personal emotional needs? Or is there something missing in our hearts and emotions?

1. *The Peace at Last Pattern:* This pattern starts in a mind that says "These children are impossible—If I can live long enough for them to grow up and get out of here, I could be happy. It must be time for bed, isn't it?—Relief is only ten minutes away!" Should you for a moment pass the thought through your mind, "At last I'll get rid of these monsters and have some peace," they will hear your silent statement.

Children are extremely sensitive to their parents' emotions and the minute you flash a feeling of "good riddance" they will pick up rejection.

Any time the child senses the parent is pushing him away, he automatically reaches out and becomes grabby. Parents pull back from clinging children who then feel more rejection and reach out again. This unconscious negative cycle causes the child to do anything he can dream up to get attention, call for water, threaten to wet his bed if he's not allowed up, run around the house, cut up the drapes, or sprinkle baby powder on the carpet.

Any one of these little acts of defiance will bring attention. As parents we seem to think "no child in his right mind would want to get in trouble." What we forget is that they aren't functioning out of their minds but out of their feelings. They are little magnets pulling you toward them. When you resist their innate tugs, they will run after you and insist you turn to them. They aren't sitting around sorting out good and bad ideas, they're acting out of feelings of rejection. "I will get her attention no matter what it takes."

Before we know what we are doing, we have established a negative cycle of bedtime behavior. The harder we push, the more they resist. Parenting is not a list of rules but a series of responses. We are not running a business but raising children.

Where does the change have to come from? Can we wipe out their need for love and attention? Not easily, and if we do we will produce emotionally bankrupt young people unfit to become loving parents themselves.

Change has to start with us. As soon as we see that bedtime problems aren't because we produced bad kids, but because we didn't realize we were transmitting a message of rejection, we can shift gears immediately. We can make going to bed a loving time, a time of personal attention to each child. Remember the time you spend tonight could save you years of heartbreak somewhere down the line.

2. *The Don't Deserve It Dilemma:* Some of us parents feel if a child has been bad today he doesn't deserve a story or time with Mother or Dad. The opposite is true, however. If he was a bad boy, he especially needs a loving time with a forgiving parent. Bedtime is not punishment time. If you refuse to give last-minute words of blessing to a naughty child, you are in fact teaching him that your love is conditional. "Only good little boys and girls get loved. Bad ones grow up alone and sad and soon become angry and bitter. Which kind of a little child do you want to be?" Logic would tell us they would choose to be good tomorrow, but often that approach doesn't work. How can we teach them that God loves us all and that He accepts us just as we are when our actions show that parents only love perfect little children? If God only gave us what we deserved, we'd be heartbroken most of the time. He comforts His people in their time of anguish and He sets the captive free. Can we do less than comfort our children? Do they have to be angels for a week before we will reach out a loving hand? Make bedtime a time of fellowship, of prayer, of joy— especially when they don't deserve it. With enough loving the child might look up and say, "I'm so sorry, Mommy. I'll be better tomorrow."

We once received the following note from Fred, Jr.:

Mom and Dad
I am sorry I have been late on getting home, and I will try to do better. Will you forgive me? Thank you for every thing you have done for me.

Fred

3. *The My Parents Didn't Kiss Me Goodnight Excuse:* As I talk with people who have problems with their children rebelling, and ask how they have demonstrated their love, the frequent answer is something like, "My parent never kissed me and I lived." So there! Recently I talked with the pre-teen children of a pastor who frequently spoke of God's love from the pulpit, but they were convinced he didn't love them at all. "He never puts his arm around us or says a kind word. He's all business at home and is happiest when we stay out of sight."

As I talked with the father about the family's craving for affection, he dismissed their needs as immaturity and a lack of spirituality. "My father didn't waste any time with physical affection, why should I?"

Obviously, if we were all perfect and ready to ascend, we would be so in tune with the Lord that His love would transcend any human need for attention. But since we as parents aren't yet on that lofty level, we can't expect our children to be that spiritually mature. When the parent does not express a warm, caring, touching love, the children either shut down their emotions or go out looking for love in all the wrong places.

If your parents didn't give this kind of affection to you, break this negative pattern. Don't be proud of it. One wife said, "I've sent the children to run and jump on their father when he comes home at night, and to tell him they love him. But he never responds. They could as well be hugging a post. He's just like his father."

We don't have to be like our fathers. We can determine today to open up our hearts and begin to love our children no matter what our parents were like. The Lord will give us a new love when we ask, because it is His will that we establish a positive environment in which to raise Christians, not just children.

Why not start tonight with a Children's Hour, a time when you put aside all else, have a pause in the day's occupation, and put your eyes upon the emotional needs of your family? If you win the world and lose your children, what have you really gained?

4. *The Some Other Time Tactic* is the one often employed by well-meaning parents who do love their children and would like

to spend some loving moments with them if they only could find the time. "Possibly tomorrow will be less hectic." "When I get off the church board I'll have a free evening." "Once Christmas is over we can settle down." "When I get this last one in school, I'll be able to relax."

I've found in my life that the nebulous tomorrow never comes.

As Shakespeare wrote,

> Tomorrow, and tomorrow, and tomorrow,
> Creeps in petty pace from day to day,
> To the last syllable of recorded time.
> (*Macbeth*, Act V, William Shakespeare)

Each busy day is followed by another one and if we wait until life smooths out before we spend time with our children it may be too late. We may get to that last syllable of recorded time and find we never had any.

I remember Lauren looking up at me one day as I rushed about doing great and wonderful things and saying, "I know what should be engraved on your tombstone."

I wasn't planning on dying, but out of curiosity I asked what she had in mind. She replied, "Not now, later." I didn't know how to respond because I realized I did say that frequently. She tried in different ways to communicate her feelings that I was always too busy "right now" but "some other time" would soon be along. I had good intentions, just "not now, later." The thought of being dead and gone with Lauren's remembrance of me being "Not now, later," did catch my attention.

Ask your children what they'd put on your tombstone. You might be surprised.

If some of us parents look at our Children's Hour as our moment of relief, if some of us withdraw bedtime stories as discipline, if some of us won't give our children what we didn't get, and if many of us mean to be good parents some other time, what can we do about it?

Realize parenting is a God-given assignment. ". . . A child

left to himself bringeth his mother to shame" (Proverbs 29:15). Our duty is to care for our children and spend time with them. "Children are an heritage of the Lord: and the fruit of the womb is his reward" (Psalm 127:3). There is no greater reward than seeing your children as grownup, well-adjusted Christian believers and know that the Lord is saying, "Well done, good and faithful father and mother. Well done." But this end product doesn't just happen; it takes purposeful planning.

Why is the bedtime hour such an important part of the day? Basically, because the last things that go into our minds before we fall asleep are the thoughts that settle in for the night and are still with us when we awake in the morning. David says in Psalm 16:7 (NIV), "even at night my heart instructs me."

If a child's last thoughts are of loneliness, neglect, resentment, anger, rejection, his heart will brood on these feelings in the night and not awaken refreshed and excited about a new day; but if he is assured of his parents' love in his last conscious moments, he will rest in peace.

How can we make this happen?

1. *Eliminate petty distractions.* So many mothers tell me that they can't get the children to stay in bed, and often I find it is because they didn't take care of some of the trivial procedures ahead of time. When you send them to get into pajamas, are there some in the drawer? Have you made sure they have gone to the bathroom before getting into bed? Do they have some water nearby?

When my Freddie was little, part of his bedtime procedure was to get his little plastic cup of water out of the bathroom and bring it to his bedstand. I never saw him drink any of it, and in the morning he'd dutifully carry it back and empty it. This cup over the years traveled many useless miles but it eliminated the cry, "I need a drink," heard nightly across this land.

If each child is in his pajamas, having gone to the bathroom with some water at his side, you have cut down on the possible excuses for getting up out of bed.

2. *Go into their room.* Often complaints of parents about bedtime problems come from those who didn't want to get out of

the chair. It's only natural that a child who wasn't tucked in by a parent is going to call for attention. If no one arrives upon demand, the child may well go on a scouting mission. If his appearance in the living room brings forth a parent who will arise like a Phoenix bird from the ashes and chase him to his room, he has achieved his goal.

Even if the parent screams and spanks, the child often prefers that to being ignored. Bad attention is better than none, but wouldn't you prefer to have Junior's last thoughts of you be pleasant and loving rather than hysterical? Remember when you are out of control, the child is in control of your emotions.

Why not get up in the first place, sit with your child on the bed, read him stories, listen to what's on his heart, pray with him, tell him you love him, and give him the security that you will be there in the morning? There's no guarantee he'll never misbehave again, but the odds are with you.

3. *Let them read.* What if they're not tired? Do you let them call their friends and talk? Do you allow them to watch TV and have their last thoughts be of gang violence in L.A.? Should they get up and play with their toys? My answer to children who weren't sleepy was, "You may read as long as you want." To do this the children must have positive reading materials available and within reach. It's amazing how quickly they drop off when they have this one freedom to read compared with your raising their adrenalin level by threats or arguments. Often when I went back to look, I'd find the child asleep with a book still in his hand and a peaceful look on his face.

4. *Give them personal attention.* Reading or talking in a group can be a positive part of your Children's Hour, but if possible give the last attention to each one privately. Even if two are in the same room, have the prayer time be with one child at a time. Children won't talk or pray about issues when they fear a sibling will tell them, "That's a stupid idea."

When your children get to an age where you go to your room first, encourage them to come in and sit on the edge of your bed and talk. Some of our most meaningful conversations with our children in their teen years came as they sat on our bed and talked on into the night. Often Fred would drop off to sleep, but if one set of parental ears was open, they'd say things they'd never bring up in the midst of a busy day. A few late nights for the right reason won't kill any of us, and it shows our children we care enough to listen. With young Fred, who has always been a quiet Melancholy, the sight of his parents about ready to drift off to dreamland turned him into a talk show host. He would come up with exciting topics and inject an occasional flash of humor. We never could figure out why he couldn't do this in broad daylight, but we were willing to take it when we could get it.

5. *Establish bedtime hours.* As with any training of our children, there have to be some standards. One of the reasons we have so many purposeless young people today is that in our permissive society there are no home rules to rebel against. We don't institute rules because we expect perfection but in order to teach standards and let our children know that nothing in life can function if there are no regulations and no one is in charge.

When we were raising our children we set all our policies at our family meetings, including establishing bedtime hours. Each child was allowed to present what he thought was fair, knowing that Fred and I had veto power. We were often surprised when one of the three would place bedtime earlier than we had in mind. When they were young, we would give them fifteen-minute warnings before it was their bedtime, but as they grew up we didn't check until it was time for them to be in bed. We felt they had to learn responsibility for time on their own.

We had a rule that if you were late getting to bed tonight you would go earlier tomorrow night. If you stayed up thirty minutes longer than you should, you automatically went to bed a half-hour earlier the next night. This honor system worked well with us and we found it was far better to be flexible in this way than to be upset over a fifteen-minute variable.

Fred's brother Dick and his wife Ruth have raised four precious Christian children. They all graduated from Wheaton College and are all active Christians. Dick wrote us when we asked him for some suggestions:

Our children knew that bedtimes were at certain hours, approximately 7, 8, 9, and 10 for the four levels. We always found that our children operated well on a regular schedule (and badly when off schedule). Most important, bedtime was made to be a happy time with Bible stories, listening to the child, prayer, backrubs, all as often as we could. We felt this personal attention was a good way to show a parent's love for the child. We started communicating with our children when they were infants and we never let up. Taking time to listen saves grief. "Do you love me?" asks the child. Listening is the answer. We listened at the evening meal, at bedtime and when driving to and from their many activities and lessons. Listening for us was expressing love.

Bob Anderson of Fort Wayne, Indiana, told us that when it was time for his children to be in bed he would go in to spend some special moments with each one. He called himself the Answer Man and the children were allowed to ask him one question a night. They tried to stump him and could hardly wait for bedtime to try him out. This added excitement to the bedtime hour and he said his favorite all-time question was, "Why do walnuts have wrinkles?"

6. *Bring Jesus into the bedroom.* Many Christian parents are running from one church meeting to the next and doing mighty works for the Lord without realizing that their children's view of God is a cloudy one. As I've talked with depressed Christian teens, I've found that few have any idea about life after death. One said, "It's just over, ma'am, just all over." Several assumed death was like a drug high, floating blissfully forever. Even the simple plan of salvation seemed confusing to some, including some whose parents taught Sunday school.

The time to make Jesus a reality in your children's lives is when they are small. Bring Jesus into the bedroom, talk with Him in prayer, let your child know He's real. I remember when my Freddie was five and he asked my mother, "Grammie, do you know if you are going to heaven?"

My mother answered, "I hope so." Freddie came back quickly, "You don't hope so, you know so. Either you're going to heaven or you're going to hell. Which is it?"

This clear-cut little message did not excite my mother, but I was thrilled that he knew this basic fact of life.

How will our children know if we don't teach them? Bedtime is a natural time to read Bible stories, to get acquainted with Jesus, and to pray in faith, believing. In 3 John 4 the apostle says, "I have no greater joy than to hear that my children walk in the truth."

Don't get so busy or preoccupied that you don't have time to bring your Friend Jesus to meet with your children that they may grow up to walk in the truth.

The poet Henry Wadsworth Longfellow sets the tone for the evening so eloquently:

> The day is done, and the darkness,
> Falls from the wings of Night,
> As a feather is wafted downward
> From an eagle in his flight.

He then goes on to suggest what we should do with our Children's Hour, whether we are the parents or grandparents, by reading poetry and singing hymns.

> Such songs have power to quiet
> The restless pulse of care,
> And come like the benediction
> That follows after prayer.
>
> Then read from the treasured volume
> The poem of thy choice,
> And lend to the rhyme of the poet
> The beauty of thy voice.
>
> And the night shall be filled with music,
> And the cares that infest the day,
> Shall fold their tents like the Arabs,
> And as silently steal away.

Part VIII

REHEARSALS

> Train up a child in the way he
> should go and when he is old
> he will not depart from it.
> (Proverbs 22:6)

VIII

Rehearsals

Teach: To give instruction, to show how.
Train: To impart proficiency by teaching, drilling.
Discipline: Training which corrects, molds, strengthens, perfects.

In order to have the cast know what to do and how to behave, the directors have to keep them in rehearsal where they practice over and over until they can play their parts automatically with no apparent effort. Thus we must do with our children. One reading of the lines, one set of directions is not enough. We need to rehearse acceptable behavior over and over again. Raising children requires repetition. Once we think we have each child in line, one of them is sure to get in trouble. I remember cycles where Lauren would feel rejected by her friends and suddenly she'd come home elated at how much they all loved her. Then Marita would bring home such creepy boys that I would be convinced she'd never have any taste in men. Overnight she got rid of them all and grew up. I'd finally breathe a sigh of relief only to get a note from Fred's school saying he was flunking math. There never seemed to be a time when all three were on a positive course at the same time.

It was somewhat like the jugglers who have all those plates twirling around on the tops of sticks. As soon as they get them all going, one begins to fall off and they have to run to its rescue.

Raising children is like twirling plates. If you relax for a minute, they'll all come smashing down around you.

We need to back up a little and realize this is only the rehearsal, not the final performance. As directors we're called to get our children ready, to prepare them for their roles in life—and we may never live to see them do it right! But we can't give up, fire them all, and hire a new cast. We must "run the race with patience and endurance" in the hope that someday we'll be proud of the results.

When I asked Heidi Fowler what she remembered from my child-raising class she attended ten years ago, she replied immediately, "The advice you gave about not taking parenting so seriously that you lost the joy. Blaine and I used to be perfectionists but we've learned to relax and lower our standards. The house isn't perfect, as it once was, but we have a lot of fun."

Remember, this is just a rehearsal; it doesn't have to be perfect!

27. Courtesy and Manners

When I grew up living in our store, we had no formal dinners, candelabra, or floral centerpieces, yet we were raised with a sense of dignity and manners. We addressed adults as "Mr." and "Mrs." and we always said please and thank you. We did these simple courtesies as a way of life even though we'd never heard of Emily Post. Yet somewhere between the '30s and the '80s manners died out and have only recently been introduced as a new idea.

No matter where any of us has been on the manners scale, it is time to realize that if we don't teach courteous behavior to our children, they won't learn how on their own. Judith Martin, Miss Manners, says:

> We are all born ignorant and oafish and it is the duty of all parents to teach their younger selves how to behave properly. The only way to do so, is by providing a good example plus tireless nagging. It takes eighteen years of constant work to get a child into

presentable enough shape so that a college will take him or her off your hands.[1]

Isn't it amazing that it takes us eighteen years to learn how to get them in shape and by the time we're good at it, we're out of a job? We must keep remembering, this is just the rehearsal, but we must press on. The sloppy, hippie-flower child attitude of doing your own thing is fortunately passé and it is once more time to bring back some semblance of civil behavior.

Perhaps some of us parents have neglected to pass on proper manners to our children. Perhaps we were never taught ourselves or didn't realize the importance of social graces until we began to reap our harvest and live in a world without them. Miss Manners has been amazed at the increase in interest in proper manners. She tells of the start of her column in a 1984 article for *Time* magazine:

> I got a very skeptical go ahead. Editors all thought etiquette was dead . . . I thought I was just writing for a bunch of old cranks like myself, but then I started getting floods of mail from young people. These were the people who were supposed to think etiquette was stupid and ludicrous, and they were all writing me and asking me questions. I found out these people had been lied to by their parents.[2]

Miss Manners goes on to explain, "The lie, basically, was the moral debris of the '60s, the sentimental notion that just about anything goes, that everything is relative or simply a personal choice."[3]

Perhaps you are one of those who were "lied" to. If so, teach yourself first. Our children learn so much by our example and if we as parents don't know how to conduct ourselves in social settings, how will our children learn?

One day in his early teenage years, Fred, Jr. came home with a new appreciation for social graces. He and some boys were invited into a friend's home for dinner. He was embarrassed for them. He said, "They talked with their mouths full, didn't know which fork to use, and they didn't even put their napkins in their laps. They didn't know anything. I guess their mothers didn't care enough to teach them any manners."

I was thrilled that all I'd been teaching had sunk in. All those lessons that seemed to just bounce off with an "Oh, Mom!" had made it past the surface. While I was thrilled with his learning, I was interested in how he translated all that teaching—". . . I guess their mothers didn't care."

Sadly, most of the current generation of parents are the product of the "lie" of the '60s and you need to know how to do things right yourself. You may be like many of the children who visited our house at mealtime. They were expected to help with the meal along with our children. When I pointed them to the silverware drawer and asked them to set the table, I was amazed at how many of them had no idea what to do. When I showed them how, a frequent response was, "I didn't know there was a right way."

Jan Frank, author of *Door of Hope*, shared with me recently that when she first came to our house as a teenager, I asked her to set the table. She didn't know where to put the silver and she guessed incorrectly. When I viewed it at dinner time, having forgotten she'd done it, I asked, "Who set this table?"

She told me she had meekly replied, "I did," at which point I showed her where to place each piece. At thirty-three she still thinks of my instructions whenever she sets the table. Looking back over the many young people who passed through my home as teens, I wonder how many of them have similar memories.

Janet Pohlhammer shared this fun idea for teaching our children good manners.

> When my daughter was in junior high her table manners were outrageous and my threats and admonitions were not working, so I told her if she would study—and this meant checking books on etiquette out of the library—and work at being more socially agreeable, she and I would fly to San Francisco for a weekend and I would take her to a classy restaurant when she and I felt she was ready. Well, it took six months, but it worked and we had a wonderful, intimate mother-daughter time that we have repeated regularly since.

If you were never taught, that's not your fault, but you can correct it now so you don't pass on your lack of knowledge to your children. Read either of Judith Martin's books, her first, *Miss Manners' Guide to Excruciatingly Correct Behavior* and her newer edition, *Miss Manners' Guide to Rearing Perfect Children*.

If you're through teaching the little ones and you'd like to interest your teens in learning to handle themselves in social settings like Janet Pohlhammer did, I'd suggest getting them a copy of a new book co-written by Joan Coles, one of our CLASS graduates: *Emily Post Talks with Teens about Manners and Etiquette* by Elizabeth L. Post and Joan M. Coles. In an easy-to-read style this book uses illustrations and examples to help teens know things like table manners, party giving and party going, dating data, and manners for job interviews. I've found it to be a helpful reference book.

Show your children your love and help them succeed. Teach them basic manners and the common courtesies of our grandparents.

Manners aren't patterns of behavior for Sundays and company, but a courteous way of life. Teach your children to be respectful of each other, of their parents, and of other people, not to win prizes but because it's the right way to behave.

They may not like your rehearsals, but when they write your review they'll praise you for caring enough to keep going.

Marita shares a recent experience:

> Recently one of my friends was having a party. It was her first, and she was in a panic. She asked me to come early to help her with the preparations. When it was time to serve the chocolate cake one of the guests had brought, she had the paper plates ready. As I suggested that she get out some forks, a look of terror came over her face. I was confused but quickly caught on when she bent down and removed a cardboard gift box from the back of one of her cupboards. She opened it up and revealed eight place settings of gold-plated flatware, much of it still wrapped in plastic. This was all she had. We had eaten the sandwiches and veggies throughout the football game with our fingers and now happily ate the chocolate cake off of paper plates with the gold forks.

Later I thought about that evening and for the first time I appreciated all the time my parents invested in teaching me how to do the things I do so effortlessly. I had taken for granted that I can set the table, that I can cook and entertain. That night helped me realize that not everyone has those same skills. If my mother had not spent trying times teaching me to cook, I wouldn't be able to entertain with ease as I love to do.

My father taught us as children that we should speak kindly and clearly and if we did, we would get jobs over rude people who mumbled. How true.

Alan Dundes, a University of California, Berkeley, professor, wrote:

> Any society that has upward mobility as a major feature pays a great deal of attention to manners. Young people today are concerned with making it, and part of making it is setting the table properly when the boss comes over for dinner. Self-improvement is a big part of the American dream, and learning manners is part of self-improvement.[4]

On the following pages are some simple basics I feel all our children should know.

28. Basic Rules of Courtesy

Don't Talk with Food in Your Mouth

When Marita was about four years old a businessman came to dinner. In the middle of the meal, he was telling a story while chewing his food. I saw Marita staring at him, and when he paused for a breath, she spoke up clearly, "Don't you know you shouldn't talk with food in your mouth?"

What could we say? She was right. Gratefully, he thanked her for reminding him, and the next day he sent us a flowering plant with a note, "I'll never do it again."

We did share with Marita that it was not our job to police the guests, but we were pleased she had learned that one lesson well. As with any instruction to our children, if we aren't doing it ourselves, it's difficult to teach them.

Often when I am at dinner with the host committee, they keep asking me questions giving me little time to eat. If I've just put some food in my mouth, I raise one finger indicating "wait a minute" or if Fred is present, I nod to him, showing that he will answer for me.

Sanguines have the most difficulty in keeping their mouths shut because they always have something to say and fear if they miss the opportunity to jump in, even with a mouthful, they might never get in again, and the world would have lost a pearl of great price.

Keep Your Elbows off the Table

Although we should not make dinner time an hour of instruction, the basic patterns must be established early with the children. One of these is posture while eating and even though little ones can't be expected to sit perfectly still, they should learn not to lie down into their food or lean on their elbows. So many adults I've observed in restaurants lean on their left elbow with their arm somewhat surrounding the plate as if they were protecting their meal from anyone who might want to whisk it away from them.

Possibly as children they had brothers who grabbed the steak off their plates, but chances are they never were taught that hanging over the table looking as if you were about to fall headlong into your dinner was an unattractive, sometimes offensive, position.

If you as parents sit correctly and remind them occasionally, the children will learn from your words and example.

Don't Criticize the Food

Would you be embarrassed if you brought your child to my home and when I placed a meal before him he said, "What is that? I don't like that"? I've had little guests who made such comments and while it hasn't ruined my evening, it has humiliated the parents. How can you prevent a child from making such remarks? You can't if they've been allowed to be critical of the food at home. The pattern they have established at home will be carried on in public. We can't expect children to be mannerly when eating out if they've had no standards set at home.

Teaching children not to turn up their noses at their dinner is an impossible task if the father is critical of what is placed before him or if the father allows the older children to scoff at mother's efforts. Little ones learn very early in life if criticism is acceptable behavior at the table.

Have an Attitude of Gratitude

One early lesson children need to learn, which will help to eliminate criticism at the table, is an attitude of gratitude. Make the first thing you do at each meal be the blessing. Establish that we are grateful we are even together, we are grateful for this food whatever it might be, we are grateful we have something to eat. If we start out being grateful, we will be less apt to be negative.

In Lauren's family, they hold hands around the table and one of the children prays. They consider it exciting to be the one in charge of thanking the Lord. They do not have memorized blessings, but are encouraged to say what they wish. Sometimes their words are humorous, "Bless the salt and pepper," but something touching, "Thank You, God, that we have such a nice Grammie who comes to see us."

Little Bryan, who is only two, already can say, "Thank You, Jesus." One night we all sat down at the table and started passing the platter around before having the blessing. Little Bryan called out, "Hold hands! Hold hands!" He was reminding us to pray.

Wouldn't it be ludicrous if after we thanked the Lord for the food we criticized the person who prepared it!

Try It: You Might Like It

One of my favorite books to read to the children was *Green Eggs and Ham* by Dr. Suess. Not only are his books humorous with an intriguing rhyme scheme, but often they have a lesson. In *Green Eggs* the question is asked, "Do you like green eggs and ham? Do you like them, Sam-I-Am?" Sam doesn't like them in a box, with a fox, on a train, or in the rain. After a book full of places Sam wouldn't dream of going to eat green eggs and ham, he's asked if he ever had any and he says no. Once he is coaxed into trying them, he is surprisingly excited, "I do like green eggs and ham." He then decides he would eat them anywhere, in a box, with a fox, and on and on.

The obvious moral is that many of us will not try something we've never had before. If we as parents are fussy eaters, chances are we'll raise children who won't venture much beyond peanut butter and Froot Loops.®

Probably because Fred was in the restaurant business when we married, he placed a high value on interesting meals and trained me to be a gourmet cook. Our children always had to try everything. They didn't have to like it or eat all of it, but they had to have three bites. By insisting they try each new item, we were able to train them to be adventurous eaters and both girls are gourmet cooks. I never had to worry that they would refuse to eat at someone's house or that they would make negative comments.

One night we were out for dinner at a friend's house and we were each served a plate of escargots that looked remarkably like what we had been killing along our front walk with snail pellets. I had never served any such items, and I looked toward Marita and Fred, Jr. Both of them had terror in their eyes, but they made no comment.

We all watched the host, as we had trained them to do, and followed his pattern. Sticking the little fork inside the shell wasn't difficult, but the little plop the snail made as he was pulled out almost undid us all. Marita swallowed hers whole followed by water, and Fred put bread in his mouth and chewed the little creature up with the bread.

When we left the home Fred and I praised them for their noble efforts and we proclaimed them to be gourmet eaters. As in any lesson, we can't teach our children what we refuse to do. Try broadening your culinary horizons at home and train your children to take a few bites of everything, without comment.

One of the most disheartening responses for me to receive from a guest after I have prepared a meal is, "Don't bother to serve the children any of that, they won't eat it." I've been amazed at how often if I get these same children alone in the kitchen I can encourage them to try something they've never had and enjoy it.

Teach them and yourselves to try it. You might like it.

Wait until All Are Served

Unless young people are instructed differently, they will usually dive right into their food the minute it is placed before them, but with a little understanding they can be taught to hold back until all are served. As soon as mother, or the lady of the house, lifts her fork, all may begin. Have your children practice this at home from the time they're young and when they are older they will not depart from it.

Let them know that sometimes a hostess will suggest they start before she is ready, if she will be busy serving for a long time. It is then acceptable to begin.

Let Them Order in Restaurants

A friend told me that when she first dated her husband, he had no idea how to order in a restaurant and she had to teach him. Don't let your children be humiliated by ignorance when they first begin to date. Teach them the difference between a completed dinner price and a la carte, each item priced separately. Show them how to read the menu and to make selections. Let them place their order and ask the waiter or waitress any questions without your jumping in with the answer.

As they grow up, tell the girls they should give their orders to their date who will order for them and let the boys know they should ask the girl what she wants and then place both orders. Even if they never use what you have taught them, the knowledge will give them confidence.

Teach Them to Tip

It is very embarrassing for teens when they go out to eat and they have no idea what to tip. Since we live in a tip-oriented society, we should leave a proper tip for adequate service. In average full-service restaurants fifteen percent tip for adequate to excellent service is expected. In grander places, fancy hotels and resorts where the service is outstanding and several waiters are hovering over you, twenty percent is expected. In cafeteria situations where limited service is rendered ten percent is enough.

Recently a lovely Christian lady took me out for lunch. We were in the midst of a convention and the line to get into the coffee shop extended to the lobby. The waitress was unusually charming and even extended extra services to us. When the lady took the check, she filled out the charge slip with little security about how to do it. I noticed she added no tip and she put nothing on the table. Even though I was her guest, I would have felt guilty to leave the waitress nothing for her services. I asked, "Did you leave a tip?"

"I never know how to figure that all out so I don't tip."

I mentioned how kind the waitress had been and would she mind if I left something? She didn't mind at all as long as I did the math.

If figuring fifteen percent is too difficult, do as I did with my children. First show them how to figure ten percent and practice. If it's $10, ten percent is $1, if it's $5 the tip is 50 cents. Once they get an easy handle on ten percent, explain that for fifteen percent, they cut their answer in half and add it on. The $10, with ten percent being $1, would become $1.50 for the tip. This sounds far too simple-minded a way for Melancholies, but for Sanguines who get nervous when they see a % sign, this little trick seems to work. Round it out to the nearest dollar, take ten percent, cut that in half, add it on to the ten percent. Voila! With this little system firmly in her head, Marita handles all our CLASS restaurant charges and adds on the tip.

Whatever we can do at home to give our child confidence when in public will be worth whatever we can dream up to help.

Although our children won't be handling luggage alone for many years, we should at least teach them as we are traveling that each bag handled by a sky cap is expected to bring a 50-cent tip. If we arrive at the last minute and need special service to make the plane, we should add an extra tip and tell the porter how much we appreciate his willingness to rush this through. Since I almost live in airports, I have become well acquainted with the sky caps at our local airport. I have found them to be men of high quality and more than willing to be helpful, but if you come late, demand service, and don't tip, your bags just might not make the plane!

29. Setting the Table

The majority of our children will never be invited to the White House for dinner, so they won't need to know all the fancy silverware placements and usages. But it is unfair to the child not to train him on how to set a simple table. Boys and girls should both learn the basics. One of the earliest task assignments I gave each of my children was to set the table. At a young age they can be kept busy ferrying forks across the room and placing them anywhere in any direction. Then they can begin to put them on each side of the plate and soon learn that the knife and spoon go on the right and the fork on the left.

Once this task becomes simple, show them that the rounded side of the knife blade heads toward the plate. Then move on to salad forks and soup spoons. As long as you praise them with each correct setting, they will enjoy learning. Teach them the principle that you set the silverware in the order in which it will be used, starting from the outside in to the plate. Also let them know if they are at someone's dinner table with extra silver pieces, they should use the outside fork for the first course such as salad, the next fork for the main course and the inside one for dessert. At a very formal setting the silver to be used for dessert will be above the plate and should not be used until that course. If their memories fail them on what to do, tell them to watch the hostess and use whatever pieces she uses.

FORMAL SETTING

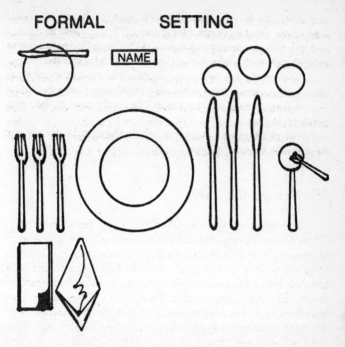

NAME

My children have all at separate times thanked me for making them learn the basics of table manners because it gave them confidence when their friends had little.

Whenever they are ready to have their plate removed, show them how to put the knife and fork across the middle of the plate with the fork tines facing down. Practicing this at home will make this step automatic in restaurants and at dinner parties.

Teach them that a linen napkin should not be spread out like a picnic blanket but left folded in half. For girls, it should be across the lap, for boys over the leg.

Ernestine Mann of Tulsa, a CLASS graduate, teaches basic manners to business executives so that they will be at ease in social situations. She is often amazed at how little intelligent, successful men know about etiquette. Her motto is, "I help them be smart," and in her class opening she quotes Will Cappy, "Etiquette means behaving yourself a little better than is absolutely essential."

Why don't you help your children be smart in social situations and encourage them to behave a little better than is necessary?

Rehearse them now so they will be comfortable in their own production later.

"Mark the perfect man, and behold the upright; for the end of that man is peace" (Psalm 37:37).

Part IX

SCRIPT

Pleasant words are as an honeycomb,
sweet to the soul and health to
the bones.
(Proverbs 16:24)

IX

Script

30. Power of Words

When actress Joanne Dru came to our first CLASS in 1981, we were in awe of her beauty and her star quality. We expected her to be an outstanding communicator and couldn't understand why she was hesitant to share her testimony. She explained, "This is the first time I've stood before a group without a script. I've had plenty of experience delivering lines that someone else wrote, but you're asking me to speak for myself from my heart. That's a different story."

Yes, what she told us was a different story; it was her story, not a set of memorized lines.

In our everyday lives we are telling our own story. We don't have writers to produce a script of clever phrases and witty repartee. We're on our own speaking from our hearts. If we are angry, bitter, resentful, depressed, we will pour out words that represent the condition of our heart. If we were insulted and hurt as children, we are apt to give similar remarks to our little ones. Jesus tried to explain to His disciples that it was not what went into a man's mouth that defiled him but what came out. "The things that come out of the mouth come from the heart, and these make a man unclean" (Matthew 15:18 NIV).

As we look at our script, the words that come forth from our hearts, we need to observe our sentences, the tone in which we say them, and the attitude behind them. We don't have a writer like Johnny Carson has; we're not reciting someone else's clever lines. We are our own script writers and we are responsible for our own words.

Solomon said, "A wise man's heart guides his mouth, and his lips promote instruction" (Proverbs 16:23 NIV).

James warned, "If anyone considers himself religious and yet does not keep a tight rein on his tongue, he deceives himself and his religion is worthless" (James 1:26 NIV).

"If anyone is never at fault in what he says, he is a perfect man, able to keep his whole body in check" (James 3:2 NIV).

As we parents consider what Jesus, Solomon, and James all said about our words, about how they reflect the condition of our hearts, we should pause and ask ourselves two questions:

1. Am I giving out kind, positive, affirming words to my children? Ones that promote instruction and are as pleasant as a honeycomb?

2. If not, where is my sarcasm, my bitterness, my pessimism coming from?

So often we need to clean out our own thoughts with a time of soul-searching and find out what negatives we have harbored from our past. As we come up with comments our parents or others made to us as children, we should write them down, look at them, and then ask ourselves if we are perhaps saying these same things to our children. If we don't know, we have only to ask them to get a quick response.

I remember how often my mother cautioned me to be sure to wear clean underwear in case I was in an accident. Once when she heard me quote her, she corrected me and stated, "I said no such thing." She paused and added, "My mother said it to me but I never said it to you."

How fascinating it is that we will pass on family homilies, warnings, and even insults just as we heard them and not even know we've done it.

On a recent airline flight Marita sat across from a woman with a two-year-old girl who was adorable and well-behaved. An hour into the trip the mother told the child to go to sleep. The little one was bright-eyed and excited and had no interest in sleep.

When she continued to chatter away softly, the mother said, "If you don't go to sleep I'm going to belt you." This so startled the child that she was jolted even more awake and couldn't possibly go to sleep. She tried holding her eyes shut and once she peeked up to see if her mother was watching. The mother was and she hit her child across the face, causing her to cry loudly. As the scene grew worse the mother scolded the little girl and said, "It's because of you I'm a nervous wreck."

By this time everyone around was annoyed and Marita got up and offered to hold the child so the mother could rest. As the precious child happily allowed Marita to carry her up and down the aisle, Marita wondered what hope this child had of ever feeling she was worth "a grain of salt" or anything else.

I'm sure those of you reading this have not done anything like what this mother did, but I'm constantly hearing comments from women on what their mothers/fathers said thirty years ago that are still crippling them today. The sample comments on page 217ff. are ones that fine Christian people have had said to them and that they have reported to me.

One beautiful young lady told me she felt ugly. I wished I could have looked like her and I had trouble imagining her thinking she was ugly. As we reflected back on her childhood, she burst into tears when she repeated her mother's frequent comment, "Why did my son have to be the pretty one with the curly hair?"

The mother didn't mean to insult the child but her repeated dirge about the death of the dream for a pretty little girl still played in her mind and every time she looked in the mirror she saw a plain little girl with straight hair standing next to a pretty little boy with curls.

We can't weigh every word we say. But if we at least realize that what comes out of our mouths has the power to bless or to injure, we might train our tongues and control at least some of our words.

Many of us don't realize that our children take what we say literally. As a child I heard my mother tell a friend, "Florence is taking elocution lessons because she has no talent." Why do I remember that sentence today when I recall few other statements of that time? Because of those two words "no talent"! Had I been a Melancholy I might have become depressed. Had I been a Phlegmatic I might have given up. The Sanguine part of me was crushed. I wanted so much to be praised. Gratefully, my Choleric nature said, "No talent. I'll show you." I worked at memorizing my little pieces, determined to succeed and today, in a way, I give "elocution lessons."

In retrospect, my mother didn't mean anything negative. She didn't intend to hurt me; I just took her literally. I thought she meant I had no talent. What was she really saying?

Considering my mother's childhood in a family full of musicians, her perspective of talent naturally focused on music. Because she studied the violin as a child, the cello as a teen, and became a music teacher and an orchestra leader in her twenties, Mother's view of artistic ability didn't go beyond playing an instrument.

Because I, as a child, looked laughable holding a violin and played the piano purely intellectually, note by note, with "no talent," my mother came to a natural conclusion. From her point of view, if you're not musical, you're not talented, therefore, her statement was a simple fact. She spoke from her background; I heard from mine.

Why am I reviewing this childhood story? Is there a lesson here? Yes. Children take our comments literally. In hearing "no talent" I couldn't review my mother's background and musical ability. I just processed her remark emotionally. A careless comment can cut down a child's self-worth forever.

Check Your Script

1. Write down the things you remember your parents saying and then compare them with the list below.

2. Pray that the Lord will reveal what you are passing on that is hurtful or degrading.

3. Sit down with your children and ask them to check off any of the statements from your list and this list that they have ever heard you say.

4. Don't defend yourself or interrupt with "I never said that." Just listen.

5. Apologize for any negative words and give your children permission to raise their hands whenever you say something nasty or negative again. Tell them you will do the same thing with them as God wants our words to be like apples of gold. Remember when they do respond to thank them for reminding you and don't argue. One defensive sentence and they'll never be honest with you again.

6. Once you have heard their comments, discuss the fact that words reflect our heart attitude and how careful we must all be to avoid hurting others with our words. Give them verses that show "the tongue has the power of life and death" (Proverbs 18:21a NIV).

7. Ask for examples of what other people have said to them that have been upsetting. You may be surprised at what comments are lodged in their minds. Let them spill out their thoughts and notice where each one is particularly sensitive.

Have You Ever Recited Lines Such As These?

On identifying self-worth:

—Your opinion doesn't count.

—You are so stupid—dense—impossible.

—You're more trouble than you're worth.

—I wish you were never born.

—You're the reason for my headaches.

—If it weren't for you I'd still be thin—happy—rich—in my right mind.

—You're responsible for the divorce.

—You children are the greatest disappointment in my life.

—You don't amount to a plugged nickel, to a grain of salt, to one iota, to a row of pins, to a pinch of snuff, to the powder to blow you to thunder.

—You were an accident.

—I'm sick of your face, your complaining, your attitude.

—You are such a slob, idiot, creep.

—I can hardly wait till you grow up and get out of here.

Instead of these lines, you could say:

—You are the cutest, smartest, sweetest, strongest, bravest.

—I'm so proud of you.

—I value your opinion.

—Having you has been the biggest blessing of my life.

—Every time you walk in the room you light up my life, give me comfort, energy, peace.

—I know I can count on you.

—When you're at home I never worry.

—You're my best friend.

—When you grow up I know you're going to be a wonderful mother/father.

As we realize how much of a child's self-esteem comes from the attitudes he receives at home, we must use words that build and don't tear down.

We must avoid comparisons with brothers, sisters, friends or what we were as children.

On Comparisons:

—Why don't you keep your room neat like _____?

—Why don't you get A's like _____?

—Why aren't you faster, brighter, more athletic like _____?

—Why didn't you try out for the play, football, track, _____?

—When I was your age _____.

On Warnings:

—If you don't say your prayers God will strike you dead.

—If you don't eat your vegetables you'll be a midget.

—If you don't wash your ears, potatoes will grow in there.

—If you swallow any of those seeds you'll grow watermelons in your tummy.

—If you tell anyone what I did I'll kill you.

—If you don't change your ways you'll end up in the penitentiary.

—If you keep up the way you're going you'll be pregnant by the time you're fifteen.

—If you ever get pregnant, don't come home to us.

—If you don't study hard you'll be on welfare for life.

We must not give warnings that are ridiculous or that might cause fear. This doesn't mean we shouldn't let them know of actual dangers in life, but odd threats are often taken as truth and some actually become self-fulfilling. A survey done on young men in jail showed that a large percentage of them had been told by a parent that they'd end up in jail.

On Reputation:

—You've ruined our family name.

—Remember you are an example to the entire church.

—What will my friends think?

—What will your grandmother think?

—What will the people at church think?

We must be careful not to let our children feel that we care more about our friends' opinions than we do about them.

On Not Giving Compliments:

—You might get a swelled head.

—If you were secure in the Lord you wouldn't need praise.

—I never know when I might have to eat my words.

—What makes you think anyone will notice you?

—You think the world revolves around you.

—It's time you got taken down a peg.

Parents who didn't get proper nurturing or receive positive comments as children tend to avoid giving their little ones praises and even defend their coldness as a Christian virtue. We don't want to lie to our children or give exaggerated phrases, but we must realize that as our plants need water to grow, our children need affirming and verbal praises to become emotionally mature. Don't be a person who has prize African violets and wilted children.

On Depression:

—Just cheer up and forget it.

—Lots of people have worse problems than you do.

—If you weren't so self-centered you'd not be depressed.

—Remember the joy of the Lord is your strength.

—You're becoming a burden to the whole family.

—Sticks and stones may break your bones but names will never hurt you.

At one time or another all children go through phases when they feel the world is going to end for some reason that we consider trivial. Telling them at that point to cheer up and get on with life doesn't cheer them up. Don't knock their tender feelings, but listen and say something like "I don't blame you. If I'd had that happen to me I'd feel the same." They don't want lectures or even scriptures, they just want someone to listen and understand.

If you feel a child may be really depressed, read my book *Blow Away the Black Clouds* and/or get some competent counseling.

The most important lesson to remember here is that our words have power to lift up or to tear down and once in the mind they are impossible to erase.

31. Creative Conversation

So many of us parents spend more time trying to keep our children out of trouble than we do making sure they're having a good time. There is no shortcut to parenting and we need to look at raising children as a challenging full-time job, but one that brings the "peaceable fruits of righteousness" to those who can endure. There is no greater pleasure than looking at your adult children and saying to yourself, "well done, good and faithful servant." There is no greater heartbreak than a child who has gone wrong.

Each week I talk with parents who have children who are on drugs, in jail, living with an unmarried friend, involved in alcohol, having abortions, and a host of other maladies not thought of in my youth. Some of these tragedies have come to dedicated Christian parents who appear to have done everything right, but most often the mother will say, "If I only had it to do over again, I'd spend more time with them. I'd talk more and watch TV less."

How can we do this?

Fred and I had an unwritten rule to make our evening time with the children so active that TV was not an obvious choice. We often sat at the table conversing for hours, and when their friends would be visiting, those who hardly ever talked at home would become verbose. The reason was twofold: 1, we listened without interruption to every opinion without telling them their ideas were stupid, and 2, we discussed interesting and creative subjects where each person would automatically have something to say. We avoided yes and no questions and topics where there would be hot controversy or it would be offensive to the guests.

The secret of creative conversation is to provide a springboard into each individual's mind and to make thinking both fun and rewarding. We would encourage new ideas and be impressed with any statement that made sense.

"I can't believe you thought that up on your own."

"That is really an exciting idea."

When the children had research projects, we would discuss the topics and ask for ideas from those present. Often a whole new perspective would open up and give a depth to the subject that the individual would not have thought up on his own.

One major prerequisite to creative conversation at the table is that you have to stay home to do it. We were an active family, but we tried not to have pressing engagements right after dinner. Nothing eliminates a free sharing of ideas so quickly as: "Hurry up and finish what you're saying; we have no time for that now; just sum it up as fast as you can." Comments such as these will have negative reactions on all four personalities. The Popular Sanguine won't be able to sum it up quickly and will be left frustrated. The Powerful Choleric will be angry when cut off. The Perfect Melancholy will feel rejected and say to himself, "I knew they didn't want to hear my opinion." The Peaceful Phlegmatic will decide, "There's no point in my ever trying to say anything again, so I'll just keep quiet from here on."

A survey was done on a group of teens who had won scholarships to determine what influence their families had on their intellectual achievement. Although there were many different contributions to their growth, the only consistent answer was that they had families who sat around the dinner table for at least one meal a day and talked. Money and parental education did not make much difference, but a nurturing time of give and take at the table gave them confidence in conversing and stimulated their young minds more than watching television would have done.

Dr. Jay Martin of USC says, "Television watching makes you so passive, the passivity itself decreases attention to anything creative or anything that establishes self. It induces us to identify passively with whatever's on TV. If violence is on, there is an increase in identification with violence."[1]

Minds that hang in limbo watching television may learn something positive but it will not be creativity. That takes stimulation and encouragement from others. Watching is passive; talking is active and stimulates the brain. Naturally, it is easier to watch television than to think, but when we realize the potential of these little minds, we should be stirred into action and ready to make deposits in their future.

Joyce Carol Oates, well-known author and professor at Princeton, had a father who had not graduated from high school. He worked in a factory forty hours a week, but he didn't waste his time when he was home. He encouraged Joyce to get an education and he engaged her in creative conversation. She says, "We could always talk in a way that I would consider intellectual. My father would listen to my ideas."[2]

Now that he has retired, Frederic Oates has started taking college literature courses and he discusses them with his daughter.

Some of you may be thinking, *What do we talk about with our children to keep their minds moving and encourage creativity?* Here are a few topics to start with that will lead to new ideas.

If you could go anywhere for a vacation, what would be your ideal choice? What would you do there?

If you could decorate your room and money was no object, what would you do with it?

If you could be in any profession you wanted, what would it be? What preparation would you need? Could you do anything about it now?

What book is your favorite, what character do you like best, and where does it all take place?

What do you think heaven is going to be like? How are we going to get there? (Follow with simple plan of salvation and description of heaven from Revelation.)

What did you learn in Sunday school? How could that lesson change your life?

What is your favorite Bible story? What is its moral?

What is the best Christmas (Easter, birthday, event) that you can remember? What happened? If you could make next Christmas into a perfect day for you, for others, what would you do differently?

All these questions, along with endless others you can create, will stimulate thinking. No answers are right or wrong but all give an opportunity for individual opinion.

Try taking one question a night and give each family member a chance to answer. If you run out of ideas, there is a creative little book, *The Book of Questions* by Gregory Stock, Ph.D. Each of the questions is designed to help you get to know the other person in a closer way and none of them allow yes or no answers. This helpful book is not written with a Christian slant, so some of the questions may be unsuitable for family conversation, but most will act as the match to start a flame of communication that will burn into a forest of creative conversation between you and your children.

Fred and I have used similar questions at dinner parties and had each person around the table give their ideas while everyone listened. This method is far better than having two or three separate groups talking or having one person monopolize the conversation.

With young people, I have found asking them a provocative question makes them feel you really love and accept them.

Some of you may have little children and feel that you aren't ready for these discussion topics, but you do want to start them conversing at an early age. In a teachers' magazine, *Learning* '87, I found an idea that may be helpful to you.

Anne Martin teaches kindergarten and she has a "class meeting" every day where the little ones talk about their problems such as lost toys, a sick little brother, and what foods they don't like. From this point she tries to lead them into concept questions such as what is love, fear, death, and friendship.

Anne writes,

> Of course, getting 5-year-olds to participate in a discussion can be tough. But several years ago, quite by accident, I came upon a way to help them listen to each other and sustain a group discussion.
>
> The school year was almost over. One day, I idly picked up a dilapidated fox puppet from a classroom toy box and brought it with me to our meeting. I casually had the fox join the discussion. I'm not much of an actor—and I'm usually uncomfortable using puppets—but the result was electrifying: Suddenly the children were ignoring me and addressing themselves to "Foxy," engaging him in earnest conversation. Of course they knew I was doing the talking, but by some magical suspension of disbelief, they imbued Foxy with a life and personality of his own. The children's response, which went far beyond the pretend games they played all day, was an uncanny mixture of whimsy and seriousness.[3]

As I read Anne's words, I realized how small children love to talk when they don't think they will be judged, reprimanded, or interrupted. Using Foxy removed the adult figure and gave them a new little friend who would listen. Perhaps you could try a puppet who could inspire confidential conversation from your child.

My grandson Randy has a teacher, Mr. Peck, who has his fourth-graders journalize their thoughts about personal subjects with great success. When asked what person he knew loved him he wrote, "My Grammie because she tells me I'm special." Based on this report I led into the subject of love with Randy and asked him what I had done that showed him I loved him. He told me first that I send him cards that say "Special Boy" on them. Next he said, "When you used to pick me up from school, you took me to Griswold's Bakery and let me pick out whatever cupcake I wanted." I realized I hadn't done that in a long time because I'm away so much, and I didn't have any idea that buying a cupcake was so memorable.

He then added, "In 1986 you gave me a bicycle for my birthday. I remember the party was in Ford Park and I looked around and saw you pushing a bicycle up the hill." I had forgotten the 1986 birthday, but his Melancholy mind had not.

"That was the best present you ever gave me." What amazing memories little children have and how they love to talk with us if we'll just ask.

When I was speaking at the North Parkersburg Baptist Church in West Virginia, I had the opportunity to converse with Larry Miller, their minister to children. He was conducting a mini-seminar for the little children while Fred and I were teaching the personalities to the parents. He had put together a program to promote personal awareness among the children and he had an adorable workbook for them to use. It was called *Marvelous Me* and was geared for ages five to eight. In the beginning it stated, "This is a book to help you learn more about yourself. There are no right or wrong answers. Work neatly. You will want to save this book and read it when you are older."

Each child was given one of these bright orange workbooks with cartoon people drawn throughout. On the page "All About Me" the child was to fill in blanks about name, address, birthday, and number of people in the family. He was to write five words that told about himself and finish the sentence, "One thing that makes me very special is _____."

He could check off little boxes next to:

I am _____ right-handed
I am _____ left-handed
My face has _____ no freckles
My face has _____ a few freckles
My face has _____ lots of freckles

On the page "My Room" he was to count and fill in how many windows, beds, lights, and drawers he had, draw a picture of a "dream room" and write the one thing he would like to change in his room.

There was a page on which to paste pictures of favorite items to make a poster, a "three wishes" page, and an "If" page.

"If I were the teacher, I would _____.

If I could make a wish for the world, it would be _____.

If I could call the President, I would say _____.

If I could be any person in the world, I would be _____.

If I could be an animal, I would be a _____ because _____."

To win the heart of the Popular child, there was a Marvelous Me Award for completing all the pages in the book.

So intrigued was I with this workbook that could make children think, analyze, and enjoy all at the same time, I ordered some for my grandsons and to have for sale on our book table.

Don't be so involved in the activities of life that you miss out on relaxing times of fellowship around the table. In Psalm 128 the man of the house is challenged to trust, revere, and obey the Lord. For his reward he will have prosperity and happiness.

"Your wife shall be contented in your home. And look at all these children. There they sit around the dinner table as vigorous and healthy as young olive trees" (Psalm 128:3 NIV).

32. What's in a Name?

In a play, names are chosen to fit the kind of impression the author had in mind, but in everyday family existence the chosen name may be for reasons that have nothing to do with how the child will come across to others.

Fred's mother was originally named Pearl Louise, but later, when her mother found "Marita" as the heroine of a novel, she had it legally changed. Grandpa claims he won money on a horse named Marita and that was the reason. We will never know the truth as they died fighting about it, both being Powerfuls who never gave in to one another.

Unfortunately, that was not the only name they changed. When Mother Littauer had her first son, she named him Frederick Jerome Littauer, Jr. after his father. Grandma and Grandpa arrived at the hospital and, upon hearing this name, immediately gave instructions that it should be changed to Grandpa's name, Richard Oelkers Littauer. No one ever bucked these two and the birth certificate was altered, leaving way for my husband, the second son, to become Junior.

My sister-in-law, Nancy, named her second son Douglas and when questioned by Grandma as to why, she said she just liked the name. That was not a good enough reason for Grandma who promptly had it changed. She pointed out that Nancy's father, Dwayne Orton, was not only the editor of IBM's *Think* magazine but an internationally known business communicator. "You must name this child after your father. It would be a shame to waste that prestige." So Douglas became Dwayne Orton Littauer who is today a lawyer in Dallas. Who knows if his name has helped!

On our side, family names were passed down to perpetuate their remembrance. My father, Walter Chapman, had a brother, Arthur, who had two sons, Walter and Arthur. Walter had a Walter and Arthur had an Arthur and a Walter.

My brother James Walter had Grandpa MacDougall's first name with his father's "Walter" in the middle. My brother who died was Arthur and my youngest brother was given two names of friends who lent my father money to buy our store in the midst of the Depression.

My grandmother was Florence Ann, my mother Katie Florence, and I became Florence Mariah after the two grandmothers. However, neither my father or mother liked Mariah so they changed it to Marcia.

Marita Kathryn was named after her two grandmothers while adapting Katie to Kathryn.

Where have the names come from in your family? Is there a grandma who had dictated choices? Is there a family tradition? Review and discuss these with your children. They may have no idea where their names came from.

Proverbs 22:1 says, "A good name is more desirable than great riches" (NIV).

What is a "good name"?

Christopher Anderson, in his report "The Baby Boomer's Name Game," tells us that "trendy names eventually work against you because they let people know when you were born . . . Most Tammys were born in the late '50's when Debbie Reynolds' 'Tammy and the Bachelor' was a hit. To be pegged so perfectly is something you want to avoid."[4]

A researcher at New York State University at Fredonia, Edwin Larson, did a study on the value of names and found that the overall best for men was Garry followed by John, Daniel, David, Kurt, and Erik. Women who were polled chose for men: Moses, Gregory, Mike, Jon, Brad, and Luke.

Lowest rated for men was Oswald. I'm so glad Oswald Chambers died before this survey was completed! Other unacceptable names were Angus, Boris, Delbert, Elmer, Melvin, Horace, and Myron.

You might want to do your own survey in your church, using both the names present and people's opinions of other names. The history of names in the Scripture would be a fascinating study along with the understanding of how important the family name was to the twelve tribes of Israel.

Anderson suggests, "Parents need to pay attention to what a name is going to do. Psychologists will say that if parents give their child a name that's going to make him an object of ridicule by his peers, then obviously those parents are either terribly ignorant of the damage that names can do, or on some subconscious level they want to make their child's life miserable. If you name your kid Lethal, it says something about your intentions."[5]

Recently I met two people in one day who had been psychologically damaged by what their parents called them. The first was a man whose mother didn't want him. When asked in the hospital what she wanted to name him, she responded with a vulgar swear word. "That's what I think of him and that's what I'll call him." And so she did. His father often quoted what his mother had said and his brothers and sisters called him that also.

Naturally, his schoolmates found it fun to use this word for his name and he never lived it down. Even though he's moved away, he's never gotten out from under the black cloud of that name. When he told me his story he began to cry.

At the same conference a lady told me her name was Eleanor. There's nothing wrong with that name except that her mother hated it and hated her. She told her daughter when she was old enough to understand, "I didn't want you and so I thought up a name I hated and gave it to you, so you'll always be reminded of what I think of you."

When I talked to poor Eleanor she had changed her name twice but couldn't run away from the "hateful name" no matter how she tried.

If you by any chance have had reason to be unhappy with the birth of a child, please don't let them know it or put a name on them which may have negative connotations.

Also, don't give them nicknames as children that if they stuck might be embarrassing to an older child. Labels that may be cute for toddlers somehow sound juvenile for adults. When I have Cookie, Twinkles, and Bootsie along with Butch, Swinger, and Spike, come to CLASS to become Christian speakers, I have to wonder how much authority or credibility they will have when introduced to the church.

There is a lot in a name, so choose it wisely.

For each of my grandchildren I have developed a title and a theme. Randy is my Special Boy and I seek in every airport for cards, plaques, or stickers that feature the word Special. He has a file folder for these items and I am having a scrapbook made for him with his picture and "Special Boy" on the cover. When this is completed, we will paste all the cards I've sent him into this book for him to look back upon in later years of self-doubt when he will need proof that he is Special.

When Jonathan got old enough to know Randy was Special, I said to him, "Randy is Special and you are Adorable." With his quick Sanguine wit, he retorted, "I am both Special and Adorable!" Later he asked me if he could be Superman and so I agreed that since he had Superman pajamas with a cape and could leap from the coffee table to the couch in a single bound, he could be my superman. I buy him any cards that have anything resembling a Superman and he is pleased with his identity.

At two little Bryan is not old enough to get into the Special-Super act, but because he twinkles with personality, I call him my Star and find him items with stars, moons, and planets. In this age when few young people have any feeling of worth, we should do all we can to give them a sense of self-value, to let them know they're Special, Super, and have Star quality.

33. Role Models

In the past children have had parents, grandparents, pastors, and teachers as role models, but in today's transient society the former feeling of family is often missing. The church may be impersonal, and many teachers may not present a positive image. Because of the lack of real people to relate to, many young people today pattern themselves after what they see on television. We've all read articles telling of the rise in suicides after a show on the subject, and we've heard talk shows and survey reports that confirm children learn about sex from what they see on TV. Since hopping from bed to bed, drinking constantly, using drugs, and having children out of wedlock are all made to look normal, acceptable, and even glamorous, our young people get brainwashed into thinking anything goes.

Michael Fox, that adorable young man in "Family Ties," has become a role model for many teens. Yet his movie *Bright Lights, Big City,* according to reviews in several magazines and the "Today" show, casts him as a cocaine addict who takes his drugs with style. Even though he ends up losing everything, a faint moral, the critics feel it was a shame to have used Michael in such a role where teens see him using cocaine and may follow his example instead of learning from the negative results.

One of the most talked about books in 1987 was Allan Bloom's *The Closing of the American Mind.* He points out that the value of literature, history, and philosophy has been lost in our practical educational system. This organism says if you can't use it today, there's no reason to study it. In Bloom's day and my day we read to have knowledge that would be stored up in our minds until we wanted to pull it out to use in reasoning and decision-making. Much of what I learned was not instantly applicable, but it gave me an intellectual cushion to lean back on and to provide me with comfort. I knew it was there when I needed it.

Dr. Bloom laments the shallowness of the young American mind and the nation that has lost its bearings and its respect for intellectual heroes.

> There used to be an intellectual class in America. In the political realm, for example, you had Dean Acheson and George Kennan; in journalism there was Walter Lippmann. These people kept the world of ideas alive.
>
> But today the distinction between intellectuals and nonintellectuals doesn't make any difference; celebrity is the only standard. If you had a direct descendant of George Washington in a class together with Mick Jagger's son, the students would probably be much more interested in Mick Jagger's son. The level of public taste—and taste is a good beginning point for serious thinking—really has declined. The cultivated person no longer has any public model.[6]

When young people have no literary or historical examples, and do not have exciting lives themselves, they fill their minds with the lives of TV personalities—the rich, the famous, and the powerful. They are apt to take on aspects of these available role models to compensate for deficiencies in their own self-image. Darwin Dorr, director of clinical psychology at Highland Hospital in Asheville, N.C. believes that emulating fictional characters is on the increase. "It's not really genuine—you sort of put on a personality like a coat. It is a personality disorder, a deficiency in identity."[7]

Dr. Jay Martin, a USC English professor, says, "The popularity of contemporary television and film characters—many of them beautiful or powerful—makes for a world in which real people have less talent, are less interesting and where it's important to play a part to be authentic."[8]

It is a sad commentary on our current society that many of the adults our children see are so dull that they would prefer to identify with a fictional character. Ask yourself what your children see in you, in your marriage, in your friends. Are you all tired, overworked, humorless, and complaining at the same time you are trying to model the joy of the Lord for your children?

So often when I speak in church services, I look out over a sea of depressing faces. No one seems to be happy there and many look as if they have literally taken up their cross daily and have it on their backs at this moment. As I see the young people working at being bored by the service, which often is not difficult, I wonder if I would want to be a Christian if these adults were my role models.

Stop and think right now about the people your children view as role models. When they think of growing up, what do they see as future possibilities? If they thought they'd be like you or your mate, or the people in church, would this be a positive image? Since relating to adults is a part of growing up, ask your children around the table some evening about the people they admire.

What adult in the family do you like best? Least? Why?

What one would you choose to be like when you grow up? Why? What one would you not want to be like? Why? What TV personality do you relate to? Which one is your least favorite? Why? What person do you know who is really spiritual? What are their characteristics? Do you want to be like them when you grow up?

If you could put together one person you would most want to be like, who would it be?

Personality _____

Looks _____

Intelligence _____

Humor _____

Spirituality _____

Values _____

Add whatever ideas you may have and put together a composite role model with your child. This kind of conversation will give you insight into the values and goals of your children. Remember in this, as in any discussion, to listen through their whole idea and don't say, "That's wrong." Feelings are personal and should not be cut off as incorrect. Otherwise our children will give us pat answers and never learn to communicate from the heart.

After you have discussed role models with your children, have a Bible study to show them that their ultimate pattern is the life of Jesus Christ. He is to be our role model.

We are to be "conformed to the likeness of his Son" (Romans 8:29 NIV).

We will be "transformed into his likeness" (2 Corinthians 3:18 NIV).

He will "transform our lowly bodies so that they will be like his glorious body" (Philippians 3:21 NIV).

"Dear friends, now we are children of God, and what we will be has not yet been made known. But we know that when he appears, we shall be like him, for we shall see him as he is" (1 John 3:2 NIV).

As you share these verses and the concept that we shall be like Him, have your children give you the qualities of the Lord Jesus as they perceive them. If your children are old enough to do a searching study, lead them into the Word and help them find the strengths of Jesus, our ultimate role model.

34. Communication Analysis

Following are two exercises to help you analyze your relationship with your teenagers:

Communication: Self-analysis for Parents

This exercise is designed to help you and your teenage children better understand how to communicate with each other. Circle the YES column when the question can be answered as happening most of the time. Circle the NO column when the question can be answered as seldom or never.

1.	Do you wait until your children are through talking before answering them?		Yes	No
2.	Does your family do things as a group?		Yes	No
3.	Do you talk things over as a family?		Yes	No
4.	Does your child think that you respect his opinion?	child A	Yes	No
		child B	Yes	No
5.	Does your child think that you lecture or preach too much?	child A	Yes	No
		child B	Yes	No
6.	Does your child feel free to discuss personal problems with you?	child A	Yes	No
		child B	Yes	No
7.	Do you feel your child is mature enough for his years?	child A	Yes	No
		child B	Yes	No
8.	Do you show real interest in the interests of your children?		Yes	No
9.	Do you feel free to discuss matters of sex with your children?		Yes	No
10.	Does your child think that you trust him?	child A	Yes	No
		child B	Yes	No
11.	Do you make it a point to listen to what your children have to say?		Yes	No
12.	Do your children know that you have confidence in them?		Yes	No
13.	Does your child feel free to disagree with you?	child A	Yes	No
		child B	Yes	No
14.	Do your children feel free to make requests of you?		Yes	No
15.	Do your children feel that you would be "for them" in a matter outside the family?		Yes	No
16.	Do you discuss things with your children *before* making a decision which affects them?		Yes	No
17.	Would your children say that you try to make them feel better when they are down in the dumps?		Yes	No
18.	Do your explain to your children the reason why you are making a negative decision?		Yes	No

Now compare your answers with your children's answers to each question. Be prepared for some "shocks" . . . they will not always agree. But, with our hearts open and ready to listen, these results can be the basis for fruitful family discussion.

Communication Exercise for Teenagers

This inventory is an exercise designed to help you and your parents better understand how you communicate with each other. There are no right or wrong answers. Circle the YES column when the question can be answered as happening most of the time. Circle the NO column when the question can be answered as seldom or never. Circle the answers which relate to your father in the first column, and the answers which relate to your mother in the second column.

	FATHER		MOTHER	
1. Do your parents wait until you are through before "having their say"?	Yes	No	Yes	No
2. Does your family do things as a group?	Yes	No	Yes	No
3. Does your family talk things over with each other?	Yes	No	Yes	No
4. Do your parents seem to respect your opinion?	Yes	No	Yes	No
5. Do your parents tend to lecture and preach too much?	Yes	No	Yes	No
6. Do you discuss personal problems with either of your parents?	Yes	No	Yes	No
7. Do your parents tend to talk to you as if you were much younger?	Yes	No	Yes	No
8. Do they show an interest in your interests?	Yes	No	Yes	No
9. Do you discuss matters of sex with either of your parents?	Yes	No	Yes	No
10. Do your parents trust you?	Yes	No	Yes	No
11. Do you find it hard to say what you feel at home?	Yes	No	Yes	No
12. Do your parents have confidence in your abilities?	Yes	No	Yes	No
13. Do you hesitate to disagree with either of them?	Yes	No	Yes	No
14. Do you fail to ask your parents for things because you feel they'll deny your requests?	Yes	No	Yes	No
15. Do they really try to see your side of things?	Yes	No	Yes	No
16. Do your parents consider your opinion in making decisions which concern you?	Yes	No	Yes	No
17. Do they try to make you feel better when you're down in the dumps?	Yes	No	Yes	No
18. Do your parents explain their reason for not letting you do something?	Yes	No	Yes	No

Part X

COMEDY

He that is of a merry heart
hath a continual feast.
(Proverbs 15:15)

X

Comedy

Situation comedies that take the most basic happenings of life and make them funny to the viewer are among the most popular TV programs. Anytime you can back up and look at your life, isn't it hilarious? Isn't your family really a situation comedy?

Without a sense of humor, directing our group could become a heavy experience. But if we keep eternity in perspective many of the happenings are funny enough for a TV pilot. Remember, your aim in family living is not to have it perfect but to provide a warm setting that will be so enjoyable everyone wants to be there. Make your family fun.

If you are a Popular parent this will be automatic with you. If you are the Powerful parent you will have to relax your authoritarian style enough to enjoy your children. Don't make them live by two standards: Fun when you're out of sight and lined up like soldiers at attention the minute you walk in. If you are the Perfect parent loosen up a little. You can have a perfect mansion in heaven but while you are here compromise your high standards to let the children have a good time in their own home. Many Perfect parents won't allow their children to play any games that might mess up the house or have any friends in who might have sticky fingers. This leads to nervous and lonely children who stay away as much as possible. If you are the Peaceful parent you let the children do what they please and you are easy-going enough to play games with them at the expense of the housework. You can always dust after they've gone off to college!

No matter which personality you are, remember to make your home a fun place where your children want to be and let them have their friends in whenever you can. In looking back at raising my children and in asking them, I can say that every extra child I entertained, every lonely teen I listened to, every party I hosted, was well worth the trouble, the time, and the clean up.

35. Make Home Fun

The difference between our home and the homes of my children's friends lies more in what *went on* in our home rather than what was *in* it. Ours was a place where everyone wanted to be. It was fun! I knew that my children were going to want to play with their friends after school or on weekends, and I always preferred to have them where I could see them. That way I knew that they were OK.

With all the horrible things taking place today, I think that every parent should aim to keep a close watch on his or her children, and the most effective way to do that is to make being at home fun, not punishment.

One of the most important places to start is with meal times. We always felt that meals were an important family time. Each day we had breakfast together. In our case it was real breakfast, a meal with some nutritional value, not just Lucky Charms and a Hostess doughnut. Somehow the smell of bacon or pancakes filled the house each day, and when Fred rang the bell to give us the one minute warning, we were all anxious to get to the table.

Breakfast was not the time to review what homework was— or was not—done, nor was it the time to disapprove of a chosen outfit. That morning meal was an important way to start the day together. We discussed what each family member had planned that day, what tests were coming up or what sporting events were taking place. Although breakfast was a brief meal, we were all together and it set the pace for the day.

We learned that this meal together was a wonderful opportunity to send our children off for the day on a positive note. They were not just nutritionally sound, but also emotionally strong. We learned that it was important to send each child out with a positive, encouraging comment. Those good words carry more weight than we think they might.

I remember what a difference this made in my relationship with Marita. When she was in junior high school, the fashions of her peers were as unacceptable to my generation as your teenagers' clothes may be to you. She went off to school each day in her father's extra large t-shirts that she had tie dyed. Her jeans barely hung on to her slender hips and they dragged several inches behind her in tattered shreds. This stunning outfit was often set off by a pair of black leather motorcycle boots. Since I'd grown up in the depression, longing for lovely clothes, I couldn't understand how she could choose to go off to school looking like a bum. She had "nice" clothes in her closet, but she chose these old rags.

Each morning I dramatically moaned about *my* daughter heading off to school looking so terrible. When Marita and I went somewhere together, there was always a battle over how she would dress. One day I had to go to her school. I noticed all the other students and how they were dressed. Against this setting Marita didn't look so bad. In fact she looked better than most!

When she came home from school that day, I apologized for my criticism of her clothes and I offered her a "deal." Although she could hardly believe that I would be able to stop criticizing her wardrobe, she readily agreed to my deal. I said that I would let her wear whatever she wanted when she went to school and was with her friends as long as she would wear what I wanted her to wear when she was with me. Her enthusiastic agreement made me aware of how she disliked my negative comments each morning, and I resolved to change.

Marita wore what she wanted to school and held up her end of the bargain by cheerfully wearing the "awful" things I wanted to see her in when she was with me. I held up my side by keeping my negative thoughts to myself, but more importantly I sent Marita off to school each day with positive thoughts and encouraging comments. The lack of negative comments and the presence of encouragement made such a difference in our relationship that we adopted this policy with each child, sending them off each day with positives.

Start each day together, start each day with encouragement. When Mom and Dad send the children off with good words, they are anxious to come home and get some more.

Dinner is another important family meal. Resolve right now to make this meal a time of togetherness. Sue Gregg told me that her husband Rick felt dinner was such an important family time he chose not to get involved in activities, church or otherwise, which required him to be away from home on weekday evenings. If you make family meals a priority, you can make it work.

Like breakfast, dinner is not the time for punishment. That should be done at another time through a family meeting or a private session. It is important that your children look forward to the dinner hour. One of the ways we did this was to involve them in the preparation. Setting the table was a treat, not a chore.

Marita remembers:

> We had many different tablecloth and napkin combinations, a variety of placemats and napkin rings, and several centerpieces for different holidays and moods. While I set the table, Lauren or Fred helped in the kitchen and vice versa. Other times we were allowed to plan the whole dinner and prepare it ourselves with Mom's help if needed. This was a great adventure for us. I'm sure most of the meals were not overly balanced, but the experience was great and as we matured, so did our menu planning and cooking expertise.

I have talked about starting each day in a fun and positive way. Equally important is the way we end each day.

Is bedtime a nightmare at your house? Do you dream of storybook children who go to bed when they are told? Proverbs 15:13 tells us that "A merry heart maketh a cheerful countenance." Many parents send their children off to bed with a fight or in anger and then expect them to wake with cheer.

Make your home a happy home. Start your day with "joy in the morning" and end it with a "merry heart"!

One of my friends, Marilyn Heavilin, and her husband, Glen, aimed to make their home the center of activity, a place where their children and their friends wanted to be. While their house was always neat and clean, it was never so perfect that children were uncomfortable and afraid to touch anything. Their children were more important to them than the paint on their cars, and they gave up the garage on their home and converted it into a game room. They put indoor-outdoor carpet on the floor, filled the shelves with games and brought in a ping pong table and a dart board. Marilyn baked cookies and invited the children in. Before long the Heavilins' home was the place to be.

As the children became teenagers, the interest centers in the garage changed, too. An old upright piano was added along with some computer games. The Heavilins invited some of those teenagers to join them on camping trips and weekends at the beach.

Glen and Marilyn knew where their children were, whom they were with, and what they were doing. Their children stayed out of trouble, they each married Christians and are active in their churches today, and Glen and Marilyn made a lasting impression on their children's friends. Many of them became Christians because of the witness of the Heavilin family. One boy commented, "Mealtime is always an event at your house. I'm so glad when you invite me to join you."

When our children were young, we lived in Connecticut. Our house had a large basement that was frequently filled with giggling girls. We also had a ping pong table and games. Marita remembers one of her favorite parts of that basement:

> As I look back on the fun we had as kids, I remember that basement in Connecticut. It was never really finished like the basement of some of my friends' houses, but I think that made it more fun.
>
> The gray cement walls and floor seemed like something we couldn't hurt. Painting pictures could be done without putting

down newspaper and roughhousing was acceptable. I remember there was an old bed down there and many extra mattresses and cushions. We used to play princess and the pea. One of us was the pea and we would lie on the bottom mattress while our friends stacked the others on top of us. Then they would lie on the top mattress and see if they could tell we were under there. Whoever was on the bottom would wiggle until finally the whole pile crashed to the floor. We laughed hysterically as several of us lay in a heap on the floor covered with mattresses.

It was wonderful to have a place to play that was just for us, not too fancy but lots of fun.

Don't make your home so fancy that fun is forbidden.

As Dr. Kay Kuzma states in her book, *A Hug, a Kiss, and a Kick in the Pants,* "The bottom line is, children don't feel loved unless they receive adequate positive attention. But it is impossible to show attention without doing things together. Therefore, many kids today don't feel loved because their parents are too busy."[1]

Once a week schedule a FAMILY FUN NIGHT. Have a different child each week select what he would like for dinner and have that child help prepare it. Have one child set and decorate the table in a special way. Since children love to decorate, let them use special dishes, different glasses, toys, dolls, or plants for centerpieces, candles, a dish of candy—whatever will make it their night. After dinner, clean up quickly and have a family activity that the children will especially enjoy. Play games, watch family movies, pop corn, do a puzzle, go bowling, build a model, and read stories. Let them know that you care enough for them to set aside one night a week for a FAMILY FUN NIGHT.

36. Special Days

One of the special times I remember as a child was our yearly "History Day." Even though my father was from England, he felt strongly that we should understand American history. We children were allowed to suggest places we would like to go and then my father would plan an itinerary and surprise us on that day. Because we never had a car, our journey started with a bus ride to the depot and then a train trip to Boston. We took the subway or walked to each different spot. My father always studied up on each place before we went so that even if there were no guide, he could fill us in on the historical background. Bunker Hill Monument was just a picture of an obelisk until we all climbed the stairs to the top. Faneuil Hall didn't sound like a marketplace until we saw the sides of beef hanging on hooks in the open square. Paul Revere was just a name in a history book until we saw his birthplace and traced his ride to warn that the British were coming.

Recent surveys show that young Americans are woefully ignorant of American history even though it is taught in school. One major reason is that history out of a book has little meaning; but take a child to see the replica of the Mayflower and he will begin to picture what those months cramped in that little space must have been like. Wherever you live, there is some history nearby that costs little or nothing to visit.

As with any meaningful experience, this kind of special day takes time and effort on the part of the parent, but the benefits could stimulate your children into a new love of American history.

Since Fred and I travel constantly, we have started a collection of mugs from each state for our three grandchildren. We carefully select ones that have the name of the state and something significant, such as the state flower or bird. We had a carpenter come into our daughter's home and build shelves just wide enough for the mugs. They now fill a wall in the family room and when the children want a drink, they can choose whatever state they want. With each cup of milk they have a reminder of a faraway state and a mini-geography lesson.

Recently I bought a map of the United States at a college bookstore and had it mounted on cork board. Lauren hung it in the children's playroom and we have all had fun sticking marker pins into each city where I have spoken. As I return from each trip, we can put in another pin and talk about that state. I hope these ideas will stir up your imagination so that you can make learning an exciting experience for your children or grandchildren.

We usually celebrate family birthdays with some kind of a party or event, but one lady gave me a suggestion I'd not heard before. Grace wrote me:

> We have what our family has labeled "Mommy-un" or "Daddy-un" time. Each month on the child's birthdate that child gets special attention for a special amount of time. Sometimes it's a quick trip for "coffee." That includes errands, but other times it's one-half to one whole day out, fishing, browsing, library time, etc. Each child eagerly looks forward to "their" special time. We try to get in as much "un" time as we can throughout the month, but this we are held accountable for.

How exciting for a child to know that he will have one day each month, not each year, that is special just for him.

Jane, a single parent, wrote to share with me how she makes sure to spend that "special" time with her children each month.

> I made a list of goals and priorities this summer and my children were first on the list. I have tried to spend one special time with Jim each month, one special time with the girls together or separately (whichever seems to be the most needed), and one special family time together. This is something that must be set up in advance or my calendar fills up and they are left out. They are important to me and I think by doing these things and setting up special times, they know they are important.

Norm and Bobbi Evans told me they make dates with their children.

> We found that our best communicating times were when we could spend uninterrupted, one-on-one times with our children. We would make a date—one child with one parent—and let the child decide on the itinerary for the evening. Once our daughter decided that she and her mother should spend the evening at the local skating rink; another "date" involved our teen-age son and his dad spending the evening looking at fishing tackle at a local sports exhibition. We found it imperative that we did what the child suggested—even if we thought something else might be more "fun"!

My neighbor Lois had a special day for her children called "their day."

One of the most valuable traditions I instituted when the children were young was "their day." With four small youngsters, it was so easy to "group" them—so, I hired a sitter for three of them each Thursday. I took one with me (rotating whose turn it was, of course), and we did the weekly shopping—groceries, clothing, etc. I also took the "chosen" child to lunch at a place of his or her choice. They had a chance to select the package of cereal, cookies, or whatever was especially important to them that day. We had time to choose something in clothing for that child—peacefully—and also time to relax together and talk about things of concern to him or her while we drove and ate lunch. Obviously, this was summertime, but we took evenings or Saturdays during the school year.

Whatever ideas you create, make some plans that can be learning experiences and some that are just plain fun. The family that plays together stays together!

37. Music and Books

There is little hope of teaching children to read books instead of watching TV if the parents don't read. Children follow what we do, not what we say, and the only way to encourage reading is to read to them when they are little and make books exciting. If you are collapsed in front of the TV each night and sending them to their rooms to read, your children will see this assignment as punishment, but if you read to them or with them, the time becomes a positive experience.

In today's busy lifestyle, we tend to ignore trips to the library, but only by showing our little children the vast reservoir of available books can we get them excited over finishing one so they can take out another. As soon as my children were old enough to get their own library cards, I had them sign up and become responsible for their card and their own books. There were occasional lapses and losses, but in general they kept track of their books and paid for overdue fines from their allowances—unless I was the one who caused the delay, in which case I paid!

Recently I donated a complete set of all my books to our Redlands Library. I took my two grandsons, six and ten, with me. I asked to see the librarian and after a few minutes' wait, we were ushered into a large office in the dim recesses of the library. The children's eyes were wide with excitement as they got to see a secret part of the building that they didn't even know existed. Gratefully Dr. Larry Burgess was very gracious in talking with the boys and they were impressed that they got to go "back stage."

Later when Randy's teacher asked for some event he had enjoyed, Randy replied, "When Grammie took me to the library." Considering the competition was Disneyland and Magic Mountain, I was delighted to hear the library ranked high.

One lady told me that she had encouraged her thirteen-year-old to read more by paying him $10 for each book he read, wrote a report on, and discussed at dinner. She had to approve of his selection, check that he was actually reading it, and spend time with him on his report. Few parents today want to bother with this or any system that takes supervision on their part, but the alternative is young people who don't read and who get their sense of values from TV.

When our son Fred was in high school, he frequently brought home his friend Cliff, a pleasant Sanguine Phlegmatic with little drive to achieve in life. I tried to inspire him to study and remember one evening when I sat with him and Fred in the living room, discussing the need for personal goals. I told him how sad it was that many people wasted their lives by eternal evenings spent staring at TV and never conversing with one another. I thought I had been close to inspirational, but after Cliff left, Fred, my deep Melancholy, said, "I was so embarrassed with you tonight." I couldn't imagine what I could have done to upset him and when I asked, he answered, "You insulted Cliff's parents."

I countered, "I don't even know Cliff's parents."

He replied, "You said you don't like people who sit every night in front of TV and never talk to each other. Well, that's Cliff's parents!"

Once I recovered from his conclusion, I was able to discuss goals with him and he agreed that mindless watching of TV was a waste of brain power.

Many of us deplore the music our children listen to as teens and yet the time to educate their tastes is when they are young. If their minds are void of any music when they're little or if they listen to their own choices unsupervised, they will be open to the lures of hard rock and its filthy lyrics. As with any temptation, we the parents must divert their attention before the activity becomes a problem.

When he bought the family home my son-in-law Randy spent extra money to install speakers in each room. He has a central radio, cassette, and CD player and he keeps classical music wafting throughout the house. Instead of conflicting tunes from each room, the children listen to the master program or shut it off if they wish. At night they go to sleep with soft sonatas playing. I can't guarantee the results, but I feel they are more apt to appreciate quality music in their later years than the person who has never heard it.

Theresa wrote me about her son Donnie:

> When he was just a baby, I would place him on my lap at the piano and sing to him and have him "match" his voice with the key that I would play. Soon he was singing and carrying a tune.
>
> At 3 ½ years old, he made a record of twenty-one children's songs. (He sang them "nonstop.")
>
> From that time he sang in churches and became interested in radio. He was a "D.J." at the age of thirteen—the youngest one in Michigan.
>
> He is now, at age 27, managing a Christian radio station and is ministering in churches singing and preaching the Gospel.

What we teach them as children does influence the direction of their adult lives. If they have good books and music available, there is a better chance that their future selection of materials to digest will be more stimulating.

Oswald Chambers wrote: "The things we listen to and read ought to be beyond our comprehension, they go into our minds like seed thoughts, and slowly and surely bring forth fruit. This is good counsel for boys and girls in their teens."[2]

38. Memory Boxes

For many years I have listened to my friend Emilie Barnes, author of *More Hours in My Day*, tell how to organize our homes into a series of numbered boxes, measuring $12\frac{1}{2}'' \times 10\frac{1}{2}'' \times 16''$, which we have dubbed "Emilie Boxes." Our daughter Lauren has put all her children's toys in these uniform boxes lined up neatly on closet shelves. Each box has a picture or label of the enclosed toys on the end of the box so that the children know the contents. They understand that you don't take out a new box until the old one is put away with the toys in it. This system teaches them order and keeps the numerous pieces of Lego and Lincoln Logs from integrating. Because these boxes have side holes for easy handling and attached covers, the children can lift them in and out and not lose the covers.

If you need to get your children's area organized so they don't have mixed-up heaps of toys by the end of each day, you could get similar boxes at places like K-Mart. If you don't have available shelf space, you could buy the decorator boxes with different prints and stack them one on top of the other in a corner of your child's room.

Melancholy and Choleric children will love the organization. Sanguines and Phlegmatics will need some help in learning to pick up after themselves. But your taking the time to set up a system of order will pay off in a neater room and in self-discipline for the children.

Judith Brady, a pastor's wife in Florida, told me that she has set up Memory Boxes for her two children. These are Emilie Boxes with file folders in them. Each child has a box set up with folders labeled "First Grade," "Second Grade," and on up. In each year's folder go their report cards for that year, school pictures, letters, birthday and other holiday cards, special reports, art work, and any other memorabilia they might want to save. This simple system teaches the children how to evaluate what to save, and it gives them an automatic place to put these things instead of shoving them in a drawer or throwing them on the closet floor. Now that Aaron is thirteen and Angela ten, they enjoy looking through their files and seeing how they wrote and drew when they were younger. Don't you wish your mother had set this up for you!

Any time you spend in helping your children to think and act logically will pay big dividends as they grow up. One system I developed to teach my children not to litter their things around the house involved a large plastic clothesbasket and about five minutes of my time each day. Once they left for school, I made a quick tour of the house and picked up any clothes or toys they had left anywhere but in their rooms. I put everything I found in the basket and sold the items back to them (for 10 cents apiece) on Saturday morning when they got their allowance. Since this money came right off the top, they saw what it cost them to litter. After a few weeks of this Basket Game, they had learned so well that we dropped the program and never had to start it again.

39. Shopping List

In keeping our home a happy place, I tried to make even routine chores enjoyable, and I always tried to make the management of the household a family affair. Not only did the children learn financial responsibility and housekeeping, but they were part of the food planning and marketing.

Fred came up with the idea of a grocery list of all the items we needed on hand at all times. He had it typed up and run off on a copier and we posted it on the refrigerator door. What made the chart fun was that we all were to check off items we noticed were running low. If young Fred used up the peanut butter, he put a check beside that on the marketing list. If Marita and her friends ate a package of cookies, she checked cookies. If she wanted a certain kind next time she could write that in. If Lauren was hosting the teen Bible study, she would note on the bottom of the chart, "Drinks and chips for 20." Any time I thought of anything we needed I'd check it off or write it in if it wasn't a regular item. Instead of forgetting what it was I had dimly in my mind, I would have it listed before me.

This method was truly one of the ingenious ideas of our lifetime because it divided responsibility for our inventory among us all and eliminated both complaints about missing items and impulse buying. If each person didn't do his part the system wouldn't work, and so they enforced each other to make sure favorite foods never ran out. They also knew if they needed notebook paper they were not to tell me about it but write it on the list.

One day Lauren got an additional idea. Why not make the grocery list in columns matching the aisles in the local supermarket? She and I took our basic list and then went to the store. We started on the far left and wrote down what we used from each aisle. Meat and dairy products were along the back and fresh produce was down the right. We had so much fun together mapping out our list to match the store. Lauren typed it up in columns, drew lines to fit the aisles, and had 200 run off at the instant printers. It was amazing how the children loved checking off items on this new chart that was a blueprint of the store—and how much faster I could do the marketing without ever having to retrace my steps!

As I would stand at the check-out counter with my organized chart in my hand, people would frequently ask where I had purchased such a list. I'd explain what we'd done and they would be so impressed that I'd end up giving them my marked up page to go home and duplicate.

Even though I'm not basically a chart-happy person like Fred, this aisle-by-aisle shopping list was a blessing to all of us and made marketing a quick and enjoyable experience.

Keeping the shelves stocked and the milk from running out became a positive group responsibility, a training ground for future organizations, and one way to make dull routines into family fun.

40. Learning to Think

One evening I asked our son, "What did we do right as parents that you can remember?" I expected him to give me some of the trips we'd taken, but instead he replied, "You made us think. You showed us how to make choices. Many of my friends haven't amounted to much in life. It isn't that they didn't want to do better. They just don't know how."

This strong statement was quite a speech for our silent Melancholy son and I would never have guessed that learning to think was something he'd thought about. Once he'd answered me so clearly he left the room. That was all he had to say. I mulled it over and recalled the times we'd discussed case histories of un-named people at dinner and had the children each give their advice in turn. They had to think about each side and come up with possible solutions.

I recalled the year the Catholic church chose two popes and we all did a study on the biographies of the candidates and re-ported on them at dinner with our personal selection and our reasons for choosing him. That exercise had made them think.

I remembered how I would read the newspaper each morn-ing before the children went off to school and give them some timely story to insert somewhere in their day's conversation. Of-ten they would report at dinner that the particular news event fit in with one of their school subjects, and they were the only one in class who knew it. This use of today's news made them think.

When I was president of the Women's Club, I would discuss the day's procedures and in doing this I was able to teach the children how to conduct a meeting without it becoming a lecture. It was during this "presidential period" of mine that we got into flower arranging. The county fair had a juvenile section and our club was encouraging children to enter their creative floral ar-rangements. As president, I felt obligated to have my own chil-dren participate and this adventure led us into a study of theme, color, and balance. One of my friends who has a real flair for flowers took ten-year-old Fred under her wing, found he had an eye for arranging, and encouraged him into winning many blue ribbons. This endeavor caused him to think in a whole new way and stretched his creativity.

My husband discussed his business at the table in such a way that the children were included and their opinions valued. When a manager needed to be disciplined, we would all give possible alternatives. Understanding the different personalities helped us to make logical choices and today young Fred runs the business so that his father is freed up to travel with me.

It has paid off to teach the children to think.

Part XI

TRAGEDY

XI

Tragedy

We would all rather have our personal production be a comedy, but for some of us it turns into a tragedy. Even though we've been good people doing good works, we are sometimes the victim of something beyond our control. It can be birth defects and brain damage, as with my boys, or it can be a child who gets on drugs or is abused.

Not one of us is immune.

41. Retardation

Each time I give my testimony and tell about my two brain-damaged sons, I have several women who come up to share their family tragedies. Not one of us expected to give birth to a defective baby and few of us have any idea how we would react if it happened to us. In my experience, I have found that our first reaction is similar to the one experienced at the death of a loved one: "This can't be true." We wake up in the morning and hope this is a bad dream. For the eighteen years that my second son lived in a private hospital, I never woke up without the shocking realization—it's not a dream, you have a dying son.

With the persistent denial of the grim facts comes a necessity to place blame: *There couldn't be a God or this would never have happened to a good person like me. Whose fault is this?*

As soon as my first son was diagnosed with a yet unnamed

regressive brain disorder, my mother-in-law did a quick family research project and proclaimed that no one on the Littauer side had ever had any "brain problems." This dumped the guilt on my side, especially when it was discovered that my mother had given birth to a baby boy who had died of "unknown causes" and she refused to discuss it. For some reason, the birth of a retarded child calls out the defenses on both sides and neither can rest until the blame is placed on the other family. No one seems to realize what this tug-of-war does to the birth mother who is already in shock and how clearly it tells her this abnormal child is a blot on our family. When she is desperate for loving support, she often gets what she takes to be condemnation for having produced such a problem.

With death comes denial, shock, and anger but with the birth of a defective baby comes, in addition, the double load of blame and shame. When the family learned of my first son's problems, they strongly suggested that I not tell anyone about this tragedy and that I not take the child out of the house where he could be seen. Before I had the time or the support to come to any healthy resolution to this traumatic situation, I gave birth to my second son. And while I was in the hospital, my husband (without my knowledge) took his namesake to a private children's hospital. There was a certain sense of relief when I came home and found the "problem" gone, but the relief was short-lived. While the families were grateful, well-meaning friends were shocked. "How could you put your child away like that?" "I can't believe you didn't even get to say good-bye." "If you were a decent (normal, good, Christian) mother, you'd have your child at home where he belongs."

All those comments were made by people who had never volunteered to spend an afternoon caring for my boy who was totally blind, deaf, and without any mental faculties or recognition of his father or mother. I was so hurt that I stopped going to church and didn't let people know I'd even had a new baby for fear I'd have more judgment heaped upon me if he had some similar problems. And indeed he did. When he was six months old, one week after my first son died, I found out that my little

Larry had the same defect. I had hardly come to grips with the guilt of the death when I was plunged into despair over the new diagnosis. I was in a double dose of shock, denial, anger, guilt, grief, and blame all at the same time.

My reason for recounting my sad tale is not to depress you, but to show that bad things do happen to good people—and that few of us know how to handle them. Almost every mother of a retarded child has been the victim of unthinking friends who felt led to drop guilt upon her in the guise of concern. In my daughter Lauren's book, *What You Can Say When You Don't Know What to Say*, she gives examples of unkind things said to others in time of tragedy, and of the hurtful words said to her at the time of a miscarriage. More important is her positive guide to what you should say when a friend is in a grief situation. Her definition of a loss is anything that falls short of your realistic expectations. Anything short of a healthy baby is a loss and is followed by the natural stages of grief. If you don't know what to say at difficult times, read Lauren's book.

What if you are the parent? I can truly empathize with you. You are in a grief situation and you need to allow yourself to work through the normal phases without self-condemnation. If you try to deny your situation, repress your feelings, or pretend you are blessed with these problems and God did you a favor, your emotions will no doubt emerge unexpectedly at a later date. Grieving does not mean that you are rejecting your child. I tried to hide my feelings and Fred and I never cried together over our mutual losses. We regret today that we stuffed our feelings away and suffered singly and in silence.

Do not let anyone put guilt upon you. When they try, be prepared to ask nicely, "Have you ever been in this situation?" The answer is almost always no, in which case they will usually drop their pursuit and often apologize. If they have been through a similar ordeal then listen as they may have a helpful thought buried in their message.

A beautiful young mother came to CLASS and told me of her extremely retarded child and the guilt people had heaped upon her. I told her not to listen to tales of condemnation and to ask if they had been in her circumstance. When I saw her six months later at another CLASS, she stood up in her small group and said, "Florence gave me the best advice I'd ever received—to not let those well-meaning people make me feel guilty."

Her child is still not well, but this young mother is not bent over with blame and shame.

The other major question that always arises in retardation situations is, "How shall we care for the child?" The first consideration is whether the child is trainable, whether he can improve with loving family attention. In the case of Downs Syndrome, the little one is often very lovable and can be integrated into the family system without major emotional injury. In my circumstances each baby, from six months on, was without any mental faculties and was screaming with convulsions night and day. The test is whether the family can function somewhat normally or whether the presence of the child brings emotional chaos on the rest of the family. My feeling is that if the normal children are made living sacrifices to the needs of the ailing one, that some alternative plan should at least be considered. I have all too often seen the other children depressed over the gloomy atmosphere, ashamed to bring their friends home, or neglected by a mother whose total focus is on the problem child. In any of these cases, we must realize that we don't want to damage the normal family members in caring for the exceptional child.

Another problem arises in the marriage relationship. The statistics of divorce after the birth of a retarded child are above the average. The mother feels guilt and blame in producing the abnormal child, and she may dedicate her life to caring for this little one who so desperately needs her. The husband often feels his manhood is threatened by this damaged child, and when the wife hovers over the baby, he feels she cares more for the little one than she does for him. This combination of hurt and rejection, when not understood, can lead to marriage problems and often the father feels that if he could leave the scene he could be happy once again.

My friend and co-worker, Marilyn Heavilin, has lost three sons, two as infants and one the victim of a drunk driver. In her beautiful book, *Roses in December*, she tells how the different personalities grieve and how easy it is for the death, or retardation, of a child to cause a split in the family. By understanding these differences and not judging the person who grieves in another way as wrong, we can be loving and accepting and have our grief unite us and not divide us.

What if you decide the child has to be placed outside the home? **First**, don't let other people lay guilt on you. If you have prayerfully come to the conclusion that the presence of the child is destroying the family fabric, don't listen to critical opinions. I have known situations where the placement was arranged only to have a grandmother threaten to disinherit the family if her grandchild was put into an institution. I've never known anyone to casually make such a serious decision as removing the child from the home.

Recently I received a letter from a woman who was the steady babysitter for a brain-damaged child. She wrote me because she had read my books and knew of my difficulties. She told me of the family she worked for who had two normal children and then a severely malformed baby. The mother had dedicated her life to this infant until she was exhausted. Her husband's parents told her God chose special people to have "hopeless cases" and that she should be grateful God selected her for this honor. She tried hard to feel honored and felt guilty when she begged her husband for some kind of help.

As the baby grew worse, she looked for a suitable place for his care and rejoiced when she found a convenient home with dedicated caretakers. When she had the arrangements made, her in-laws, in the guise of loving Christian counsel, told her she could do no such thing. She turned to her husband for support and he took his parents' side, even though he had previously agreed to the placement. Faced with total opposition, she went into a deep depression. Within a few weeks she packed up the other two children and left the baby with a sitter, the woman who wrote to me.

At this point, the mother has been painted as a neglectful, heartless, self-centered person by the in-laws and the church, and the father is now trying to find a home for the dying baby. The in-laws who intervened want no part of the child's care and the private home no longer has any room.

Why is it that people who are not responsible for the special child's care seem led to pass judgment on the ones who are bearing the burden? Why do I still today, after giving my testimony, have well-meaning people come up to me with suggestions of tests, exercises, or treatments that I should have had done on my babies over twenty years ago?

I cannot bear this heavy burden and I don't have to. I've prayerfully given it to Jesus who died to relieve my guilt and shame that I might live abundantly. If you have a heavy burden, seek the Lord's will, do what He directs, and don't let people make you feel guilty if you decide to find alternative care.

Second, when it is time to take the child to the home, do not whisk him away as we did. We thought we were doing our two daughters a favor by not having any tearful farewells, but in retrospect they always felt cheated that they were not allowed to say good-bye to their brothers. Explain that sister or brother needs hospital care and that they can later go and visit. Have a memorable dinner or dessert in honor of the child and keep it as positive as possible. Children are usually resilient if we tell them the truth.

Because Fred and I kept the departures secret, they made a negative impression on Lauren especially. We didn't tell her where the boys were and she would sit tearfully at the piano and play and sing "Goodnight, my someone, wherever you are."

I wish there had been someone to give us wise counsel, but no one even talked about such things at the time. I wish there had been books and articles dealing with problems and solutions as there are today, but there weren't. That's why I share with others that from my mistakes you might receive help and hope in times of trouble.

"There hath not temptation (problem, tragedy) taken you but such as is common to man: But God is faithful, who will not suffer you to be tempted above that ye are able; but will with the temptation also make a way of escape, that ye may be able to bear it" (1 Corinthians 10:13).

42. Substance Abuse

It would be nice if, at the time you signed your marriage certificate, you could also fill out a questionnaire that would effect the right choices you'd make throughout your married life. You would choose things like:

_____ Happily Married
_____ Healthy Children
_____ Nice Home
_____ Rewarding Jobs

You would certainly select a comedy, not a tragedy.

But that is not the way it works, and not every home is like the Cosbys'. Even in "nice homes" where the parents are "happily married," where the children are healthy, tragedy can strike. The purpose of this chapter is not to scare you but to make you aware that, yes, even in good homes with good parents and good kids, we need to watch out.

As I have already written, our family has been touched with tragedy through the death of my two sons. We have had to live with the hurt and the heartache. We learned to come to grips with the realization that our dreams for those boys would never come to completion. We would have selected a comedy but we got a tragedy.

Although our lives had more drama than we would have chosen, we were still blessed with many happy scenes. Our home was untouched by many of the tragedies that are so prevalent today: drugs, alcohol, and sexual abuse. It would be natural to think that these extreme episodes didn't happen in nice Christian homes. I'd like to believe that this chapter didn't have to be included in a Christian book, but history, research, and my own personal experience have shown that it is an essential.

I have known many good Christian families whose children struggled with drugs, homes that have been torn apart with a drug-overdose suicide, while other well-meaning parents looked the other way thinking this would never happen to their children.

Parents want so much for their children to turn out well and do the right things that they will frequently not notice when trouble is right before them.

Kathy, a girl whose parents are well-known in their Christian community, told me how busy her parents always were in doing good works for the church. She felt rejected and even though they would take her out for dinner, they would always have someone else with them and ignore her. When she went away to college, she became very depressed. She felt unloved and sensed her parents were glad to have her out of town and off their hands. By complaining to the college doctor about her depression, she got a Valium prescription and one night she took the whole bottle of pills. Her roommate found her and got her to the infirmary. Two days later the doctor called her parents and they told him to send her home. After driving exhausted for hours, she got home expecting to be reprimanded, but when she arrived her parents greeted her as if nothing had happened. They whisked her out to dinner where they had ten of their friends waiting. They all had a party, basically ignoring her, and never brought the subject up again. Even in attempted suicide, Kathy couldn't get her parents' attention. It was easier for her parents to deny problems and look the other way than it was to sit down and talk about the cause of Kathy's depression.

None of us wants to face the possibility that our children aren't happy, but when the signs are there, we must find out the reason before it's too late. Kathy was begging for face-to-face time with her parents who chose to ignore her needs in the hope they would go away. When I met Kathy she had just returned from three months of psychiatric care where they were trying to figure out why she had no feeling of worth and was constantly depressed. It doesn't take a psychiatrist to see the roots of Kathy's problems.

One of my CLASS staff members, Becky Tirabassi, grew up in a religious home and yet by the age of twenty-one she had to face the fact that she was an alcoholic.

Becky's behavior was following the pattern she'd seen in her own home. She came from a background of alcohol. A recent *People* Magazine cover story states that "Children of alcoholics are also 3½ times more likely than others to become alcoholics themselves."[1] These behaviors are passed on and on. I recently met a lady who is working on a book on multiple-generational alcoholics. She told me that it touched her grandfather, her mother, her, her children, and her children's children. While she was not an alcoholic herself, she suffered from the dysfunction and carried it almost like a recessive gene. Through her, alcoholism has carried into the next generation.

This lady can probably relate, as perhaps you can, with Suzanne Sommers when she shared, in that same *People* issue, about her alcoholic father and the sickness that consumed the entire family. Suzanne said, "In their teens my brother and my sister started drinking and eventually became alcoholics too. It's a mystery why I didn't start. But I was just as sick."

Maybe like Suzanne you were the lucky one, the one who didn't fall prey to alcoholism, and maybe like comedian Louie Anderson said of his relationship with an alcoholic father, "Drugs and alcohol weren't my choices for escape. Mine was food. If I was under stress I'd get a couple of Big Macs, while an alcoholic might pick up a couple of beers." Near the time of his father's death, Louie discovered in a rare intimate conversation with his father that his dad's father and mother were both alcoholics. You may not realize that being brought up in an alcoholic home has affected you. You may have responded like Susan Sullivan, Maggie on "Falcon Crest." Her brother became an alcoholic and a drug addict, while she "learned to survive by being in control."

Did you grow up in a home where drugs or alcohol was a fact of life? A home like Suzanne Sommers', "A pretty house with green shutters, a friendly green door and a white picket fence." A home that outsiders would have been shocked to know what went on inside? Are you the struggling survivor? The eater or the controller?

Before you pass the danger on to your children, look at your past, and look at your present. Was your mother or father an alcoholic? Are the lives of your brothers and sisters a mess? Have you dealt with the root of your difficulties? Give your children the best mom and dad they can have. Don't think that just because you are not an alcoholic or a drug addict that you don't carry the scars and that you won't pass on dysfunctional behavior to your children. Get some help today.

A 1986 article in *Christianity Today* quotes a director of a drug-abuse resource group. Dr. Thomas Gleaton says, "Youngsters with loving, caring parents, who live in nice homes in wonderful neighborhoods, are almost as likely to become involved in drug abuse as those from deprived backgrounds."[2]

We as parents need to be careful. We need to do everything we can and we need to be aware of potential problems. In this section I will cover some signs to watch for and suggestions for prevention. If after reviewing this material you feel a cause for alarm, please research further. I have included a research and reference list at the end of this chapter to assist you in your study. Raising children today is not an easy task and raising Christians is even more of a responsibility.

Drug Abuse

I remember twenty years ago, Fred was teaching Junior Church. There were two boys in the class who were the children of one of the leading families in the church. Their father was a deacon and their mother a Sunday school teacher. One Sunday after Junior Church one of the boys came to Fred and shared with him some of the horror stories of what went on between him and his brother when their parents weren't home. In those days of naiveté, Fred went to the father and shared what he'd heard. This well-meaning Christian man accused the boys of lying and insisted that such things were not going on in his home. The issue was dropped there.

Time wore on. We moved away and forgot about the stories of the older brother chasing the younger through the house with a butcher knife. We forgot about the deacon who wouldn't look at the danger signs in his own home. We forgot until one day we saw a piece in the paper that said that John had died. This boy whom Fred taught, with whom our girls had played, this boy who had reached out for help to an adult who didn't know better, had killed himself with a drug overdose.

We need to be aware. As parents we need to know what to

watch for and, more importantly, we need to know what we can do to set the stage for solid, healthy children.

First, we need to be aware that our Christian homes are not immune to these social tragedies. While parents are looking the other way, children are experimenting. An interesting study reported in *USA Today* showed that out of 600 high school seniors, 67 percent said they had used alcohol in the last 30 days. Their parents, when questioned, felt that only 35 percent had used alcohol in that same time frame. The same study showed that 28 percent of the students had used marijuana in the last 30 days while only 3 percent of the parents thought their children were involved.[3] Numerous other studies bring forth frighteningly high figures such as 64 percent of twelve-year-olds in affluent Orange County, California, have drunk beer in the last three months.[4]

Drug and alcohol use is all around us, and sooner or later our children will have to make a choice. We can help them say "no" by openly discussing the problem with them.

Our school systems and our government have engaged in major campaigns to teach our country's young to say "no." But research indicates that these campaigns don't sway the decisions of too many. Jeanne Gibbs, a San Francisco-based school consultant on drug education, says, "There is no one single program that on its own can be proven to prevent drug abuse." While it would be easier to lay the fault for this tragedy on the schools, the responsibility falls back on us, the parents. Education Secretary, William J. Bennett, "suggests that the best prevention efforts are comprehensive ones that involve parents, peer counselors, and community leaders as well as schools."

Not only have the school programs proven to be largely ineffective on their own, but a UCLA study has shown that "in fact, kids who turn down drugs base their choice on their self-image, not on school drug programs."[5] As parents we need to build a strong self-image and high moral values into our children. As this same study shows, "To be effective, programs have to delve into this deeper area of values and identity." We need to have our own "program" in our homes. We need to "delve into the area of values and identity." Don't just put this off onto the schools as their responsibility.

My daughter, Marita, is proud that at twenty-nine years old she has never tried marijuana, cocaine, or any other drugs. She says, "It's not that I haven't touched them; I have. I've been in places where a joint was being passed around. I took it from the person next to me, said 'no thanks' and passed it on. I've been there when the cocaine was being cut and carefully lined up. Again, I've passed on my turn. When my husband and I lived in Los Angeles, our next door neighbors were dealers. Nice guys with nice cars and even nicer cars stopping by on a regular basis. I remember when Chuck told me they were dealers, I didn't believe him. But one day I came out our front door and there was one of the brothers with another man admiring the visitor's brand new Porsche. As I was introduced to him, I also admired his new car and I noticed a fine white dust along the edge of one nostril. Chuck was right. These nice guys next door made coke very accessible to us, but again I said 'no.'

"As I look back on my opportunities for drug use and reflect on why I never got involved, I can see that my simplest answer is I didn't need it. I wasn't trying to escape from anything and I had too many plans for my future to take a chance on ruining my mind and my life. I had been brought up believing that I was valuable and had something of worth to contribute to the world. I knew my family loved me and that they were there if I needed them. This strong foundation gave me the ability to say 'If these people only like me because I do drugs with them, then I don't need them.' Because I didn't do drugs I wasn't invited to their parties very often, and before long they weren't my friends and my social sphere had changed."

As parents, providing this strong foundation is the major role we can play in our own drug prevention program. We need to help our children feel secure about our family and themselves. We need to help them have a future.

Jesse Jackson, who has emphasized anti-drug crusades in his presidential campaign, relates an experience he had. He was in jail for protesting South Africa's policies. While spending the night in jail, he talked with the twenty-five young men in his holding cell. They were all there on drug-related charges. He said that one of the most depressing things was that "None of them had a father at home and only one had a dream."[6]

A pamphlet titled "The Drug Crisis, A Word to Mom and Dad," offers these helpful suggestions:

1. Provide teens with as much love, understanding, and approval as possible.
2. Maintain good communications between you and your child.
3. Create an awareness of the parental family influence in developing values and standards.
4. Set a good example for your child.
5. If necessary, seek professional help early.[7]

While we don't want to think this could happen to our child, it is possible and we need to do all we can to prevent these heartbreaking situations. These simple suggestions focus on the key things we as parents can provide as preventative measures.

Another simple suggestion comes from Dr. Michael DeWitt of Children's Hospital in Washington, DC. He says, "Not enough parents are willing to say to kids, 'You're not allowed to take drugs.'"[8]

We can't look the other way. We must take a stand.

Dr. DeWitt's comment reminds me of a discussion between Dr. Art Ulene and Bryant Gumble on the "Today" show. They were talking about safe sex and the use of condoms. Dr. Ulene said, "Why isn't anyone talking about abstinence?" He shared that he is telling his children to wait. Bryant scoffed and said, "Certainly you can't expect them not to have sex." Dr. Ulene replied, "I can't expect them not to if they've never been told not to. At least if I tell them no, then I know I have tried."

Even when we are aware of the dangers of drugs and we have provided a firm foundation for our children, there is no guarantee that they won't stray. Research shows that children from families with strong emotional bonds and respect for one another are less likely to get involved in drugs and alcohol, but it does happen.

One friend, who is a Christian speaker, wrote me about her sons. Both of them have now been arrested for dealing in drugs. Her oldest son got the younger one started on marijuana in second grade. She says, "I learned later that Scott smoked a joint every noon through sixth grade . . . I have suspected not only drug use, but dealing, lately."

In a later letter she shared, "We came home Saturday to a mess. Locked in my den was a satchel of drugs. Scott called later from the county jail . . . We have not bailed him out, nor have we hired an attorney. He is eighteen and will have to be responsible for the mess he has made for himself." Gratefully, this boy is now doing well having recommitted his life to Christ and admitted himself to Teen Challenge.

Another friend's son has stolen everything he can from his parents and from any job he's had. "He has been in detox programs and jail more times than I can count. Still, the grip the drugs have on him controls his life."

These are only two of the thousand of similar stories taking place in fine homes all over the country. If you know what to watch for, you can stop this cancer from spreading and destroying your child and your family.

The drugs crisis pamphlet I mentioned earlier offers these key things to watch for:

- School work drop off
- Carelessness about personal appearance
- Withdrawal from the family circle
- Paranoia (very suspicious attitude)
- Forsaking old friends—association of new ones
- Exhibiting a nasty attitude in the home.

Watch for these symptoms. If your child begins to display several of these characteristics get help immediately before it's too late. In addition to these traits we can also educate ourselves as to the language of the drug-user and the equipment that goes with it. The words and items are so foreign to most of us that we could hear our teen carry on a drug-related conversation and not know enough to be suspicious. If you heard your kids talking about "flea powder," would you know that they may not be making reference to the family dog but rather to heroin? Or if you heard mention of a "business man's special" would you know that what they had for lunch may not be a sandwich but diethyltryplamine, a drug that causes LSD-like hallucinations?[9]

In an effort to fight drugs, many public and private agencies have made material available to help you be more informed as a parent.

I have listed some of them at the end of this chapter. Many of them provide free brochures and helpful booklets. Take advantage of their research and learn all you can today.

It's far better to be safe than sorry.

Although I have not seen a study relating drugs to different personalities, I have been alert to what grieving mothers and recovering teens have told me; also I talked with a high school counselor in Dallas who had applied our four personality types to what she had observed. Even though we have no conclusive evidence, I felt the generalities would be worth mentioning.

The counselor explained that in years past, marijuana was the only drug a young person could afford. Twenty years ago "important people" were saying that marijuana was harmless and we should legalize it. Testing and research since then have shown brain damage in many cases, and experts are now stating that marijuana is far from harmless.

One of the consistent underlying results of drugs starting with marijuana is that they remove our natural God-given guilt system and we no longer feel responsible for our actions.

We are always dumbfounded when some good boy, who was brought up in the church, beats up a helpless old man, rapes a girl, or blatantly defies any sense of morality. What we as Christians don't realize is that the boy has probably taken some drugs which may have obliterated his inborn sense of responsibility. This allows him to freely do something with a clear conscience that he would not have dreamed of doing before. Marijuana gives the person a boldness and daring attitude that he would not have had without it.

My counselor friend told me that the Peaceful Phlegmatic in high school who has a poor self-image and is perhaps considered a

TEEN DEPRESSION AND SUICIDE

NEEDS Love: Acceptance, Approval, Attention
Security: Support and Stability

Every 90 minutes a teen kills himself.

CAUSES
Early Rejection
Family tension
Frequent moves
Sibling rivalry
Lack of support systems
High standards
Rigid rules
Lack of love
Learning disabilities
Poor communication
Poor eating habits
Lack of goals

Low self-image
Desire for revenge
Rejection by friends
Rock music/TV violence
Dungeons & Dragons
Alcohol and drugs
Homosexuality
Pregnancy
Fear of nuclear war
Availability of weapons/drugs
Lack of faith in God
No concept of eternal life

Teen suicide up 300% in last 20 years.

SYMPTOMS
Behavior changes
Lowering of grades
Different friends
Depression and hopelessness
Change in eating habits
Dazed look

Extreme fatigue
Withdrawal
Talk of suicide
Written signals
Giving away possessions
Attempted suicide

PREVENTION
Recognize the problem
Restore the family
Revitalize the community
Revive God

50% of teen suicides are drug related.

An estimated 20,000 teens committed suicide in 1984.

wimp by the tough guys will reach for marijuana to increase his masculinity. The pushers recognize the insecure teens and let them know what drugs will do for their self-esteem.

Cocaine is now available in any city and many towns in this country. The few shipments intercepted by our Drug Enforcement Agency are but a drop in the bucket compared to what flows in daily from Colombia, a poor country that we have gifted with foreign aid. Raw cocaine has to be prepared to be used, but Crack is cocaine already cooked and gives an intense jolt of excitement although shorter in duration than cocaine. Because it makes the individual feel like a star and gives an illusion of power, teens are attracted to it—but especially those who are Popular and Powerful. My friend told me that in her experience Crack provides these two personalities with what they are desperate for in life—popularity and power. Experts say cocaine products are not habit-forming, but each counselor I've talked to tells me they are psychologically addictive. When people stop taking them they become insecure and powerless.

Speed or amphetamines appeal to the Powerfuls because they help you move faster, stay awake longer, and feel in control.

The Perfect Melancholies tend to reach for downers, sedatives that help them to withdraw emotionally even in crowds and give them a feeling of peaceful solitude.

In seeing the reasons why our teens reach for drugs, basically to make them feel better about themselves, shouldn't this spur us all into finding positive ways to elevate the self-image of the shaky teen? Understanding their personalities is only a beginning but it does provide a tool for analysis and open a door to personal discussions where we might uncover some deep-seated hurts and resentments we weren't aware of before it's too late.

For information on teen depression and suicide, read my chapters on this subject in *Blow Away the Black Clouds* and *Hope for Hurting Women*. The chart on page 274 is a summary for your convenience.

For more information on subjects addressed in this book, contact:

National Child Abuse Hotline
(800)4-A-Child

Office of Alcohol and Drug Programs
565 N. Mt. Vernon Avenue
San Bernardino, CA 92411
(714)383-1525

Do It Now Foundation
2050 East University Drive
Phoenix, AZ 85034
(602)257-0797

Pamphlets available from the Do It Now Foundation:

Sniffing: A Parent's Perspective
Comprehensive Drug Knowledge Test
T's and Blues: Double Trouble
LSD and the Market Place
Dusted: Facts about PCP
All about Speed
All about Sniffing: Good Smells and Bad Smells
Gunk: All about Drugs and Pollution
All about Marijuana
Pot: A Guide for Young People
Cocaine Papers: From Freud to Freebase
MDA/MDM: The Chemical Pursuit of Ecstasy
The Second Generation Lookalikes
Amyl/Butyl Nitrite and Nitrous Oxide
Coke-Alikes: A Close-Up Look at Lookalike Cocaine
Garbage: A Report on Street Ripoffs
The History and Use of Peyote and Mescaline
Junk: A Look at Heroin Treatment and Alternatives
Acid: LSD Today

Ludes: *New Facts About Methaqualone*
Mequin *AKA Quaalude*
Fresh Garbage: *A Guide to Street Drug Bummers, Blunders, and Burns*
Loads/Four Doors: *New Wave Narcotics*
Downers: *The Distressing Facts About Depressant Drugs*
All About Downer Drugs
Barbiturates: *The Oblivion Express*
Drugs: *Information for Crisis Treatment*

The Benjamin Rush Center
672 South Salina Street
Syracuse, NY 13202
(315)476-2161

Pamphlets available from the Benjamin Rush Center:

Hallucinogens and PCP
Inhalants
Sedative-Hypnotics
Marijuana
Stimulants and Cocaine
Opiates

The American Council for Drug Education
5820 Hubbard Drive, Dept. A
Rockville, MD 20852

Koala Centers (Specializing in the treatment of alcohol and drug abuse)
Fidelity Bank Plaza
Tower Two, Suite 330
11350 N. Meridian Street
Carmel, IN 46032
(317)573-6272

American Educational Materials, Inc.
P.O. Box 2613
Anaheim, CA 92804
(714)761-8661

Parents Anonymous of Texas, Inc.
2602 Dellana Lane
Austin, TX 78746
(800)252-3048

43. Child Abuse

Like the abuse of drugs and alcohol, sexual abuse is also something we as Christian parents need to recognize. I'm not suggesting that we become preoccupied with fear and lock up our children day and night to keep them from exposure, but I do want to show you several aspects of this national problem.

First, you need to be aware that it can happen to your family. In 1986, the *Los Angeles Times* reported that "99.83% of last year's cases involved familial, not institutional abuse."[10] We hear stories and read bizarre reports and often think that these abusive situations happen only to someone else, only on the other side of the tracks, or only where people are sick. But that kind of thinking makes us and our children vulnerable to trouble.

After I wrote *Hope for Hurting Women* and began speaking on some of the topics discussed in it, such as incest, I was inundated with letters crying out for help. Many were from nice girls who grew up in nice homes and yet were molested from childhood by a father, brother, or a close friend of the family.

One woman wrote and told me this story:

> I have been married 29 years, and have four daughters (27 – 24 – 17 – 15) and I found out one month ago my husband has been having sexual intercourse with all of them since the age of six— each one did not know about any of the others. My oldest left home at age 21 to marry, my husband was still forcing the 24-year-old after she got married.

I am and so are the children all born again, Spirit-filled Christians. The Lord has kept us all through this tragedy. (We found out my oldest daughter had an abortion at age 13 and three months later was pregnant again, and my husband was forcing her to take bottles of Castor Oil to lose it.) It didn't succeed, so he proceeded to do the abortion himself with a salt solution.

He is a very smart man in man's eyes and knows the Bible very good, in fact, he preached for four years while this was still continuing.

I hear so many stories like that. Good Christian homes are touched by this tragedy as much as those from the other side of the tracks. In fact, some research indicates that the strict, legalistic, moralistic, religious father is more likely to be abusive than any other.

Linda Goldston points out in a 1987 article in the *Dallas Morning News*, "Researchers have discovered that 90% of the time children are molested by someone they know, love or trust; their parents, their neighbor, their teachers, their ministers."[11]

Keeping our children in the church or in the home is, sadly, not the answer.

The most important step in protecting our children from abuse is to make sure that we are whole and healthy ourselves. While some researchers disagree, I have found that in my personal experience, 100 percent of the abusers I talk to were victims themselves.

Zena Rudo, director of the Exchange Club Center for the Prevention of Child Abuse, says, "Abusive parents are not monsters. They are usually depressed, isolated, lonely and under tremendous stress—women with almost no self-esteem. Almost all of them were abused as children."[12]

As some of you are reading this, scenes from your childhood may flash across your mind. Some may remember well-meaning parents who were too busy to direct the show, leaving you to write your own lines and do your own thing. Some may have had parents who took the time for family discussion, weighing the pros and cons of debatable issues before making conclusions and teaching you how to make healthy choices. Some may have grown up under a controlling parent who allowed no one to offer a different opinion and who became abusive at the hint of an insurrection.

Contrary to what we intelligent Christian adults might assume, we tend to raise our families with the same negatives that were put upon us. Few of us have taken child-raising courses and even if we did and had perfect plans in our minds, we would still react out of what we learned as children. In many tense situations our emotions take control of our minds and we respond in a manner similar to how our parents did.

Psychologists agree that children who were abused in any way repeat the same actions with their children. We continue to follow faulty behavior patterns. Jan Frank, sexually abused as a child, was shocked when she felt herself heading for her child with an uncontrollable rage. She tells how she overcame this urge to abuse in *Door of Hope*. Kathy Collard Miller tells of her child abuse in *Out of Control*, and Stormie Omartian, locked in a closet as a child, writes in her biography, *Stormie*, about her own sufferings and then about her urge to hurt her children. Patsy Clairmont, in the emotional instability chapter in my book, *Hope for Hurting Women*, didn't remember any specific problems from her childhood but she found that in many cases the punishment she doled out to her boys was far worse than the crimes they'd committed. When she looked back at her childhood she could see a dysfunctional pattern and found many gaps in her memories, usually an indicator of some childhood trauma.

All four women are Christian leaders who know intellectually and spiritually that any abuse is unacceptable in God's sight. Yet the emotional reactive tug has been so strong they could hardly control it. By admitting they had a problem, seeking Godly counsel, and working through their childhood traumas with a competent therapist, they were able to emerge emotionally healed and to function as "normal parents."

Evaluate your family background and see if there were any faulty behavior patterns as you were growing up. If any come to your mind, ask yourself if you are repeating anything that was done to you. So often this repetition is totally unconscious and yet if we prayerfully seek God's vision, He will show us what we are doing that we didn't realize at all. Is there something one of your parents did that you might be reliving with your children? Remember, the sins of the parents are visited upon their children up to the third and fourth generations.

As you hear these brief capsules, some memories may be pricked in your own mind. My experience has shown me that an uneasy feeling is often the way God speaks to us to let us know that this is an area we need to deal with. "The secret things belong unto the Lord our God, but those things which are revealed belong unto us and to our children forever, that we may do all the words of this law" (Deuteronomy 29:29). Take some time and think about your past. Are you a victim of emotional, physical, or sexual abuse? When you think about a certain brother, cousin, or neighbor, do you get a strange feeling, or are there some rooms that bring about a negative memory? Or, like Patsy, do you have large gaps in your memory? As Oswald Chambers says, "Never be afraid when God brings back the past. Let memory have its way. It is a minister of God."

As your memories, or lack of them, kick up uncomfortable feelings, let that be a sign to you and get some help before "you pass this sin on to the next generation."

Jan gives some excellent, practical steps to help you find freedom from the past. While some Christian leaders such as Jimmy Swaggart teach that no outside help is necessary, that all we need to do is pray and read the Bible, we can see the folly of this theory from his example. Numerous articles point out that he had prayed over his addiction to pornography for years and yet its grip still haunted him. You may have prayed about your past. You may have forgiven the abuser, but still feel bound by those emotions. Get some help before it's too late. Work through the steps in *Door of Hope*. Start journalizing your feelings. Share with a Christian counselor what you've never told anyone before.

Once we have cleaned our own house we need to look at the other options. There are those cases where we do all we can do as parents and discover that in spite of our efforts our child's privacy has been violated.

One of the members of our CLASS staff, Georgia Venard (also the author of the drug addiction chapter in *Hope for Hurting Women*), came from a dysfunctional family herself. Many of those same dysfunctions were passed on to her children and as Georgia began to deal with her past and worked to restore her relationships with her children, she warned and urged them to be especially careful with the new generation of little ones. Since Georgia is now a counselor who spends much of her time dealing with sexual abuse victims, her children thought she was overly cautious until one day their four-year-old reported what had taken place between her and her seventeen-year-old uncle.

Even being careful and cautious, Georgia's family has again been touched with trauma. Since her little granddaughter knew right from wrong and she knew all the correct anatomical names for all the body parts, she knew what to do and she knew how to describe what happened.

A *Family Circle* article offers several suggestions to help protect our children. One of them is to "use the correct anatomical names for the reproductive organs of the body and teach your children to use them. Similarly, don't fail to let them know that it is not shameful to talk to you about any of these organs."

This same article encourages us to "teach our children that no one has the right to ask them to keep a secret from you and specifically to touch them in their 'private' or 'bathing suit' places, or anyplace they don't want to be touched. That lesson has to begin with not having to kiss Uncle Joe if they don't want to or not having to play wrestling or doctor games with him or anyone else."

One of the speakers we recommend through our speakers service, Colleen Weeks, teaches Christian sex education classes in Christian schools. She suggests that as soon as our children are old enough that we teach them to wash their "privates." Not even Mommy or Daddy should touch these areas because they are private. Colleen has taught her own daughter in this way and has told her to let Mommy know if anyone ever tries to touch her "privates." We need to let our children know from a very early age that those areas are private and no one should ever touch them.

Of course we need to be careful about childcare. Remember

the profile of the abuser is often someone who loves children and is religious. Debra Kanof, a prosecutor from El Paso, Texas, commented on the practice of looking for "a good Christian woman with a kind face, who loves children" to care for our kids. Daycare centers check for criminal records to determine "good" and church attendance to validate the "Christian" part. She says she has "never prosecuted an abuser who has a prior criminal record. Neither has she ever prosecuted an abuser who was not a churchgoer. So one has nothing to do with the other."[13]

If you must use a daycare center, be cautious. Get references of other parents who use that facility and talk with them. Be sure you are comfortable with the facility before leaving your child. Stop in unannounced on a semiregular basis to be sure things are as they should be.

Always keep an eye on your children. Watch carefully for any signs of abuse (see chart). If you suspect any foul play, carefully question your child. If you have previously laid the suggested foundation they will be able to tell you what did or did not happen. It is important that you listen carefully to whatever they say and never discredit their comments by saying things like "he'd never do that to you." Many victims don't tell anyone what has happened because they tried once and no one believed them, or they were told they were wrong and were lying so they hold it all in and suffer silently.

If, after reviewing the "symptoms" chart, you are talking with your child and your worst fears are confirmed, it is important that you get your child to a counselor who specializes in childhood abuse. The sooner you discover an abuse taking place and the quicker you get help, the easier it will be for your child to continue to live a normal life.

I often wish I could go back inside my bubble. Back to the days when I thought everyone who smiled in church was happy. Back to the days when bad things didn't happen to good people. But I can't go back, that's not reality. Tragedies do happen and as much as we'd rather look the other way, we as Christian parents need to be aware of these pains so we can protect and prepare our children.

INCEST OR CHILD ABUSE

SYMPTOMS

As a child:
- Fear
- Helplessness
- Inferiority
- Blame and guilt
- Bedwetting
- Nightmares
- Hiding away
- Asthma

As a teen:
- Early rebellion
- Acute depression
- Looking downward
- Feeling worthless
- Talk of suicide
- Running away
- Promiscuity
- Prostitution

As an adult:
- Gaps in memory
- Perfectionism
- Sacrificial work
- Lack of faith in God
- Repeated victimization
- Overweight
- Nightmares
- Flashbacks
- Migraines
- Allergies

As a wife:
- Poor choice of mates
- Accepting of abuse
- Frigidity
- Extreme anger
- Abusive to children
- Controlling
- Lack of emotion
- Lack of trust
- Suspicious
- Promiscuous

PROFILE OF OFFENDER (Usually a victim himself)

Rigid, religious, legalistic, high morals
Quiet, well-mannered, withdrawn
Believes in obedient children
Believes in subordination of women

STEPS TO HOPE by Jan Frank

Ten-Week Incest Support Structure

Face the problem
Recount the incident
Experience the feelings
Establish responsibility

Trace behavioral difficulties and symptoms
Observe others and evaluate self

Confront the aggressor
Acknowledge forgiveness
Rebuild self-image and relationships
Express concern and empathize

3/4 of offenders are friends or relatives.

When I first wrote the chapter on incest in *Lives on the Mend*, now republished as *Hope for Hurting Women*, I had no idea how it would be used. What emerged was a checklist of symptoms that I pulled out of the chapter and began to use as I spoke on the subject. Women asked for copies and soon I was printing up the symptom page by the hundreds.

By reading over the symptoms of childhood abuse, divided in sections—child, teen, adult, and wife—women have been able to identify past problems and realize why they are having migraine headaches, nightmares, and stomach problems, why they have gaps in their memories, why they have poor sexual relations in marriage, and an urge to abuse their children. Mothers have been able to spot abuse in their own children that would not have been understood before.

The profile of the offender, usually a victim of some childhood trauma himself, has been eye-opening to many who have assumed all offenders are weird perverts lurking in dark alleys in some other city far away, when in fact 75 percent of the offenders are friends and relatives. The description has helped pastors to realize that just because a man is in church and preaches high morals to others doesn't mean he could not have harmed his own child. Many newspaper accounts of child molesters say "he was a good church-going man who appeared harmless."

Pamela came to me at a large women's retreat and said she had listened to my symptoms of child abuse, and she was concerned for her three-year-old. Little Patty had within recent months started wetting her bed and screaming out in the night. When Pam would go in to her bed, the child would cry, "Don't hurt me, Mommy." As I questioned Pam she revealed that Patty wouldn't let her put panties on her and said she hurt while clutching onto herself. She kept her head down and wouldn't look anyone in the eye and was found hiding in her closet. Since all of these behavior changes are symptoms of abuse, it would appear that somewhere recently the child had been harmed. The question was where, when, and by whom.

We started by naming any time that she was out of her mother's sight. This narrowed down to her grandmother's house, an unlikely place to be harmed. As we discussed who else lived there, Pam came up with her teenage brother who took care of Patty if the grandmother had to go out.

When Pam went home she took Patty over to the grandmother's house to watch her reaction. She cried when she saw where she was and when Pam's brother came into the room she screamed and clung to her mother. When questioned, the young man, active in his church youth group, admitted that he and a friend had "experimented" on Patty. "I didn't think it would hurt her," he said in defense of several acts that could mar Patty for life.

At least the molestation was stopped, Pam is having counseling with Patty, and the brother/uncle is in court-ordered therapy. This case is one of many that I have personally dealt with which have been brought to light through use of the chart on page 284. For further study get *Hope for Hurting Women* and Jan Frank's book *Door of Hope*.

Part XII

REVIEW

> Her children rise up and call
> her blessed.
> (Proverbs 31:28)

XII

Review

44. Proud to Have Lasted through the Curtain Call (by Florence)

After each performance comes the review, an evaluation by an objective critic on how well each character has played his role and how effectively the director pulled his people and his plot together. Awards are given in each category and the backers are paid off.

As parents we have the leading roles, we are the directors, we establish the theme, and we create the setting. We run through daily rehearsals, encourage positive lines, and try to make the whole production fun. We bear responsibility for financial support, try to hold the lives together in times of tragedy, and seek insight from the author and finisher of our faith when we don't know which way to turn.

There is no Broadway production that would dream of investing so much power and responsibility in the wisdom and creativity of two people—and yet year after year we keep trying!

For some of us these multiple roles may seem overwhelming and by the time we have a handle on what we're doing, the show closes and we're standing on an empty stage wondering what the review will be.

No one could be expected to be a perfect parent but we want to be remembered for having done our best.

A *Family Circle* survey asked, "What kind of upbringing

provides children with a firm foundation for success as adults? What nurtures the creativity, self-confidence and love of learning that contribute to a high achievement?" Those 237 interviewed were adults who had reached the highest levels of distinction in their chosen fields. The conclusion showed that success lies in the childhood foundation, "but it has nothing to do with fancy schools or even the size of the paycheck." The results showed two distinct patterns in the homes of successful children: "The expenditure of parental time rather than money and on respect for children's independence and individuality rather than on force-fed lessons at an early age."

In this book I have tried to set the stage for spending creative time conversing with our children, for encouraging them in reading, music and artistic talent, for providing a setting of warm Christian love and fellowship. To assist you with the second desired pattern, understanding and respecting the child's individuality, I have provided the tool of the four personalities so that we can understand ourselves and then learn how to live positively with those who may be nothing like us.

What a dull show it would be if the whole cast was one big clone of Mother! God gave each one of us his own personality and as the family director, our charge is to bring the best out of each one and not try to change our children to become what we had in mind.

Dr. David Elkind, professor of child study at Tufts University, writes, "With gifted and intelligent children the best thing a parent can do is give them encouragement and follow their lead instead of deciding what they ought to be interested in and urging them to pursue it hard. Kids need time to expand their imagination, time to play and provide their own stimulation instead of having it bombard them from the outside. When they learn to read, they need the time to explore books by themselves without a specific goal in mind . . .

"Certainly, parents play a crucial role in the lives of individuals who are intellectually gifted or creatively talented. But this role is not one of active instruction, of teaching children skills . . . Rather, it is the support and encouragement parents give children

and the intellectual climate that they create in the home which
seem to be the critical factors."

How important encouragement is to the development of
our children. Let's throw away the old script of critical comments
and encourage each child. Let's provide a setting "where never is
heard a discouraging word and the skies are not cloudy all day."
Let's show them that the theme of the Christian life is one of
excitement and challenge and let them know with David that "All
the days ordained for me were written in your book before one of
them came to be" (Psalm 139:16b NIV).

When the review comes from our children, not every opinion will be positive but the Lord will reward us for our good
works and faithful direction and in the long run when our adult
children are struggling with their own performance they will look
back in amazement at how well we held the cast together.

They will rise up and call us blessed.

45. Proud to Be a Chip Off the Old Block
(by Marita)

"Sketches of mother/daughter relationships bear witness to
the fact that a daughter's growth into selfhood requires direct or
indirect affirmation from her mother."[1]

As I have spent the last ten years traveling throughout the
country speaking to women's groups, I receive one comment
more than any other. It is the highest compliment I could get.
As I finish speaking to a group many people say, "You are a chip
off the old block." My mother is not too thrilled to be thought of
as the "old block," but I am proud to be the "chip."

You've heard the stories of Bette Davis and her daughter,
Joan Crawford and her daughter, and Lana Turner and her
daughter. All these famous mothers have had terrible relationships with their daughters who want nothing to do either with
their mothers or their professions. Often when movie stars' children are in the movies you'll hear them comment on the
"Johnny Carson Show" that they made it on their own. Of

course, as we sit and listen to this nonsense we know that the only reason they were in that movie is because they are a certain famous person's child. The typical relationship between a famous parent and a child is too often distant and detached at best.

The first time I was asked to speak on mother/daughter relationships, my first thought was, "No! I can't do that, I'm not a mother." But as I thought about it, I realized that I have a mother. I have a mother who is famous in her sphere and I have a mother whom I am proud of. She is my best friend. The more I read about famous mothers and their daughters, the more rare I realize our relationship is. I began to wonder why had we escaped the typical scarred relationship. As I looked over my childhood, I realized that there were some specific things she had done that have made us best friends today. Since I was the second child, I guess that my mother had caught up with this parenting program by the time I came around.

Ann Taylor, the author of *Twinkle, Twinkle Little Star*, says of her mother, "Who ran to help me when I fell, and would some pretty story tell or kiss the place to make it well . . . my mother." In an overly simplified way that sums up the crux of why my famous mother and I are best friends today.

A major factor is that my mother was there while I was growing up. She was there to help me when I fell, she was there to tell me stories, and she was there to kiss me and make it well. This does not mean that she was there around the clock, that she home-schooled me and never left me with a baby-sitter. What it does mean is that when she was there, she was there. My mother made me feel important. She didn't start her full-time ministry until we were all grown up. She was involved in various church and social activities and occupational pursuits that kept her away from home some of the time, but when she was with us we knew she was glad to be there.

Talk

As I look back at my youth to see what specific things my mother did that made me feel important, one area is her talk: the things she said to me.

I remember one time when I was nine years old. My mother must have been to some seminar that told her to tell her children that she loves them. Out of the blue she asked me, "Do you know that I love you?" My response was, "I know that you would if I get good grades." From that point on she made sure that she sent me off to school each day with, "I love you, Marita." Even during my difficult teenage years when I looked atrocious, she would say, "I love you." While I struggled with my identity as a teen, I knew I was loved and that I had a place that I could always go home to where I was accepted.

I have a friend, Connie, who has thirteen-year-old and ten-year-old daughters. As I watch their family I see that same rare close relationship between Connie and her daughters that I have with my mother. I've been impressed as I've dropped in for a few minutes to find them all working together in the kitchen and for no reason Emily, the thirteen-year-old, will reach over, give her mother a kiss, and say, "I love you." I've been with Connie when she has called back home to check in. The last thing she says as she hangs up the phone is "I love you." Sometimes I hear her say "I love you, too" because her girls often say "I love you" first. I asked Emily why at thirteen she is comfortable with this kind of relationship. She told me, "It's always been that way."

As I talked with Emily I discovered our mother/daughter relationships had another factor in common: Both of us have mothers who tell us we can do it. Both of us are encouraged. I remember when my mother took me to art classes. She never told me that the teacher told her I had more creativity than talent. She continued to take me there each week and she proudly displayed my works. I was on the swim team at our country club. At that time I didn't realize that I was only on it because I was the only one in my age group who was willing to swim. I didn't realize that the reason I got third-place ribbons was because there were only three in the race. I swam in each race and was proudly cheered on by my mother. She encouraged me.

My friend Emily is on a swim team. Just last week I dropped over and, in front of Emily, Connie enthusiastically shared with me how many seconds Emily had taken off her record in the last meet and that she had Olympic potential. Amanda, the ten-year-old, plays the violin. I played the violin, too, but I never took to it like Amanda. Every week she has lessons. Connie encourages her to practice by frequently sitting with her and listening. Connie has enthusiastically invited me to attend a recital of Amanda's. Connie encourages her girls; she is proud of them.

One day I was watching Marlo Thomas on the "Donahue Show." As she was telling about her family, she said that the reason why all the children in her family have been successful is because her mother encouraged them. She told them they were the best in whatever they did.

Philippians 4:8 tells us, "Fix your thoughts on what is true, good and right. Think about things that are pure and lovely. Dwell on the fine good things in others" (TLB). Through my childhood my mother dwelt on the fine good things in me. She encouraged me, she told me I could do it.

I know my mother loves me. I know she thinks I can do it and I know she thinks I am special. If you have ever attended a seminar or program where both my mother and I are speaking, you know my mother thinks I am special. She sits in the front row and watches me intently while I am speaking. She breathes with me and nods for me. We constantly get comments about how Florence watches Marita. She could use that time as a good chance to go to the restroom or go talk with some friends but because she loves me, because she encourages me, and because I am special to her, she chooses to stay there and listen to the same thing she's heard me do over and over again.

When I first started speaking I knew that my mother believed in me and told me I was special by telling groups that invited her to speak that I was available. If they would let me come, at no charge, I would teach a workshop on wardrobe organization and color coordination. Together we traveled all over the country. Together we taught seminars. She believed in me and told me I was special.

Even before that time, my mother laid the groundwork for this close relationship when she started speaking, and with my father taught marriage seminars. I was only eleven at the time.

Mom and Dad took me with them to these programs. They had me pass out papers and occasionally I went up front and shared a story. They made me a part of their life when I was young. They made me feel special and that they would like to take me on this trip with them. It wasn't a punishment or it wasn't because they couldn't get a sitter. It was because they wanted me with them. I felt special. As the pace of my mother's ministry picked up, she did not have the time to spend at swim meets or PTA meetings like she used to, but we still spent quality time together. Again she brought me into her life. Through those marriage seminars Mom and Dad taught, Mom ended up doing quite a lot of marriage counseling.

When she had spent the day in the office counseling, that was our dinner conversation. We all ate dinner together each night and Mom would tell us the situation of the couple she had worked with that day. We never knew who the people were, but we knew their situation. She asked us what we would tell them they should do. Each one of us gave our suggestions. Sometimes Mom would say, "That's exactly what I told them" and other times she would say, "What a great idea. I'll suggest that to them next time." Again we were encouraged by her positive response to our ideas and we were made to feel special because she brought us into her life, she cared enough to ask for our opinion.

When I booked Connie to speak at her first women's retreat her first reaction was, "Can I bring Emily?" Connie chooses to spend time with Emily. Emily is special to her mother and she knows it. Her mother tells her she loves her, she encourages her and tells her she is special. Connie is involved in Emily's life but she also makes Emily a part of her life.

Listen

One day I was in a restaurant. At the table next to me was a woman and two children. The lady and the older child were talking away. The young boy kept pulling on her sleeve saying, "Mommy, Mommy," but she kept ignoring him. Finally she got irritated enough with his constant interruptions to stop talking and see what he wanted. He said, "You never listen to me." "What do you want to say?" she snapped. He pulled back and replied, "Nothing. You just never listen to me."

How grateful I am that my mother listened to me. She'd listen to my dreams and ideas, she'd listen to my stories, and she'd listen to my secrets. When I came home from school I would share with her my ideas and my dreams. Because she listened to me as a child, I am comfortable sharing with her as an adult. Two years ago I shared a dream with her. I told her that I had finally decided what I wanted to do with my life. I told her that in ten years I wanted to make CLASS the place to call for Christian speakers. At that time my dream was not as well defined as that, but together we talked about it and she helped me define my goal. Shortly thereafter I quit my job and went to work full-time in my parents' ministry. Today I am living out my dream. I run the part of our ministry that provides Christian programming, singers, speakers, and dramatists for churches and other Christian groups across the country. Thank you, Mom, for listening to my dreams and taking a chance on me.

Another friend of mine, Colleen, has an excellent way to encourage her daughter to tell her what she's thinking. It lets her know she's listening. When her daughter says, "Mommy, I want to tell you something." Colleen says, "Good, I want to hear it." Sarah knows she can talk to her mommy.

I remember my mother listening to my stories and I was a great one for telling stories. Since I was a constant talker, a Sanguine, there was a lot to listen to. Most of my stories had no real point but merely reviewed every event of my day. I sat on the kitchen counter while my mother cooked dinner and filled her in on every detail. I was famous for my book reviews. After reading *The Cat in the Hat* or *Green Eggs and Ham* I had to tell Mom every detail of what went on. Although she would laugh and tell me she could read the book herself in less time than listening to my review, she always listened anyway. I trailed around behind her as she vacuumed and cleaned, telling all about *Green Eggs and Ham*. Telling her about them "in a box with a fox, in a house with a mouse, or in the rain on a train." Of course she'd read me the book a hundred times herself and knew the story backward and forward but she still listened. Today if we are feeling down or discouraged, reciting "I do not like green eggs and ham, I do not like them, Sam-I-am, I do not like them here or there, I do not like them anywhere" will get us laughing quicker than almost anything.

Not only did my mother listen to my dreams and listen to my stories, but she listened to my secrets. Since my mother developed a pattern of listening with me from a very young age, I knew I could tell her my secrets, my innermost thoughts, and my feelings. I remember one summer I'd been away for two weeks at church camp. When I came home my parents eagerly took me to the back yard. There stood a life-size playhouse. It was real wood with a white Dutch door and a glass window with a window-box out front. It was one room inside that was big enough for adults to stand in. In my enthusiasm I ran down the street to my friends' house to tell her my good fortune. Instead of being excited for me Cindy said, "So what, I got an Easy Bake Oven." She didn't even want to see it. Now we adults know that as a sign of jealousy, but we children don't always see those logical explanations for another's hurtful behavior. I'd dragged myself home and cried to my mother. She could have told me I was silly to be hurt or that I was thoughtless to share my news with Cindy since she was less fortunate, but instead she listened and taught me one of my first real lessons in jealousy. Once I understood, I wasn't so hurt.

When I struggled with those junior high and high school years I could come home and tell her how I felt. If I was feeling left out because I wasn't invited to a party, we could talk about it and while that didn't change the invitation, being able to talk it out without being told my feelings were stupid was an emotional release.

In more recent years, I've shared my secret desires with her. I told her that I thought that God had given me a new career goal. I felt so silly about my ideas that I didn't tell anyone for many months. Finally, I told her. Not only did she not laugh at my plans but she encouraged me and over the last few years she has helped me with my ten-year plan.

When I asked Emily why she and her mother had such a good relationship she gave me reasons much like those I had come up with. But, one that struck me the most was that she said, "I can talk to her." Emily went on to explain that she could tell her mother how she was feeling and know that she would not be ridiculed for those thoughts. Emily told me about one of her friends at school who had gone home and told her mother how she felt about something and the girl's mother had told her she was immature and that if she were really a good Christian she wouldn't feel that way. While the mother's comments may have been true, they surely didn't help to keep the lines of communication open.

Like Emily, I am glad that I've been able to talk to my mother and know she'd listen. I can tell her my dreams. I can tell her my stories and I can tell her my secrets.

Pray

While the words you say and the way you listen can have a major impact on the relationship between you and your daughter, I believe that for us, the icing on the cake was my mother's regular prayers. While I was never a horribly bad kid, I also was not the most perfect. I did, and still do, speed too much. I dated boys who were not my mother's first choice and, as I mentioned, I did spend two hours in jail.

Each day as I headed off to school and later to work, she'd tell me that she had prayed, "Bring her home, Lord, just one more day." He always did.

I remember when I was waitressing the graveyard shift. I got off work at 6 A.M. Some days I then went straight to college and other days I went home first. I remember many times that I fought to stay awake during the fifteen-minute drive home. I didn't always make it.

One morning I woke up in a parking lot. I wasn't really sure where I was as I lifted my head off the steering wheel. After just a few seconds I realized I had been so sleepy that I had pulled over into this parking lot and fallen asleep with my head on the steering wheel, even before I turned off the engine. I was awakened by some concerned passers-by who had seen me slumped over the wheel with the engine running.

Yes, I did some stupid things. I lived like that for nine months before I finally quit that job.

When I finally got married my mother told Chuck, "She's yours now. I've been praying for her every day and now she's your responsibility."

I'd forgotten all her prayers until one day I was asked to give my testimony. Since my life has not been too exciting, I tried to convince them that I was not the one, but they were sure they wanted me so I began to prepare my talk. My friends tell me that I lead a charmed life and I looked in my concordance to find a scripture that fit my life. I found a verse I liked but thought another version might say it more clearly. I got out my old Living Bible, the one I'd used in high school with the dark green cover that wrinkled with age. Mine has a luminous fuschia "One Way" sticker on the back, left over from my "Jesus freak" days. I opened it to Psalm 32. There at the top of the chapter, in my mother's handwriting in an olive green Flair pen, it said, "God's Psalm for Marita." I have no idea when she wrote it. I haven't seen her use olive green Flair pens for years and I had not really used that Bible since high school.

As I read those verses I knew why I'd had such a "charmed life." She'd underlined verses 7 and 8: "You are my hiding place, you protect me from trouble and surround me with songs of deliverance. I will instruct you and guide you along the best pathway for your life. I will counsel you and watch over you." I had a "charmed life" because every day my mother prayed for me. She prayed that God would "watch over" me and "guide me along the best pathway" for my life.

I am so glad that as I was growing up my mother told me I was special and encouraged me. I appreciate all the times she listened to my incessant chatter and my broken dreams. I am thankful for her prayers, for making me what I am today.

I love you
Not only for what you are
But for what I am when I'm with you.
I love you
Not only for what you've made of yourself
But for what you are making of me.
I love you, for the part of me that you bring out.
I love you, for putting your hand into my heart
And passing over the foolish weak things
That you can't help dimly seeing there.
And drawing out into the light
All the beautiful belongings
That no one else had looked quite far enough to find.
I love you because you are helping me to make of the lumber
    of my life
Not a tavern, but a temple;
Out of my works, of my every day
Not a reproach, but a song.
I love you
Because you have done more than any creed could have done
To make me feel my goodness.
You have done it.
With your touch, with your words, with yourself.

                                          Roy Croft

Recommended Books for Further Reading:

*Personality Plus by Florence Littauer (Fleming H. Revell).

*Your Personality Tree by Florence Littauer (Word Books).

*Hope for Hurting Women by Florence Littauer (Word Books).

*Blow Away the Black Clouds by Florence Littauer (Harvest House Publishers).

*Roses in December by Marilyn Heavilin (Here's Life Publishers).

*Becoming a Woman of Honor by Marilyn Heavilin (Here's Life Publishers).

*More Hours in My Day by Emilie Barnes (Harvest House Publishers).

*Survival for Busy Women by Emilie Barnes (Harvest House Publishers).

*Complete Holiday Organizer by Emilie Barnes (Harvest House Publishers).

*Eating Right by Emilie Barnes and Sue Gregg (Harvest House Publishers).

**The Challenge of Raising Cain by Debe Haller.

*My Utmost for His Highest (Special CLASS Edition) by Oswald Chambers (Barbour and Co.).

*From Rejection to Acceptance by Barbara Taylor (Broadman Press).

---

*If not available at your local Christian bookstore, these books may be ordered by contacting:

    CLASS Book Service

    1814-E Commercenter West

    San Bernardino, CA 92408

    (714)888–8665

**May be ordered by writing:

    14811 Monroe Street

    Midway City, CA 92655

End Notes

Program Notes (by Marita)

1. *Time*, 22 June 1987.

Part I. The Cast

1. David Feldman and Lynn T. Goldsmith, *Nature's Gambit: Child Prodigies and the Development of Human Potential* (New York: Basic Books, 1986).
2. *Houston Post*, 13 January 1987.
3. Ibid.
4. Barbara Taylor, *Fullness Magazine*, "Overcoming Rejection," excerpt from *From Rejection to Acceptance* (Nashville: Broadman Press, 1987).

Part III. The Directors

1. *Los Angeles Times*, 19 January 1978.
2. Ibid.
3. Nancy Cornwell, *Learning '86*, "Encouraging Responsibility," (Cornell: September, 1986) 47–49.
4. Ibid.
5. Ibid.

Part IV. The Plot

1. *Family Circle*, 5 April 1988.

Part VIII. Rehearsals

1. *Time*, 5 November 1984.
2. Ibid.
3. Ibid.
4. Ibid., 69.

Part IX. Script

1. *Los Angeles Times*, 27 March 1988.
2. *USA Today*, 29 July 1986.
3. Anne Martin, *Learning '87*, "Encouraging Youngsters to Discuss Their Feelings," (Cornell: July/August 1987).
4. *Los Angeles Times*, 13 January 1988.
5. Ibid.
6. Allan Bloom in *U.S. News and World Report*, "A Nation That Has Lost Its Bearings," 11 May 1987, 78.
7. *Los Angeles Times*, 27 March 1988.
8. Ibid.

Part X. Comedy

1. Kay Kuzma, *A Hug, A Kiss, and a Kick in the Pants*, 119.
2. Oswald Chambers, *The Best from All His Books* (Nashville: Oliver Nelson Publishers, 1987) 277.

Part XI. Tragedy

1. *People* Magazine, 18 April 1988.
2. *Christianity Today*, 7 March 1986 (Editorials—Kenneth S. Kantzer and Paul Fromer).
3. *USA Today*, 28 April 1986 (Emory University study of 600 Atlanta High School seniors).
4. *The Sunday Express News*, San Antonio, TX, 23 March 1986 (UCLA Study conducted in 1983 of secondary schools in Orange Co.).
5. *USA Today*, 20 October 1986 (UCLA study of 17,500 California seventh, ninth, and eleventh graders/Psychologist Rod Skager).
6. *USA Today*, 10 February 1986.
7. The Spirit of Freedom, P. O. Box 50583/New Orleans, LA 70150.
8. *USA Today*, 23 June 1986.

9. *Dallas Morning News*, 27 January 1988 (Dictionary of Street Alcohol and Drug Terms, University of South Carolina Books/Dr. Peter Johnson).

10. *Los Angeles Times*, Sunday, 2 March 1986 ("Band Aids for Child Abuse" by Nancy Amidei).

11. *Dallas Morning News*, 23 June 1987 ("Children Who Molest Children" by Linda Goldston).

12. *Family Circle*, 13 August 1987 ("True Life Drama" by Joan Heilman).

13. *El Paso Times*, Sunday, 20 April 1986 (Tim Palmer).

FLORENCE LITTAUER is an internationally known speaker and author who exhorts, excites, and entertains all at the same time. Two of her twelve books— *Personality Plus* and *Your Personality Tree* —have been recognized by Religion in Media with *Your Personality Tree* winning the Silver Angel Award. For years her Bible teaching has delighted audiences across the country at women's retreats and church services. At present she is the founder-president of CLASS— Christian Leaders and Speakers Seminars. She has earned the Certified Speaking Professional designation and received the CPAE (the Hall of Fame award) from the National Speakers Association, and she is a member of the Council of Churchmen at Azusa-Pacific School of Theology.